In for the Kill

A True Story of Hunting Evil

C. J. HART

MAINSTREAM
PUBLISHING

EDINBURGH AND LONDON

Fo   n.

First published in Great Britain in 2012 by
MAINSTREAM PUBLISHING COMPANY
(EDINBURGH) LTD
7 Albany Street
Edinburgh EH1 3UG

ISBN 9781780575636

A catalogue record for this book is available
from the British Library

Printed in Great Britain by
CPI Group (UK) Ltd, Croydon, CR0 4YY

1 3 5 7 9 10 8 6 4 2

Acknowledgements

Thanks to my brilliant editor Ailsa Bathgate, whose dauntless efforts on behalf of this book leave me speechless; to Bill Campbell, whose unique mind made everything possible.

Thanks to Graeme Blaikie, who eased the way. Thank you to my art director, lovely Claire Ward from Random House for her truly great cover design. The following people must be thanked for their support: Glyn Powell, friend and life coach; my oracle, who shall remain nameless; Nick Davies for his idea; to Richard Hugh Burnett, my beautiful friend; the 'rock star' Reid Meloy.

To my dear friend Alex Martinez and our Los Angeles mornings. The beautiful women from my Wednesday morning group. To Barry Bernfeldt, to Susannah De Fere and to the great Ron Dreyer who told me, *'carpe diem'*. To my new friends who wrote to me to say keep writing – I love you. To all the victims of adoption, childhood abuse and neglect – my heart is yours. Thanks to all the journalists and editors I have had the privilege to work with on Fleet Street – for we have known the days. To my amazing son, without whom the sun would never shine.

Author's Note

This book is a work of non-fiction based on the life, experiences and recollections of the author. In many cases, particularly in respect of those connected to the IRA or Real IRA, names of people, places, dates, sequences or the detail of events have been changed to protect the privacy of others. The author has stated to the publishers that, except in such respects not affecting the substantial accuracy of the work, the contents of this book are true.

Contents

One

The Lost Princess

Is there no pity sitting in the clouds, That sees into
the bottom of my grief?

Romeo and Juliet, Act 3, Scene 5

After being abandoned by my 14-year-old so-called mother at
a Crusade of Rescue Home, shortly after I was born, the fairy
stories I was told as a child seemed to have a special resonance
for me. Her sloping hand had written me a wish in blue ballpoint,
like a wicked fairy at a gathering.

> I am giving this child a chance in life. I am seeing that she
> never wants for anything. I am doing a work of CHARITY by
> giving her up.

As I grew older I became particularly fascinated by Rapunzel, the
story of a golden-haired lost princess who was removed from her
kingdom and taken to a tower by a fake mother who turned out
to be a wicked witch. Looking back, it seems that is just how the
next stage of my own story began: with a journey to the tower,
which in this case was an old stone house near Guildford.

After three years in the orphanage, a good-looking Irishman,
Liam Hart, and his English wife, Georgie, took me in as their
daughter. Georgie Hart could not have children. The couple had
already adopted a little boy they'd called Nicky, who was two years
older than me.

Home was now a Victorian terrace in the Surrey countryside
with dark green shutters on the windows and cool, high-ceilinged,

9

cream-painted rooms with floral curtains and leather wing-backed chairs. Our village was in a well-to-do, quiet area with big Mercedes parked outside sprawling mansions. In the side streets, the modest Victorian and Edwardian houses stood alongside the affluent larger homes. In many ways it was a start just like Harry Potter.

'Is this my home?' I asked, as I gasped in happiness, twirling around, gratefully appreciating it. At the orphanage I had longed for a family, thinking of myself as a lost princess waiting to be found by her real parents.

My new dark-haired mother, Georgie, who had not uttered a word to me on the car journey home, now spoke. 'Your name's Christine Joanna now. Christine's a name that'll remind you all your life to keep Christ centred.'

I had no idea what she meant – my name, as far as I knew, was Lucy – but I gazed up at her beautiful face with its alabaster skin and rosebud lips, longing to kiss the skin that smelt of wet flour and almonds.

'Thank you, Mummy.' I felt afraid of the strength of my need for my new mother.

'Don't you go calling me Mummy! Your mother didn't want you. Understand?'

I did not understand and I felt very, very afraid of her cruel words. As I looked around me, I saw a man I later discovered was the Pope staring back from pictures in every room in the house. They were a strict and devout churchgoing Catholic family. The hallway was cramped and the stairs had a scarlet carpet. All the way down the stairs were paintings of religious events in the lives of the saints.

The years passed and I came to learn the Hart family ways. In the summer months, the hallway always had a large vase filled with lily-of-the-valley from the front garden giving off its delicate perfume. Liam would duck down to see himself in the hall mirror while he combed back his blond hair with Brylcreem, patting his golden waves and fussing over their position. He would then cover his fairytale blue eyes with dark aviator sunglasses and give out a low howl of appreciation.

Liam liked to mimic the matinee idols of the day, with their flamboyant dress and behaviour. I would hop from one foot to another, enjoying the soapy clean smells coming from this handsome man whom I loved to call 'Daddy'. I stared at him, trying to work out how to secure this kind-hearted dreamboat for myself.

He turned and caught my admiring glances.

'Put that record on I was playing earlier, Chris, love.'

The crooning voice played out in the dusty living room that Georgie had grown too fat and depressed to clean.

My adoptive mother disliked me greatly, which she showed by either ignoring me or hitting me. By the age of five, I had accepted it as the norm, though life was lonely. If anyone mentioned that I was pretty, Georgie would tell them that I was illegitimate and adopted. One day she came along with a sharp pair of scissors and chopped at my long, dark-blonde hair that was silky and fairy-like.

'Oh, Mummy, I don't want my hair short,' I cried as I saw long silken strands pool around my feet. But she cropped it, finishing it off by cutting around a pudding bowl placed on my head as I squirmed and wept.

As I grew older and prettier, my father paid me more and more attention.

'Don't be telling anyone I'm Irish. You'll get on better at school if you don't,' he said, in his put-on posh English accent. 'And don't be telling anyone we got you from an orphanage either, or they'll think that you're beneath them for ever. Bastard's a dirty fucking bastard and so low-life it's beneath everyone.'

'Yes, Daddy. Sorry, Daddy.'

'Don't you ever forget where you come from neither, Chris!'

'No, Daddy. I won't ever forget where I come from.'

'Sex, filth and shame.'

'Sex, filth and shame,' I repeated, and swallowed the fear and feelings that rose up to tell me something awful about my father that I didn't want to recognise.

When I was 11, I passed the 11-plus and was sent to a very middle-class all-girl grammar school. Georgie was tight-lipped and acted as if she was angry, but my daddy was pleased. The problem was that the school was twenty miles away, meaning two changes on buses. I was up at six and home late every night, then I had to face a curled, hairy fist under my nose as I did the two hours of homework.

'Get the fuck on with that homework, shite! Friends won't get you anywhere in life! You can forget them right now. Friends mean nothing. I've none and you don't need them.'

'I know. I'm trying to do it neatly, Daddy.'

'Pass the pen here. I'll do the maths.'

'Please let me do it, Daddy. Please. We've been doing it all day – please.'

'I can do this maths as good as any Englishman. Are you saying I can't because I'm a low-life Paddy?'

He pushed his fist into my face threateningly, then pulled it back and punched me hard in the jaw. The pain shot through me.

'Oh Daddy, Daddy, please – please!' I pushed my maths book back towards him and sobbed in agony, clutching my chin.

I eventually got to bed by midnight, jaw throbbing, my book blotted by Liam's heavy-handed, miscalculated algebra. Sleep did not come and then it was morning again, bringing the long journey to school, where I still hadn't been able to make any friends. The others girls were all daughters of doctors or lawyers and ate tuna fish and drank pineapple juice at break times. My father was a cleaner for an airline company and I drank budget orange squash and ate peanut butter sandwiches.

On the way home, the local schoolgirls would grab my straw boater off my head, snatch my hockey stick from me and call me a snob. At school, because I was a bookworm with no confidence, I began to get bullied by the bright, pretty girls, who called me Margot, after Margot from *The Good Life*, because of my posh speaking voice and because I was a shy nerd.

At weekends, Liam would attend to himself in the peach-coloured bathroom mirror for hours, plucking the tiny dark hairs from inside his oval nostrils, trimming his golden moustache, fixing his hair just right. He would croon to his reflection in the mirror and splash on Brut aftershave, sometimes holding conversations with himself in an American drawl.

'I told you, I love you, doll face. I said it and I meant it, baby,' he said, clenching a cigarette between his teeth and admiring the reflection of his yellow silk cravat and grey slacks.

Liam would often rage at the TV as he watched the news, frowning at the IRA bombs that were going off in London.

'IRA scum! IRA filth!'

On the settee sat my overweight mother, Georgie, and Nicky. Nicky was almost two years older, a good-looking, clever boy. I was afraid of him. Once he had whispered in my small seashell-shaped ear, 'I'm going to fuck up your life, you little wanker.'

The Lost Princess

I had no idea what the word wanker meant and hoped that it was something nice.

The next day was a Saturday and the weather was tropical. A bright blue sky hung above the still day, with the tarmac giving up wavy lines of heat. I helped Daddy wash his second-hand gold Bentley in the sunny afternoon. He'd invested his savings in the car and planned to use it to start a chauffeur service. When it had reached a high shine, he washed his hands.

His usual Saturday-afternoon ritual was to sip whisky while watching westerns but that afternoon Georgie had commandeered the TV.

'Mother, where's my sweet girl gone?'

'She came in and then went up to her room to read a book, I suppose, like the bookworm she is.'

Georgie stuffed another piece of fudge into her mouth and turned up the sound on the television. Liam laughed and called up the stairs, 'Come back down, Chris. Let's show off all that hard work and polishing.'

He winked at me as I came downstairs, then put on his dark glasses and grinned, exposing long, tobacco-stained teeth. I slipped on my pale pink ballet pumps and grinned back.

We drove too fast in the gold-coloured limousine with the radio blaring 'Can't live, if living is without you'. Daddy had his arm thrown around the back of my seat with a lustful look on his unshaven face, sometimes silent, sometimes singing loudly. A cool summer breeze blew in the window; the countryside outside was honeysuckle lush and full of forest. We sailed on for miles and ended up in Maidenhead.

'Are these sexy, Chris?' Daddy asked me, holding up a lime-coloured satin thong. We were standing in the underwear section of a large department store.

'Yep, pretty. Are they for Mummy's birthday?'

'No. I've a little scrubber on the side.'

'A scrubber? A cleaner?'

'Something like that.'

As far back as I could remember, Liam would make frequent trips over to Dublin to see his family, the journey made possible by him being allowed to fly on standby with the company he worked for. I had accompanied him from about the age of six. Daddy and I would fly over and stay in the slummy, yellow-bricked terrace where he had grown up with 11 brothers and sisters. The only one of the large family who would stay at home to nurse their blind mother was Ruth. Ruth was in her 50s, had white hair, a quick smile and had never married.

'Oh, Chris, it's so lovely to see you, pet. Will I give you a pound and watch you out the window while you run over for some chips?'

'Ooh yes, Auntie Ruth! I can get over the road without being knocked over, don't you worry.' I thought of the hot, golden-fried chips drenched in salt and white onion vinegar, wrapped in newspaper.

I loved Ruth. I also loved the small crumbling house and the imposing blue-gated Guinness factory that always gave off the heavy smell of yeast just before it rained. It was a rough neighbourhood. Next door lived a poor family – the Clearys. They had a washing-line full of grey sheets and three boys spilling out of their tiny terrace. My brother Nicky was terrified of the Cleary clan, particularly their eldest, Val – a muddied-kneed, good-looking blond boy, with thick lips and an air of insolence. I found him absolutely fascinating and would stand and stare until his mother caught me.

'Hello, Chris. How's your mother?'

'Oh, good, Mrs Cleary.' *She thinks you're the dirt on her shoe, Mrs Cleary.*

'And your daddy, Chris?'

'Good too, Mrs Cleary.' *And he'd probably like to buy you lime-green knickers and see you do a twirl in them.*

I stared at Mrs Cleary and saw something lovely in her moss-green eyes. My throat choked with need as I watched her putting out her grey sheets. Black smoke smelling of burning wood billowed from their chimney. Something in me wanted to have the woman hold me. I would have liked to live with Mrs Cleary and call her 'Mummy'.

Liam's mother, Nanna Hart, was old and blind and would sit by an unlit fire trying to keep warm with her threadbare woollen shawls in dark colours. Even in the baking-hot month of August, she still sat wrapped in a forest-green shawl, listening to the Angelus, mumbling repetitive prayers. Like a white-haired lump, she hardly spoke or smiled, noisily slurping endless cups of sugary tea in the living room with its dull-brown linoleum floor. Her dinners were frozen pastry wrapped around fish or boil-in-a-bag cod and frozen vegetables cooked by Ruth.

The tiny terrace had a Sunday-best, icy-cold front parlour full of pink plastic geraniums. It had a smelly, cold outside loo with no toilet rolls and massive hairy black spiders. It overlooked a small concrete back yard with tall weeds and stinging nettles.

Liam would always drop his English accent and put on his thick Dublin brogue after he had been in the country a few hours (and had a few winning bets on some horses). I wondered where he put his British accent, but he always found it midway on the journey back.

I adored my Irish uncles and aunts.

'Chris, love – d'ye want some cheese and onion Tayto crisps, love? Some Club orange too, Chris?'

The tiny front room would now be hot, filled with smoke and sweaty red-faced relatives. I soaked up their warmth and felt less afraid; it felt so much warmer in Ireland than in England.

'Look at this Flamenco doll we got from Sardinia last year.' Uncle Jim was short and kind. 'Would you like it, wee Chris? Go on, just take it out of the glass cabinet – careful now. Go on ahead, love. It's all yours, love – just take it.'

'I've never owned anything quite as nice as this, Uncle Jim.' I fingered the doll's long, black lace dress appreciatively and sat it on my knee as I sucked my ice-cold orangeade through a paper straw.

Liam's face got hotter and redder as he drank glass after glass of Guinness. He plonked happily away at 'Magic Moments' on the piano in the front room. Uncle Paddy, with his dark hair slicked wet with Brylcreem, smiled. I sucked down some more of the cold, fizzy orange juice.

One hot, sticky day in late July, the summer before my 13th birthday, Val Cleary cornered me in front of the house. I knew a bit about boys and tongue kissing from the girls at school, but I hadn't done anything but practise on the back of my hand. As Val came nearer, the gold in his hair became brighter and I could smell his strawberry bubblegum breath.

'D'ye want me?' he whispered up close to my face. 'D'ye want to make love to me? I know you do.' He pushed his warm mouth against mine and I felt myself tighten between my legs. I pulled back and wiped my mouth of his bubblegum spit. I knew it meant I had to marry him now he had kissed me.

'I want to marry you, Val!' I whispered hopefully in his ear.

'I want to marry you, too.'

In for the Kill

He jumped on the back of his red Chopper and rode off across the recreation ground with a sarcastic yodel. I turned towards the house, bursting with joy. I could smell my aunt's eggs frying in the tiny kitchen and my mouth watered. A deeper sniff brought the stink of outdoor toilets and bad plumbing.

I ran inside and stood in the steamy kitchen, watching Ruth's fried eggs spitting furiously in the pan. The news of my peck of a kiss was on my lips and I was waiting for the right moment to share it.

Ruth turned and when she spotted me standing there she slammed the milk jug down with a loud bang.

'My God, I couldn't believe it when I just looked out of the window just now and saw that little shit-bag kissing you, and you letting him.'

I opened my mouth to reply. Then I stifled a huge sob and went running upstairs to fling myself on the bed. After an hour of sobbing, I sat up and nosed through the drawers I had respectfully regarded as private. In the lined drawer of Ruth's bedroom I found a book all about aliens. I was surprised at my aunt and then remembered she had always loved sci-fi on the TV.

The book listed different types of aliens and claimed that these creatures had existed for all time and now lived beneath the earth and were plotting how to get the planet back from humans, who they felt were warlike and evil. They were even, according to the author, abducting some of us and replacing us with their own kind.

What a lovely thing, I thought to myself. *I want to be abducted. I hate being alive; it's so terrible and no one cares about me.*

That night I let sleep take my exhausted body, and I dreamed. I felt hot tears sliding down my face. I knew I wasn't wanted; I knew there was worse pain to come. I realised I didn't much like living.

Whoever you are, please abduct me and let me die. I want to die. Take me. Go on, take me and replace me. I'm all yours.

Two

My Father, the Rapist

The wild cruel beast is not behind the bars of the cage. He is in front of it.

Axel Munthe

It was early August and there had been a sticky and relentless heatwave in Dublin.

'Chris, baby, are you already in bed? Daddy's coming up now.'

I often curled up cosily with my daddy in the comfortable, creaky, oak double bed that Ruth vacated during our visits. The front bedroom had a triple-panelled mirror that I loved to sing in front of with a hairbrush, pretending to be one of The Three Degrees.

A honey-coloured moon shone into the front bedroom, then the clouds moved past it, covering it with a mist of black velvet. A cool breeze blew in the open windows and with it a heady aroma of sweet william from Ruth's flowerbeds. My father's warm, whisky-smelling body in the bed was familiar.

All of a sudden: 'Just touch me. That's it, rub my cock a little, darlin'.' He grabbed my little hand and illustrated the milking motion. 'Wank me off, darlin'. Come on, Chris. Just do it.'

I was filled with horror – it was starting again. Years ago, when I was tinier, he had touched me down below. It had stopped and I was glad. I had put it out of my mind and told myself that everyone's fathers did the same. Now it was beginning again. This time I felt as if I was the one doing wrong. Guilt ran through me.

I'm bad, I thought to myself.

'That's good, so it is, Chris.' He lay back satiated.

In for the Kill

He turned over, pulled the pink blanket over his large, ginger-freckled shoulder and fell straight asleep. I lay beside him with the silvery moonlight streaming through the window, my eyes locked on the ceiling and the weight of the world atop my shoulders. I felt I had done something terribly ugly and it brought up memories of earlier times, other incidents that I had buried but which now seemed to gather like storm clouds.

A figure came into my head, scarier than any memory I had stored up. Georgie! Georgie hated me. She would kill me after this. The thought of suicide went around in my head grimly until I heard the birds twittering playfully and let sleep overtake me.

The next day the warm morning sun shone through the streaky windows, lighting up the dusty mantelpiece and grubby patterned linoleum and sending sparkling white shafts of sunlight fingering their way along the brown peeling wallpaper on the bedroom wall. I sat up and looked around at the sun-filled air. Liam had already risen early.

I got out of bed, pulled a blue cotton sundress over my head and padded downstairs. It looked quiet and silent. Nanna sat by the unlit fire, pale-faced and unsmiling. I stared at her, then tried to imagine what it was like to be blind by shutting my eyes and walking around the front room, stumbling over everything then giggling. *She'll be dead soon*, I thought with the heartlessness of a child, as I bounced my tiny red ball hard against the fireplace.

It was a lazy, late-summer Sunday morning and the house was cool and quiet. A bee thudded against the sun-drenched dusty window and buzzed in frustrated zigzags. We were going to Mass in the next hour or so and I was dreading it: the service was hollow and boring. I bounced the ball against the wall again and felt resentful about having to go to church.

Out of the window I could see the centre of the Victorian terraces and the patchy green that the locals called the 'plantation', full of prickly green gorse bushes and weeds, and surrounded by iron railings. That morning it was discovered that some of the local boys had burned some newborn black and white kittens in a cardboard box in the middle of the plantation. The neighbours were all shocked and upset after hearing about the discovery of the bodies.

'Cleary did it, I'm sure of it, the evil bastard,' Aunt Ruth announced over breakfast after Mass in a voice that dripped loathing. 'He's evil through and through. But Jesus will punish him.'

'I'm sure Val didn't do anything so horrible, Auntie Ruth.'

My Father, the Rapist

'Chris, you would stick up for evil. It'll be because you're illegitimate.' She pursed her lips and looked me up and down as she slapped down a plate of fried food in front of me. I stared without enthusiasm at the runny fried egg with its bright yellow yolk that ran over the black and white pudding. I realised then that Ruth did not love me and that made me want not to eat. The thought of her loathing darkened something inside my mind. They thought I was evil both in England and Ireland now; there was no escape. I clasped my new identity – evil! I cut into the egg on my plate; it tasted like plastic. *I am evil.*

Ruth spoke. 'Vera Cleary has just put out all her dirty bed sheets on the line. It's a wonder the lazy slut is bothered. There they are all grey and torn – how shameless is that?'

Liam nodded his head at her in a puppy-like way. 'Aye, no morals. Fucking dirt.'

I felt overwhelmed by something as I stood up, wiped my mouth on a serviette and ran off upstairs. It was still morning and the sun's warmth was not yet strong enough to heat up the salty Dublin air. From the bedroom window I could see Val and some others spinning around a girl with carrot-coloured hair. I tried frantically to push up the window but it was old and firmly stuck. The clatter of my attempt alerted Val and the others.

'I've a real girlfriend here – Irish, like me – you're an English snob!'

I could just make out his voice faintly through the glass. I backed away from the window. Somehow Val must know that my father makes me milk his willy and that's why he's stopped loving me.

I want to die – I so, so want to be dead. I want the higher beings to take me over like in Ruth's book.

I lay on the bed and tried again to offer myself up to the higher beings. I lay whispering to them until I heard Ruth calling me to come downstairs for Sunday dinner. I was so hungry, having had no breakfast, that I tucked into the roast beef and Yorkshire pudding covered in beef-dripping gravy and a pile of cabbage. Conversation was non-existent over lunch, and I was glad of it. They always slagged everyone off, and it made me feel afraid.

At four o'clock, our family dressed up and left the house for their monthly visit to see Uncle Edward in his psychiatric hospital in the country. Liam pushed his blind mother in a wheelchair. The large chair would not fit on the pavement, so he pushed it along the busy main road. Cars honked mercilessly as we slowed down the traffic. Liam's face was red with tears.

'Shut up, losers! My mother's fucking blind,' Liam shouted at the cars.

'Daddy, why don't you push her on the pavement? The cars won't beep then,' I offered.

'It's too fucking thin for the chair, you stupid little cunt!' he yelled, glaring at me coldly. 'Shut that smartarse mouth of yours and walk faster. WALK FASTER!'

Dublin in the '70s was rife with IRA activity. The walls were daubed with signs: 'UP THE PROVOS'. I found it curious.

'What's PROVOS, Daddy?'

'You're making me fucking sick.' He leaned over and punched me hard in the side of my head. The world went darker and I wept quietly.

It was an impoverished Dublin street that we walked. It stank from the Guinness factory, the Liffey and too many pubs. Uncle Edward had been committed to the psychiatric hospital as a child after he had wrapped himself in his bed sheets and set fire to them, then jumped out the bedroom window. He had been ten years old when he was committed and now he was forty. To me, he looked exactly like my father.

St Brendan's was a crumbling Gothic monstrosity just outside Dublin, set in acres of landscaped garden and surrounded by a high, yellow-brick wall with barbed wire on the top. Entering the grounds via a large blue gate, I saw facing us a large sign in black on a white board: 'Trespassers Will Be Prosecuted'.

The sandstone building was like a medieval castle, its long, thin corridors were icy cold, winding and mysterious. We sat in a large room filled with chairs and tables and relatives visiting the other inmates in the asylum. It stank of hopelessness and medication.

'Aren't you cold in here, Uncle Eddie? I'm freezing cold. It's practically icy.' I shivered visibly and smiled at Edward, who looked the twin of my father.

'It's cold all the time. We don't ever have any heating on, Chris. It's to save the government money.' He took a long, hard drag on his cigarette butt, watching me carefully with his shocked-looking eyes that were the same fairytale blue as my father's. Edward tapped his ash into an open Coke can he had been sipping from. I looked at his pale bare arms. He had a barbed-wire scar running down one arm from another childhood suicide attempt. I felt filled with an all-consuming love for him, poor man, and longed to take care of him.

He looked at me carefully.

'How are you keeping, Chris? You've grown so big since I last saw you. It must be nearly a year or so since you big shots deigned to come over from London.'

'Yes, nearly a year, Uncle Eddie.' My father hadn't bothered to come and see him the last few times that we had been over.

A blue haze of smoke formed between us and we stared at each other.

'It's awful about the cold, Uncle Eddie.' I turned to my father. 'Daddy, it's awful, isn't it?' I put my cardigan around Uncle Edward's shoulders.

'Shut up, cunt!' Liam snarled out of the corner of his mouth.

I stood up and paced off along the corridors to escape the threat of his hard, heavy fists. The corridors smelt of school dinners and disinfectant. Each corridor seemed to get thinner and thinner, and I suddenly felt afraid, as though caught in a maze.

Through a crack in a door I spied a man sitting on a bed. I stopped and peered at him in silence. He was a good-looking, dark-haired young guy, dressed in blue striped pyjamas, but I could tell from the movement of his shoulders that he was sobbing. My stomach flipped in excitement to see someone emoting; it just wasn't done in our house. I stepped backwards then turned and jumped with fright as a tall figure in a white coat put a hand on my shoulder. I had wandered a long way from the visitors' room into the lock-up corridors of the men who were criminally insane. Doors that had been left open were locked by the doctor as he walked me back.

Back in the visitors' room, Liam and Edward were hugging each other. Their mother sat in her wheelchair, seemingly oblivious to their presence, wrapped up in her own diminished world. I watched cool-eyed as Edward sobbed like a baby, like the man in the lock-up ward, while my father remained stiff and silent.

Monday was a cloudy bank holiday. Outside in the street, children were shouting and dogs were barking. I stayed in with my father watching television, as the dogs in the plantation were vicious.

In for the Kill

Val Cleary was out in the street; I could hear him. With his too-big clothes and dirty face, despite his rejection he still fascinated me. He was so very different from my own brother Nicky, who hated getting dirty and showed no interest in climbing trees.

Through the window I could see Val was riding too fast on his bike. He flew off the muddy hill in the late afternoon's weak sunlight and landed with a crash on the pavement, getting a bloody knee which he wiped with his dirty T-shirt. I stared admiringly out of the window at Val, then sat with my father and watched *It's a Wonderful Life*, the afternoon matinee. I knew not to make a noise, as it would upset Daddy. He was watching the TV – rapt – in a wingback armchair pulled too close to the set. It was hot in the terrace. I wandered in and out of the front parlour and counted the pink plastic geraniums then played jump on the stairs.

I came back into the living room and watched my father. He was wearing a clean white vest yet still had some rough blond stubble. He held a cigarette in his right hand and tapped it into a nearby ashtray. He laughed now and again and seemed excited.

He is content here in this house with his blind mother near, in a way he never is in England. Laughter echoed from outside. *I remember last night.* Memories of sex came in flashbacks. *I do not want sex; it revolts me.* I looked sideways at him. *How nice it would be if he were to die in pain. Maybe some rat poison or a nasty car accident. Val might want me then, if he knew that my father was dead.*

Daddy suddenly turned to me and caught my look of hate. I knew then that he knew what I was remembering. He turned away, half amused, and resumed watching the screen.

I turned and took a long last look out of the window, through which I could hear the Clearys playing. I could smell the sharp scent of lavender from the bush as it pushed up against the polished pane. I watched Val as he shinned up the side of the muddy plantation. Inside was the smell of another of Ruth's fry-ups.

Suddenly Val looked towards the window and his lovely, intense grey eyes locked onto mine. I could barely breathe. In the flicker of a second I felt the taste of hope – of a saviour. I looked at Daddy, turned back and Val Cleary had vanished into the rough scrub of the plantation. It was six o'clock and nearly time for supper. Soon nightfall would come and then the dark.

Upstairs, dressed in my white lace nightie, I lay down on the

My Father, the Rapist

floor of the bedroom and thought about the man in the asylum. I prayed again – this time more desperately – to the aliens. It didn't matter to me who they were. After all, I would be gone someplace where there were no penises.

Use my body, take my body. If there is anything out there, take over my body and do with it what you will, even if I end up in the insane asylum.

In my dream they came – transparent reptiles with clear yellow eyes. I woke up with a start when I heard my father's foot on the stairs.

Three
Return to the Orphanage

For frequent tears have run
The colours from my life.

E.B. Browning

Iwas 13 years of age. I was excited by boys and yearned to wear make-up. My father seemed to have grown afraid of me and the tiny breasts that perked out of my hammock-like pink junior bra.

That early December day I was wrapped in my yellow quilted coat, wearing my worn-out ballet pumps, shivering and staring up at my father. He had driven me to the local children's home a few streets away, the one he'd taken me to every Christmas, to give away some of my old toys. This time it was me who was to be given away.

Daddy took a deep breath and went on in a matter-of-fact way.

'You see,' he said to the administrator, 'we know it's nearly Christmas and it's probably the wrong time to hand her back, but we don't want to ruin our marriage. I wish I'd never heard of the Crusade of Rescue, but Georgie was upset when she couldn't have her own babies.'

Matters had come to a head one day when I tried on some scarlet lipstick, drawing it messily onto my childish lips. When Georgie saw me, she attacked me with a sponge, clawing at my face and telling me that I was a whore just like my real mother. The physical violence wasn't a new thing, but this time, when I ran to my friend's home in fear, she refused to have me back in the house.

As I now listened to Liam's excuses for handing me back, I

25

could no longer contain the anguish I was feeling and heard myself groan, 'Oh, no, no. No. No.'

He turned and looked straight into my eyes. 'I even offered to leave home myself, but Mummy forbade it.'

I gazed up into the blue eyes of this man that I so profoundly adored, the face that was my whole world, and pleaded, 'Oh Daddy, my Daddy – please don't leave me here, please.'

He looked back at me impassively.

'Mummy wanted this, not me. You know it's not me, don't you? I'm not guilty; Mummy's the bad one! We've talked it over with a priest and the best thing is for you to come into care to please your mother and keep the peace at home.'

Peace! I was too scared to even open my mouth.

My father closed the door behind him with a final betraying click.

I'm alone, I thought to myself in anguish and terror. I was going to become one of the sad kids dressed in second-hand clothes that I had always felt sorry for. I was no longer the smug orphan who had found a home, I was back down a snake and would be forced to smile at strangers as they came to pity me and hand in their old toys.

Four

Letters to a Vampire

I have suffered too much in this world not to hope for another.

Jean-Jacques Rousseau

A year had passed. I had turned 14 and been moved to a home for older children, Greengage House. A series of plummy-voiced university students had come to do their placements at the home, and since the latest of these had arrived, James Stratford-Barrett, life seemed bloated with possibility.

James was apparently busy writing a thesis titled 'Behaviour in Young Adolescents Undergoing Parental Separation' for his sociology degree. He was a good-looking young man with silky dark hair, navy-blue eyes and fine bone structure that made him look refined. James had taken a particular interest in me and we had grown close, probably closer than was appropriate, given the difference in our ages and his position of responsibility in the home. But I lapped up the attention. He would recommend books for me to read, like Sartre and Tolstoy, and in this way continued some form of education that I'd otherwise pretty much abandoned, despite the early promise that I'd shown at grammar school.

In the summer months, we spent a lot of time in the garden, reading poetry underneath the trees. One day, James took me off to Cookham Wood in his car. He had already taken me to pubs in the countryside and given me my first taste of lager. I was young, nearly 15, and excited about the future.

We went on to Shere to see his childhood home, Coverdale. We drove in his beaten-up blue Spider under tight archways of trees that were so hard to drive two cars through that we had to wait for the others to pass. Coverdale was a crumbling mansion with two grey stone dogs standing outside and iron gates barring intruders from the long private drive. It had a long yellow-marble hallway and a garden laden with black tulips. I adored the purple black of the Queen of the Night that stood tall, in full bloom. Velvety white butterflies and large Red Admirals flitted around the stems. We made love in his father's bed and I hated every minute of it, as it brought back the horror of my father.

He left Greengage House not long after this, to head back to Oxford. I watched broken-hearted from the upstairs corridor window as he drove off. He rang me later to say that he hated goodbyes, but the pain of him leaving led me to a suicide attempt: an overdose of paracetamol followed by having my stomach pumped. It was a cry for help but in the orphanage there was no answering call and no caring adults.

After this, my adoptive parents were approached to see if they might take me back. I had stayed in intermittent contact with the Harts since my return to care and my mother sent me my *Jackie* comic every fortnight. It made me wonder if she felt guilty about what had happened between us.

The staff in the orphanage thought I would benefit from the stability of family life, and so I went back for a few weekends as a trial run. Everyone seemed to think that it was working out, and so one day I found myself sitting with my suitcase at my feet by the gate, waiting for Liam Hart to collect me for good.

Liam drew up in his Bentley. I felt need for my abandoning father slip into my heart and squeeze it. I opened the car door and climbed in. He threw my case onto the back seat, then got back in, lit a cigarette and leaned over me to fasten my seat belt.

I looked out of the car window and waved goodbye to the other kids. It hurt like hell to leave the only place I had known as home for the past couple of years of my life.

'You have no idea how I'm feeling, Chris. I'm so happy. Mummy's a bit off with me about it all, but she'll come round. We'll just stay out of her way in the house and it'll all be OK.'

He grinned at me. 'Kiss?'

I felt weak and nauseous as he came near to me. He smelt of amber and musk.

'No.'

'Oh, come on, please! I'm wearing the Brut aftershave you like.'

of salad for her and Liam. My mouth watered hungrily at the sight and smell of the perfectly browned potatoes and their crispy skins. Georgie turned and could see that I was hungry, but she looked at me coolly. 'I haven't done anything for you. You'll do your own. Have it in your room by yourself.'

I went back upstairs; it was exhausting having to continually defend myself against her hatred. I grew so tired of it that I began to identify with her and believe that I deserved to be disliked and had a blackened soul. But I also needed psychic protection from her colossal hatred of me. Ah. I know! The vampire!

I lay on my single bed, tore out a page of lined paper and began to write another letter to what the book called an other-worldly demon. I wrote in hate for my adoptive mother and my birth mother. I fantasised that he could swoop down and destroy them with the supernatural killing powers the book said he possessed.

> *Dear Ian Brady,*
> *I have written to you before from my kids' home, hoping you may be my real father. I don't know if they let you read my letters. My name is Chris. It's not my real name. I was called Lucy at the start. But I don't really have a name. I read in the book about you that you did not have a name either and your mother left you on the street, where you were picked up by another family. I bet they were horrible – adopted families always are. I think being adopted is a terrible thing.*
> *Who do you pray to for protection against people who don't like you?*
> *Please write back to me, if this letter ever reaches you.*
> *Chris*

Although once again I received no response, I continued to write to Brady regularly after that, telling the vampire what I was doing that day. I began to enjoy my new hobby. It was like keeping a diary, but there was a real-life serial killer on the receiving end of my needy childish scrawl. I desperately needed to be rescued from my pious Catholic torture chamber with its copious prints of Jesus and the Pope; Brady, according to *Beyond Belief*, was superhuman enough to be able to do it.

Five
Cinderella

I don't know. It looks like some kind of glass shoe . . .

Prince Charming

Being back at 'home' with the Harts was a form of hell. I fell into a deep depression and my mother seemed much happier around this very cowed version of me. I was scared to express myself in any way, even adopting the dowdy clothes I knew she preferred, as I was terrified of upsetting her and being thrown out onto the streets. The lost princess had died, and in her place was a numb robot who pleased Mother, while I watched from a glass coffin.

The Harts had wanted a daughter like them: someone who wasn't very bright or dominant, someone who laughed at banal game shows and was enthusiastic about life.

In order to survive, I became her. I lost myself. I got a dull job in an accountant's office, and life started to take on the quality of a grey nightmare. I felt suicidal each day, and a heavy grey dust seemed to settle over everything.

One day, however, I put on a tiny bit of make-up, which was forbidden, and my mother attacked me badly again and threw me out into the street in the cold dark night. She seemed to hate any hint of my budding sexuality; it enraged her. I ran in terror back to Greengage House, and a worker arranged for me to stay in a nearby bed and breakfast. I was 19, and I felt completely lost in life. I felt like a ghost who would at any moment float away. I needed someone to tell me who I was.

The next day, I stood in the callbox, shivering in a thin cotton

33

dress. I took ten pence out of my red ladybird purse. I only had a pound left, and I had changed it into loose coins in the sweetshop. I picked up the receiver and dialled the number slowly. A voice at the other end said, 'Who's that?'

'It's Christine Hart. I'm a friend of James.'

'He's not here. He lives in my flat in Belgravia, but he'll be back down for the weekend.'

I assumed it was his father. I gave the number of the hostel, mentioned Greengage House and then hung up.

Two weeks after that call, James drew up with a skid in front of the paint-peeling hostel like a white knight in a chocolate Corniche that crunched noisily in the gravel. I was lying on the bed, sweating in the early afternoon heat.

I stared at James as he stood in the doorway. It was four years since I'd seen him and around his eyes I saw the marks of age. In his expensive-looking grey trousers and smart cotton shirt, with his hair slicked back, he made my stomach flip.

'Chris, I was so pleased when you rang my father, but he didn't take down your number, so I had to find out where you were from one of the kids at Greengage. Why the hell didn't you ever look for me before?'

I felt like crying. He was my only hope and he was saying he cared. I felt like a character in a Dickens novel.

He sat down and lit a cigarette. I barely let him speak as I was so desperate to blurt out my news. 'I bought some Miners frosty green eye shadow and some lipstick; it was only cheap, pearly pink stuff. Mum caught me with it on and dragged me screaming into the street, calling me an evil little home-wrecker. She made me leave after she took me up to my room to pack my stuff, and I cried, James. I packed my Beatles records in between my clothes to make sure they didn't break.'

James tried to comfort me, but I got up from his embrace and started to brush my tangled blonde hair.

'She scrubbed my face so hard it bled,' I said in a flat voice as he opened the window to let fresh air into the room. 'I'm so alone in the world, James.'

'I've had this idea for you, Chris,' he said, brushing the furry dust from the windows with the tips of his fingers and then dusting them on the front of his trousers.

'What do you mean? Marriage?' I went over and wound my arms around his neck. It sounds so childish of me to think he'd propose to me, but it was a fantasy of mine and fantasies were about all I had left.

He laughed aloud and clasped his arms tightly around my waist.

'No, something far more exciting than marriage. It's something that most people dream of in life. I'm hoping to train you into a career that will stand you in good stead for the rest of your life.'

James watched me as I went into the kitchen and poured us both tea from a red-spotted teapot into cracked red cups. I spread six chocolate digestives onto a plate. He leaned against the kitchen sink, cup in hand with biscuit stuck to his front tooth, and watched me.

'You won't understand this yet, but I'm involved in special duties for the government.'

'Oh,' I said, wondering what had happened to his sociology degree.

He looked out of the window and paused as I admired his handsome profile.

'What sort of things are you doing, then?'

'I'll tell you more about it sometime, but would you be interested in helping me?'

'Yes, I'd enjoy helping you.'

'I knew you would.'

I took a sip of hot, sugary tea from the chipped red mug and watched him warily over the rim. I was thrilled to see him again, but I hadn't forgotten how quickly he'd dropped me after leaving Greengage House, and I wasn't entirely convinced he'd always had my best interests at heart.

He pulled out another cigarette. 'I'll set you up, Chris.'

James barely smoked unless he was stressed. My eyes wandered over his fine bone structure and his blue eyes. I bit into the rest of the chocolate biscuit.

'It's exciting stuff, Chris – deniable operations.'

'I don't understand what you mean.'

'Well, you've no alternative. What's it now for you? A hostel for the rest of your life? Or your humdrum job as an accounts clerk? You'll never find a profession without qualifications, and it'd be a shame, as you're a very smart girl.'

I nodded my head. James was right – I was on a fast train to nowhere.

An hour later, after I'd had a hot shower, James headed for

London, driving us too fast, brushing hawthorn bushes on the hot, sticky, summer afternoon. I had all my worldly goods on the back seat in a black bin liner.

'Where are we going?'

He looked elated as he grinned at me. 'Let's go get *clothes*!'

I looked at him in shock. 'Clothes for me?'

'Not just any clothes – the *fanciest* clothes. The *designer* clothes the actresses and models wear. We're going to Sloane Street and we're going to spend, spend, spend, and by the end of it you'll look so hot you'll turn every head on the King's Road!'

I felt a bubble of excitement rise in my gut.

'Why? What for? Is this *your* money, James?'

He winked at me and pulled out a gold Amex card from his breast pocket.

'Company card. As I said, I'm the man with a plan.'

We passed the green canopies of Harrods and parked in leafy Lowndes Square. In warm and drowsy Knightsbridge, we walked up and down Sloane Street. I felt light as a feather. The shops had marble pillars and frontages, with big windows and doorways guarded by fierce bouncers wearing smart dark suits. I looked with awe at a large, fake silver fox-fur coat that hung in one of the windows.

'Gosh, look at that. Very Bette Davis, isn't it?'

'Would you like it?' he muttered, half to himself.

'Course I'd like it, dafty! I'd think I'd died and floated to heaven on a cloud in a coat like that. Any girl would kill for it.'

James smiled at me and left me outside with my nose pressed against the glass, eating a croissant out of a crinkly white paper bag from the bakers in Harvey Nichols.

A few minutes later he emerged with a large box tied up in purple ribbon. I opened it in the sunlit street. Inside lay the stunning grey fur coat. I buried my delighted face in the soft, kitten-like fur.

'Oh, thank you, James. Oh, my God! Look at it – it's out of this world! I look like Bette!'

In Prada, I tried on a jade silk evening dress. I twirled in front of James and smiled shyly, the silk slipping off my shoulder provocatively. He turned away, smiling.

In the heavily scented cubicle of the next boutique, I tried on evening dresses in red silk with deep-cut cleavages. I slipped on glossy killer heels and silky sandals with jewels sewn into them.

Cinderella

Shop assistants moved around, helpfully advising as I tried on high-heeled shoe after high-heeled shoe.

I fingered the cold sparkling red stones sewn into scarlet silk sandals with a six-inch heel. 'Can I really have these ruby shoes? The price tag says 600 quid!' I asked, poking my head around the velvet curtain in the changing room.

'You can have the lot,' James said, smiling at the shop assistant and passing her his Gold American Express card. 'Box the red dress and the tops and all of the shoes, especially that *Wizard of Oz* pair with the rubies on the front.'

I watched him. So! He had come back to save me after all. I knew then that I would do anything for him as a reward for such heroism. I felt sick with love for him.

Later, as a glowing sun set red and low in the sky, the chocolate-coloured Corniche took us to James's father's Eaton Square apartment. It was a part of London replete with white stucco-fronted houses.

I showered in the cavernous bathroom with its roll-top bath. James had picked out a new dress from the bags, to match the new red shoes.

'Where are we off to, James?' I asked as I emerged from the elegant bathroom in the new Katharine Hamnett dress.

'An exclusive country hotel. You'll love it. I'm going to bring you into a world of smokescreens and mirrors.'

I wondered what he was up to as I settled back into the front seat of the Corniche I glanced at myself in the wing mirror; life had taken on a scary air of unreality.

Chanel Cristalle wafted from me as we rolled through country lanes. *La Bohème* played loudly on the car stereo. The luxurious smell of the leather seats of the Corniche made me feel special. The sky-high red sandals matched the low-backed sequinned dress; my legs looked tanned and polished poking out of the slit. I felt proud of my tight body and feminine curves.

As we entered the drive to the magnificent seventeenth-century house built on the Thames by the Duke of Buckingham, James leaned down and kissed my shoulder. I imagined us both in the outdoor pool, swimming up and down, sipping Pol Roger at the edge.

Black-suited butlers greeted our car in the drive that was lit by large golden cones of fire. We were ushered into Clivedon's Great Hall, with its magnificent fireplace. There were silver suits of armour and tapestries hanging on high-ceilinged walls beside a great winding dark oak staircase. It was a world I had never dreamed of entering.

An elegant grey-haired man in a beige suit stepped forward out of the shadows and James introduced him as his father, Julian Stratford-Barrett. I knew I was entering a world of money, and I felt anxious and uncomfortable.

I sipped an icy champagne aperitif over the dining table and eyed Julian. He had a plummy voice and an impressive bearing, grey hair and green eyes that bulged like those of a frog. Julian wasn't as good looking as his son, but he made me feel very at ease.

After small talk, he finally got to the point during the main course.

'James has brought you here so I can have a look at you,' he said as he sliced into his fillet steak and it oozed blood.

I stopped eating and dabbed at my face with my napkin. *What is this guy talking about?* I thought.

'I used to be in the Intelligence Corps.'

Something about his tone worried me. and I started to think that James had nothing good planned for me, that the clothes had been an attempt to sweeten me up.

James spoke up. 'Look, Chris, after he left the army, my father used to work in Whitehall for MI6.'

'MI6? And is he still with them?'

'That's his business, Chris, but he also has his own outside outfit. It's top-secret work, and I can't tell you much about it. It's what's known as black-bag stuff. It's operations in, say, Sudan and other trouble hotspots that the government can't touch for obvious reasons.'

'Dirty work?'

He smiled. 'No, not dirty – the most interesting work and the most dangerous, but we get paid a hell of a lot of money. Some people call us MI6's commercial arm.'

'I'm not sure I get it, James.'

'Don't worry about that; focus on what we can do for you. You'll come to like money, Chris; it's a real power base.'

Julian, who was staring at me, spoke next. 'We have offices all over the world and people who investigate things – like the IRA.'

'Doesn't the government do that?'

'The government is tied by rules and regulations, so we do all the exciting stuff for them.'

Cinderella

James spoke. 'If you're interested, we could train you up to work for us – sound exciting? We would set you up, my darling, in a smart little Mayfair flat. That's if you're interested. There will be lots more clothes, of course, and flashy holidays on private islands in the Caribbean with me.'

Did I have a better option?

'I've no other offers, so, yes, I guess.' I gazed at them both. It seemed like I was in a fairytale for real, only not Rapunzel but Cinderella. James flipped back his dark silky hair and licked his teeth.

'Next week you can go along to the offices and let the boys interview you. Rob'll love you, but let him think it's his idea to take you on. He's stuck an ad in the *The Times* for a graduate, but the job's yours.'

'OK.'

After dinner we sat in the large drawing room and sipped brandy in front of the fire, then James booked me into a wood-panelled suite in the main house.

'Live here until I can find a suitable flat for you, Chris.' He looked around the old-fashioned suite approvingly.

'I'm so, so grateful, James.'

'I promise you, darling, that with me by your side you'll fly.'

He leaned me back on the bed and covered my mouth with his. After he kissed me, he got up and left.

I lay on the bed, thinking. Then went over to the fur coat he had bought for me and wore it naked as I sprawled across the giant bed and looked at my reflection in the gilt mirror opposite.

I looked around the suite. There was a four-poster bed, dark-wood furniture and a marble bathroom. A trunk of designer outfits and La Perla nightwear had been left by the four-poster bed, replacing the black bin liner I'd previously used to transport all my possessions. In the beautiful brown leather trunk with distinctive gold lettering there were suede Jimmy Choo boots in a deep plum, with a high stiletto heel. There were handbags: a large Gucci black day bag and a green velvet shoulder bag, both smelling strongly of leather. A black Chanel evening bag encrusted with stones glinted in the bottom, poorly hiding a pile of classy underwear in every imaginable colour: bras of scarlet silk, black thongs as light as a feather adorned with creamy antique lace, and suspender belts in jade silk.

I looked at them all. Did he want me to make love to men to get information? It was clear that he had recruited me for my looks and my lack of ties. He would be disappointed if he did. I would never let any man use me as my father had when I was a little girl.

I called room service on the ivory phone. The butler brought a tray bearing a bottle of thirty-year-old Cognac, some Bendick's mints and some dark chocolate.

I turned on the gold taps and drew myself a bath. I glugged back a brandy and then sank back, relaxed underneath the scented bubbles. *I'm entering a world of polo, yachts, apartments in Cap Ferrat and the French Riviera.* It appealed to the powerless abused orphan that I remembered myself to have been before tonight.

I got out and lit a cigarette, standing naked in front of the floor-length mirror, dripping bath water. I admired my body – I was a knockout. I saw a confident look in my eyes that I barely recognised. I was on my way up and nobody was going to stand in my way.

Six

The Spy Game

I can assure you my intentions are strictly honourable.

James Bond to Honey Ryder, *Dr No*

James set me up in a very smart flat in Shepherd's Market near to their offices. I painted it dark red and put up some prints of nudes to put my stamp on it. I jogged to the office every day in a smart navy tracksuit. The Stratford-Barrett Ltd Company organised investigative and surveillance operations both in Britain and abroad. In other words, they were spies. Overseas, they hired former army intelligence men to work on security operations, helping the owners of goldfields, diamond mines and oil refineries fight terrorism and piracy. Their contracts included work in sensitive zones such as Sudan, Albania, Angola and South Africa. Most of the staff were ex-intelligence or former cops, and I enjoyed mixing with them.

My first week's training took place at the national shooting centre at Bisley. On early winter mornings, we lay in the snow and fired rifles into targets about 500 yards away. Karate was also a discipline I had to learn and excelled at.

I was taken out and asked to obtain names and details from strangers. I was taught how to carry out surveillance on foot, in a car and in a group, and how to do counter-surveillance to see if anyone was tailing me. I was taught how to get information out of someone's head and how to turn someone into an asset to garner information for me. I was taught how to go undercover for long periods of time and how to adopt another identity. I particularly enjoyed undercover operations, as I liked escaping from myself and pretending to be someone else.

One of my teachers, an old guy called Adrian, told me he had been in an elite ex-military club called the 'Feathermen'. A film was later made on the Feathermen called *Killer Elite*. Adrian told me that it was all true.

My first job was planting listening devices in trading offices at midnight; we had to break in to do it. I liked the work as it was challenging, and it probably suited me as I had no idea who I was. You had to be a ghost – an inquisitive ghost who finds things out but leaves no trace. I felt that I had left no trace throughout my life so far.

Sometimes I played the wife or girlfriend of the guys on undercover ops, but soon moved on to solo missions, as it was discovered that I had a huge talent for undercover work and getting people to open up to me. Most of the time we were checking what other people were up to – usually high-level people. I would set up a scenario where I would meet them and get them to reveal the information we were looking for. I was good at looking at them or reading a file on them, then figuring out how to play the situation. I would look at someone and get a feel for them. I would know how a person would react to me, and this helped me a lot. If I was in a group of people, I would be able to work out who was the weak link. When I later came to work with terrorists, I would be able to spot undercover operatives from other agencies. My bosses used to say I was amazing, and so I came to trust in my unique espionage abilities.

But throughout this time that I was building up my career I had my own dirty secret. I had continued to write to Ian Brady and even travelled to the house where he and Myra Hindley had lived and carried out two of their terrible murders. I wanted to find out whether he was pure evil, to uncover what went on in such a twisted mind. I felt that if I went to the house I could somehow figure it all out, and I was also convinced that if I took photos of the outside of the house then I could lure Brady into speaking to me. Part of me now wonders whether this drive came from a need to understand the abuse I had suffered at the hands of my adoptive father, but I also feel that deep down there were more profound motives at work. I wanted to find true evil, examine it and find out what it actually was. Was I evil like my parents had taught me I was? Or were my parents evil disguised as respectable and good?

The Spy Game

The local people that I met were very helpful. They told me that kids crept into the house at night and had reported terrifying presences. I looked up at 16 Wardle Brook Avenue from the safety of the local pub The New Inn opposite. It seemed to seep with menace. I knew I was on the right track. It was like the house in *The Amityville Horror*.

For years, there had been no response to my letters, but then one day, out of the blue, an official-looking brown envelope landed on my mat. It was from Brady. His interest had apparently been piqued by the photos that I had sent him, and he said they had brought back many memories, some good and some bad. While he didn't usually enter into correspondence with people who wrote to him, something about me interested him.

From then on we corresponded regularly, and a shoebox containing his letters quickly filled up under my bed. Friends and boyfriends tried to dissuade me from continuing this contact, but I had nothing to intellectually chew on in my life and Brady was a mystery I felt that I could solve.

But I was naive to think that I could enter into any kind of relationship with a criminal as notorious as the Moors Murderer without attracting attention, and after I visited Brady in prison a headline appeared in a national newspaper: 'Mystery Girl Visits Brady'.

My secret was out, and I was like a rabbit to the hounds of the tabloid press. The *Sunday People* said I was his long-lost daughter. Brady had said he remembered sleeping with my mother, Olivia, in a letter to the newspaper, which they then published.

James told me it was untenable for me to continue in my job now that my face was all over the papers, and I ran away to America to get away from the press who were hounding me night and day.

I went to live in New York for a few years but didn't do very well; I was working in a bar as a cocktail waitress along 52nd Street and living in digs in Queens. I came back to the UK where I drifted and tried to do some freelance writing for newspapers, but I also resurrected the connection with Brady.

The truth was that I enjoyed digging about in Brady's mind. His letters were full of discourse on literature and political writing. He wrote about Jules Verne and Edgar Allan Poe, Shelley and Sylvia Plath, Flaubert and Rimbaud. I didn't get this kind of intellectual stimulation from my friends or boyfriends. Brady also let me feel a sense of superiority. For all my self-loathing, despite the shame I felt about my father's abuse, I had found someone who was much worse than me. With other people I felt worthless and inferior, but with Brady, he was the beast – the lowest of the low.

Now he wrote asking me to visit him again. He told me that his visits were unsupervised and that he was allowed time alone with visitors. I found it extraordinary that the asylum would agree to his having hours alone with a beautiful young blonde – after all, he was Britain's worst serial killer – but I had no reason to doubt what he was saying. He seemed to like to try to frighten me, enquiring whether I was worried he might bite me when alone with him.

Bite? I knew he wouldn't bite me.

I wrote back immediately, agreeing to meet him. I would visit the monster and feel superior to it.

Seven

Beauty and the Beast

Were you in love with her, Beast? Did you honestly think she'd want you?

Gaston, *Beauty and the Beast*

How could I ever forget my very last visit to see the Moors Murderer, Ian Brady? As I approached the heavy, navy, wrought-iron gate of Ashworth Hospital on that gloomy, cold day in the winter of 1995, I shivered with fear and anticipation. It was so foolish to be there but I felt as if I was just about to solve the mystery of evil. Although I had screwed up my education, and with it my dreams of becoming a psychiatrist, I felt as though I could somehow cheat and make something of my life as a writer, if only I tried hard enough. I thought of myself as some kind of intrepid investigator and evil was the specialist subject that I would one day write a book on.

Once inside, I was taken to the main visiting room near the canteen.

'He's in there already,' announced a skinny blond nurse crisply as he walked out, shutting the door.

The room was dark, as the day was grey and the light was going at four o'clock. I had arrived late and the regular visiting appointment had already ended. I saw Brady immediately as I entered: a dark-haired figure in a black suit, his appearance far too smart for the white-walled surroundings. He looked like a solicitor waiting patiently for a mad client to come back from their medication time. As he had promised in his letter, it was just me and him.

In for the Kill

I sat down on an uncomfortable wooden armchair and said, 'Hello.'

'Make yourself at home, Chris.' Brady did not look up to meet my eyes. Dark glasses covered his own, so I could barely see them. I knew that he could still see me. This was his way.

It didn't strike me to be afraid, as he always looked so normal. I did however feel a burst of anxiety and wonder what we would talk about – how it would be. I wanted to get some top-secret information out of the visit – to walk away knowing all his undisclosed thoughts. From my readings of numerous psychiatric textbooks I had borrowed from the library, I naively saw myself as able to plumb the depths of his mind. I looked around the small, overheated room we were sitting in and tried to relax. This was a new league. Brady exuded an effortless air of dominance.

His armchair was positioned very near to mine. A coffee table was pushed to the side, so our knees would be nearly touching. The room had the feel of an intimate candlelit restaurant.

'I hope you don't mind it strong and sweet,' said Brady as he poured and fussed like a maiden aunt with the tea things. The navy flask had BRADY carved into the side of it.

'I don't.'

I stared at him in silence. He was 57 years old. We had been writing regularly since he was 47 and I was 19. The years of letters and previous visits made it feel as if I had known him for a lifetime. Sitting so close to him, I could smell his smell: Hai Karate aftershave and mint. I could also sense the intense aura of fury that lay beneath his surface charm. I was penetrating his layers – all the hard work I had put into burrowing close had been worth it.

'You're extraordinary,' said Brady, still not meeting my eyes.

'Am I? Why?'

The similarities between him and Liam were amazing. Both men were rapists who liked young girls, and both were very good looking, well-spoken and clever. Brady was a handsome man, angel-faced with innocent eyes, but then so was my father. I had to remind myself that this time I was in control. This wasn't a man I had to beg for somewhere to live. This was a man in a cage, dependent on me.

'Your intriguing spy job, the things you write, your need for adventure and the way you really think for yourself – it impresses me. I've kept all your letters,' said Brady.

I stared at the floor. It was like being reminded about a guilty secret by someone who knew you well. Only Brady knew about my perverse need to pick him apart and see what he was made of.

'I'm glad,' I lied.

He pulled off his glasses and his stare burned through me, letting me know he knew all my secrets. His eyes were such a watery-grey they appeared colourless and other-worldly. After what felt like several minutes of enduring his stare, he put the glasses on again.

I looked around the room and the intimate feel of the place dissipated as I focused on the bare white walls and institutional furniture. Brady looked shy all of a sudden, and I struggled to find a way to keep the conversation going. Then I remembered: he had read books. *I must talk about books, make him feel relaxed, then move in for the kill.*

'I read a novel once with a mass murderer in it called Brady. But it wasn't you.'

He tried to smile but it didn't reach his bright-red lips.

'Perhaps it was a psychic writer.' He was being sarcastic.

'It was some old book, don't remember who by.'

'Perhaps he invented me!'

'You think?' I fidgeted with the hem of my skirt.

'Aye, the audience always waits with baited breath for the villain of the piece to appear.'

'Perhaps they do, but doesn't it depend on which villain?' I fidgeted uncomfortably again.

While reading his letters, I had wondered whether his terrible crimes were the result of childhood sexual abuse. In her books about child maltreatment and abuse, psychologist Alice Miller talked about 'the crime that was committed years before, that had gone on in secret and had never been punished'. Miller believed that serial killers were acting out what had been done to them by their care-givers. Sitting there with Brady, that was the energy that I was picking up from him – that he had been struggling with something all of his life, a dark secret.

He was speaking. 'You came here to get something from me. There's always a motive, isn't there, with you, Chris? Not one of life's givers, are you?'

'I bought you some soap. I left it at the gate. I saw it in a shop on the way here. I thought, *Oh, he probably needs one of those and so I went in and bought one.*'

'Hmph.'

'Did I do wrong?'

'I don't need fucking soap. It itches. Don't use it. I bathe in plain warm water.'

'Sorry.'

'Forget it.'

'Did you buy me my smokes?'

'Oh God – no.'

He stared at me open mouthed, as if he didn't believe me. Then . . .

'It's OK.'

'I'm so sorry.'

I was back in control; I had deliberately forgotten.

'I want to write a book examining my need to dissect you like I'm searching for something. What is it I'm searching for? Is it evil itself, do you think? Perhaps it's to seek the tiny golden nugget of good inside my evil adoptive parents?' (I had told him about my life with Georgie and Liam in my letters.)

'Evil? If you like evil creeps, then there's plenty in here to chose from.'

'Really?'

'The staff.'

'Are they?'

'Aye.'

He let his mouth form into a wide grin. 'By the by, I'm getting out of here. I'm going on hunger strike. I intend to die. Quickly as possible is my aim.'

'Don't.'

'What's it got to do with you?' his voice was cool as ice. 'In what way are you connected to me?'

'No kind of a way.'

'I find your expression of pity suffocating. Your pity's wasted on me. I, myself, don't emote. Ever since I was first put in a cage, I switched off anything to do with feelings. I don't even watch films where I'm likely to emote.'

'You sent me a DVD of *King Kong* and told me you'd cried to it.'

He looked at me speechless for a minute – then . . .

'When I was fucking seven.'

'Oh, I'm sorry.'

He chuckled. 'You do amuse me, my little eagle.'

He leant over and reached out his pale, bony fingers and held onto my hand. He took off his glasses and looked deep into my eyes as he squeezed my fingers. I felt uncomfortable under so much scrutiny. He was holding my hand so tightly that my rings pinched into my fingers.

He then got out a cigarette for each of us and looked around for a way to light them. He stood up to peer through the tiny slat of a window into the hall to look for one of the staff, then said, 'Shit, they're lining up for medication. It must be late – I have to take my fucking medication. They give me enough to knock out a horse.'

As he went out of the door, he turned back and said, 'Hang on.'

I sat alone, half expecting him to return and say we had to wrap up, but when he returned he looked really dazed, as if he'd drunk a bottle of whisky all in one go.

'Do they give you bromide?' I asked. I don't know why I said this but I had heard that they gave bromide to male prisoners to stop them getting aroused. I suppose I wanted to dissect him. One way I knew to do that was to strip him down. I hadn't intended it as a flirtation but he seemed to take it that way.

'No, leave off. There'd be an outcry if they did that to us. I'll prove it to you if you like; I've no bromide in my system.'

'How? Oh. No. No thanks.'

'Oh, shame, from where I'm standing,' Brady laughed.

I tried to change the subject. 'The cops are asking you to go back up onto the Moors again, so it said yesterday in *The Independent*.'

'Aye, I read it in *The Guardian*, the only decent newspaper. You'll remember, when I went back last time, it was all over the news.'

He paused to pick up and light the cigarettes he'd abandoned before going to get his medication. 'We were searching!' he said as he lit them both and then handed one to me.

'You looked hard. The terrain had changed. You really, really tried,' I said as I smoked the cigarette he had lit for me. 'I know you're desperate to help – but . . .'

He leaned back in his chair. 'When they arrested me, word got to me that they'd found the Downey girl. I was in the cop cell and I thought, *Yeah, they've found her*. I was glad it was all over.'

I felt faint. Brady was talking about Lesley Anne Downey, whom he had raped and strangled. It was like being stuck in a scary dark fairytale, unable to get out. I didn't want to face what my father had done to me. How he had murdered the soul of the little girl that I once was. He was just like the man who sat in front of me and yet he had walked around free – a respected member of society – and so did many other fathers who had raped and murdered the souls of their daughters, daughters who lived on in an agony of self-hatred and fear, minus their womanhoods.

I raised my head. 'Were you upset that they found Lesley?'

'No.'

'No?' My head swam.

'This last time, I tried to help that know-it-all cop and his team. But I need another chance to go up there again. They wouldn't let me.'

He drew hard on his cigarette. 'I know I can find him.'

The room seemed to become smaller. I felt out of my depth and dizzy. Murder wasn't real; it was something that only happened in films and books. It wasn't real; children didn't suffer. I wanted to run. What was I doing here? Was I trying to find my missing inner child that my father had taken? *Yes, you can help them find Keith, but me, what about me? Who will find where my father buried me? Will you Ian?*

'It's time now, though. I don't want her to suffer any more!'

'Who?' I wiped my brow and swore softly to myself. Christ!

'The mother!'

'Bennett's mother?'

'Yes. Her. Yes. She wrote to me. I've still got her letters. Nice woman.'

'You've decided to help her?' I stubbed out my cigarette in the ashtray.

'Aye.'

He really was a weak, controlling piece of shit who seized power in any way he could, even over a mother who had lost her child. He could never give Keith back alive, and that was what his mother *really* wanted, not a tiny coffin.

He stood up and came and stood very near to me. It was so hot and airless in the room I felt as if my neck would drip with sweat.

'You don't own me. No one owns me,' said Brady.

Own you? I have long ago burrowed under your bars, Brady, you ice-man. At night when you go to sleep, I'm the last thing on your mind and the first thing as soon as you wake. My father wanted to fuck me and so do you.

Beauty and the Beast

I wanted to have some kind of power over him, yet I had played it all wrong. Serial killers are like reptiles: they observe others as a predator would do. When I first got in touch with him, Brady had groomed me, preparing me for this moment when I would be all alone with him. While I dug to find the real Brady, he was busy showing me his fake masks, like he did to all writers who foolishly thought they had really met him. Throughout that time, he was moving me closer and closer so he could feed on my beautiful young face. I was food.

Ian Brady, the Monster of the Moors, pulled me close, his hands gripping around my waist as he ground his hips against mine. He pushed my hair back off my face and mentioned *Now Voyager*, a Bette Davis film he had enjoyed that I had also liked. Bette plays a lonely ugly duckling, unable to function in relationships because of the way she had been treated by her bitchy mother, who had flattened her self-esteem. She falls in love with Jerry, but they cannot be together as he is married. Brady said, 'Remember the line, "Oh, Jerry, don't let's ask for the moon. We have the stars."' He cupped my face in his hands and positioned his long legs either side of me so I couldn't escape. Then he brushed back the strands of blonde hair from my face again and stared at me. I looked up into his amused grey eyes. He gripped my arms, pinned me up against the window and leaned down as if he was about to enjoy a good meal.

He shoved his tongue into my mouth and explored me with the hunger of a man who hadn't kissed a woman in decades. I pulled away and wiped my mouth. I was shocked. He had gone too far, this was not part of my plan of being a pretend shrink. I was drowning in a sea where I had swam much too far out. I felt sick – to me he was an old man. My stomach churned. I wiped his spit from my mouth and started to feel really weird and spaced out. My mind started to spin.

Oh, no, no, what have I done? Don't be afraid, he's just a man. But he's not just a man. He's a devil. His life experiences are the most demonic on this planet. Just a man. No, no, he is the Daddy of the Devils.

'Don't be afraid,' he said.

He leaned for me again. *Now I know what it would be like to fuck the Devil*, I thought to myself. *A long kiss, then all of a sudden you feel the weight of the guilt about all the bad things the Devil has done crashing into your mind.*

I backed away from him over to the other side of the room. I expected to look up and see him grinning, but I looked at him and saw that he was dazed. So! The monster had overestimated itself. Beauty had overwhelmed the beast. I felt smug. I had underestimated my power. I was in complete control of the killer. I had achieved my goal.

I went to the hospital bathroom and looked back to see another guard leading him back to his cell. He seemed to fade like an old photo. The sight depressed me. What a loser he had been in his life. With his mega-intellect he could have easily been a university professor; instead, he had wrecked his own life as well as those of others.

What's your secret Brady? Whose was the hand that soul murdered you?

After coming out of the toilet, I found there was no one around, so I went down to his room and found him sitting on his bed. I put my arm around him like a nurse might, saying nothing about what had happened. He pushed me off. I felt the power high of victory. I had won. And yet how had I?

I looked at him on his bed and felt infused with a desire to hurt him. *Who fucks over the rapist?* I thought to myself. *Me – I do.* He looked so upset I knew that I had him, like a butterfly collector scooping up a dark specimen and pinning it down under a glass cover. His kiss had been like the insertion of a cold pin into his soft weak flesh. Brady was now mine to do with what I wanted. I walked off down the corridor, my high-heeled shoes echoing on the stone floor of the asylum.

Looking back now, I can see that my contact with Brady and my visits to see him were part of some kind of attempt to get revenge on my abusing father. I hadn't been able to hurt Liam or make him suffer for what he had done to me, so instead I'd tried to exert some kind of control over Brady. I had also wanted to get into his mind, to find out who he really was and uncover the reason for his heinous crimes. I believed that, having done this, I would then record it all and be respected as a great writer. In some amateurish way, I had achieved my goal. But I was never going to write a book about him. I lacked the necessary psychological training, the terminology and education to fulfil my writing ambitions.

One day, three weeks after that last visit, and after a total correspondence numbering dozens of letters, I received the one and only note where he actually showed himself to me. He said that he was allowing me to see the 'real' him. Why? Because he trusted me now, he said.

From that letter I knew that I had not wasted the years I had spent writing to the monster. I had got close enough to smell that Brady was a victim of some kind of childhood abuse. I could feel his terror and his loneliness. Evil had used him, rather than the other way round.

What must the little ones have suffered out on the dark freezing cold moors, all alone with the beast? Brady told Fred Harrison, who later published a book called *Brady and Hindley: Genesis of the Moors Murders*, that when he saw the warm green of the moors, he was reminded of picnics he went on with his foster family, the Sloans, in Scotland. What was Brady trying to re-enact? There was however an onlooker, a woman who stood and gloated at the suffering and torment of children – Myra Hindley.

The evil ground zero lay in the foot that had stamped Brady's mind into a deadly broken clock and Myra Hindley, who assisted that broken clock as it ticked its foul, psychotic tick-tock – all the time dis-owning her dark-side and seeing herself as good.

I sent two letters to Hindley to try to get in to study her, but Hindley was crafty, as befits true evil. I heard nothing back.

The time I'd spent following the wrong path only made me more hungry to find true supernatural evil, to nail it down, examine it and discover its capabilities.

Eight

A Replacement Self

No one is from this planet; everyone is from God or consciousness, everyone on earth is actually a space being.

Ruth Montgomery, *Threshold to Tomorrow*

I knew if I were to make a real life for myself I needed to clear out the anger I felt towards my adoptive parents. I knew it wasn't normal to want to pin down a serial killer like Brady and get control over him or collect him. I was curious about evil, but how much of this was due to the damage that had been inflicted during my childhood? I had let a serial killer groom me to fulfil his sexual needs for youth and beauty – I was clearly a vulnerable fool.

I felt as if I needed to book myself in for a service like a car. I wanted someone to check out my mind and, if it was broken, to repair it so that I could function at my full capacity. I went to the library to look for information but found nothing helpful. I was about to leave when the idea came to me to go back and check in the psychology section. Something made me reach forward to take a book from the shelf and, without looking at it, I checked it out at the desk. It was called *The Primal Scream* and I had heard of it before in passing. It was about a radical and some have said dangerous therapy created by an American psychologist and psychotherapist called Arthur Janov. Janov believes that negative emotion stored up in childhood can lead to a person becoming distanced from their emotions and cut off from their real self. In Primal Therapy, you smash down the ego defences built up in an abusive childhood and let the stored emotion come out to reveal a soul that has been hidden – the inner core.

While I was aware that there had been some criticism of the therapy, I was desperate. I was lost, alienated and angry. I wanted to know who I was and why I was here. I knew I wasn't a bad person, but I had nothing and no one to cling on to. I found a clinic on Santa Monica Boulevard in Los Angeles that practised Janov's techniques but had to pass a detailed written test to check that I would be able to cope with the rigours of therapy before being accepted. Following confirmation that they would see me, I packed up all my things and travelled to LA.

After I had been there for about six months, I experienced a breakthrough. After a retreat in Santa Barbara with the Primal Institute, I came back to my flat in LA and lay on the bed. My head was spinning and I saw a vision of a creature with a gold face that wasn't human. Then I had a thought in my head that told me that I wasn't the same person I had been. From then on I felt connected to something strong. I felt like a heater had been turned on inside me. I started to find out who I was and what I liked to eat and drink, whereas before I had just copied others. It was like I had been in a wheelchair and then found out that I could walk, or had been blind and was now able to see. I felt as if I was a completely different person. I had no idea who the other me had been but I was happy to let her go. It was like taking off an old overcoat. My therapist told me I was letting go of the false self. This is a self that we form in order to please our parents.

All I knew was I had gone into the clinic as a Morris Minor and come out a Ferrari. I was now ready to rock and roll.

It was a brand new C.J. Hart that looked up for the details of my return flight to London in Los Angeles Airport. Janov's pioneering therapy had ripped down the walls of my ego defences and pulled out what was there. I felt re-born and like a completely different person. I was hot to trot. I was ready to shake off the past, where I had acted like a victim. My previously long blonde hair was now darker and cut into a smart bob, my dress demure yet classy. I had lost the anger and I had lost the victim mentality. I felt the world was mine for the taking.

As soon as I returned I was like a late train trying to go as fast as I could to catch up. I quickly formed my own investigations agency – Warner Security Services – to mimic Stratford-Barrett's set-up, and it flourished. I introduced myself to elite lawyers and stuck an advert in the Yellow Pages advertising myself as an ex-military security specialist and surveillance expert. I re-established my skills and found I had developed new ones. I could carry out most investigations and believe it was my training as a spy and my new confident state of mind that proved phenomenal.

My success continued and I recruited staff. I had more money than sense but it meant little to me, so I frittered it away. I drove an open-top ghost-silver Lotus around London and had my evening meals in Harvey Nicks or Harrods. I drank cocktails on the King's Road and lunched with my rich clients at The Ritz. I was being sent CVs from former cops and military men looking to become investigators, and I put them to work for me. I was the best spy in London and became known for solving cases where other agencies had failed. I had a beautiful rented penthouse right next to Tower Bridge with a spectacular view of the Thames and a thriving agency that included clients such as the Israeli Intelligence Service. I had finally arrived.

But after working non-stop to build the business, I started to become disillusioned about what I increasingly saw as the sordid world of spying. It had always been a dream of mine to become a great writer, and I had continued to submit stories to some of the newspapers, hoping to find a way to break into journalism.

Then, out of the blue, I got a phone call. It was James. He had been working in Thailand and I hadn't seen him for years.

A week later, James Stratford-Barrett lit a cigar in the In and Out Club in Mayfair and exhaled slowly. I sat opposite him and sipped at a glass of vodka on ice. He narrowed his eyes with the indolent, prosperous air of an oil magnate.

'I've been back in London for quite some time and I've been hearing all about you on the ground. What a star in the night sky you've become, and all from our training.'

I looked at James. I had missed him; he was still a very good-looking man. I also felt a bit insulted that he hadn't come looking for me immediately.

I regarded James carefully. The days when I was small-fry for the company were long gone. I was a totally different animal. On the many undercover spy missions his father had given me in the years after my training, I had nearly been murdered on several occasions and beaten up on others. I had done my time and now

In for the Kill

I was moving up in life on my own terms. I wanted to get it across to James that I had no intention of staying in the world of espionage. I wanted to be a journalist and I was particularly interested in writing about conflict and conflict resolution.

'This week I'm going for an interview with a chap called Greg Miskiw for a place on the *News of the World*. I've been sending him stories and he's impressed with me. If I get the job, I want in as an investigative writer.'

'This is great. The sky's the limit for us if you become a Fleet Street journalist. We can use you to get in anywhere once you've got a press pass and some bylines under your belt.'

'I like it – writing. I like that whole world. I want to write books one day. Don't worry, not on anything the company's done.'

I saw a flicker of anger in his haughty blue eyes.

'Do me a favour and ransack the newspapers' libraries to see what they've got on one of the rabid dirtbags in the IRA I'm looking at.'

'OK.' I felt angry. He was acting as if he owned me.

'There's an IRA leader we're interested in – a man called Sean Flynn [not his real name]. He's going places. We know he's tipped for the top, but he's got a bad habit.'

He had a cheek, but I was curious. 'What's his bad habit?'

'He likes to hurt women. That's the nature of the beast, I'm afraid. We're up against something so difficult to penetrate. No one gets close to the IRA, let alone this little band of diehards at their core.'

'This man's a sadist?'

'Yep, likes to tie 'em up and treat 'em mean in the sack.'

'In the senior ranks of the IRA?' I was barely listening and had gone into some kind of a dream of remembering my father.

The evening ended and James said he would ring me in the morning. He kissed me on the cheek and I felt attracted to him again, but I was afraid of my need for him.

Early the following morning, James rang me as I was out walking around an antique market in Bermondsey.

'I had no idea you had your heart set on becoming a writer, but this is all great news. I can even help you by feeding you stories, so you'll shine. You can then be in place to spy for us. You could even have a codename for us – how about Faith?'

'Faith?' I pushed my sunglasses up on my nose, looking intensely at an antique silver teapot through the dark lenses.

A Replacement Self

'James, I want to become a bona fide journalist, not just use a press pass to spy for government agencies.'

'I own you,' he said, and I could hear him smiling down the phone before the line went dead.

I wished that he would respect me and we could be equals. But then I never felt quite good enough wherever I ended up. I told myself that although the *News of the World* was a tabloid, I could use it to make my way up to *The Independent*. I naively thought that while I was lowering myself to work for a tabloid, I would somehow be able to use the opportunity to clean up the industry. I wanted to protect the vulnerable and teach others how to behave with kindness.

Nine

In Bed with the *News of the World*

Tracy: Suppose I were to kill you for a thrill?
Bond: I can think of something more sociable to do.

On Her Majesty's Secret Service

It was an Indian summer. A fragrant breeze blew in the window as I lay on the comfy double bed in my apartment in Shad Thames with the enigmatic news editor of the *News of the World*, Greg Miskiw. The light was fading but we were still talking shop as we lay naked after a particularly energetic round of lovemaking.

Greg spoke.

'You love it, don't you?'

'Love what?'

'What we do.'

'How do you mean?' I licked his shoulder.

'The kill? You're in for the kill, Chris. You have a knack for it – the instinct for blood, the moment when we swoop down on someone, and for them, that's it – it's all over. We ruin lives.' He began to suck my nipple. I groaned.

Greg was right. In the couple of years that I had been working for the *News of the World* I had lost all the scruples I had held about journalists' behaviour. Instead of somehow cleaning up the industry from the inside, I had become exactly the kind of journalist I had once abhorred. I was now responsible for destroying lives with the stories we peddled, and I could no longer pretend, even to myself, that I didn't get a kick out of it when it was an attack on the rich and famous. When it involved ordinary people, on the other hand, I used to tip them off that they were being investigated, as long as they weren't hurting anyone.

After carrying out a painstaking investigation, sometimes lasting months, we would do what is known as 'the kill'. This was when we drew blood from the victim in a grand finale.

Most of us knew that we struck terror into people's hearts when we arrived on their doorstep and told them we were from the *News of the World* – particularly celebrities and major politicians. Bob Geldolf looked at me in shock one time when I arrived at his door and told him who I was. Ditto Mick Jagger, who stripped me down a peg or two. But when I arrived with another reporter called Dennis Rice at George Harrison's house, George liked Rice and gave him an exclusive interview.

On one occasion I remember we were due to confront a well-known celebrity who we had been investigating for ages in relation to drug use. A colleague went off to do the kill and came back grinning. 'He denied it. I showed him the evidence – he's going to talk to us and give us something on his co-stars.'

I glared at him from across the news desk.

'You killed without me? After all the work we did together on that case?' I was livid.

Another time, the kill was all mine. We had investigated claims that three Catholic priests were using sex chat lines. Their parish officers had grassed them up to us by showing us the phone bills that had come in. On the morning of the first kill, I washed off my make-up, dressed demurely, got into my silver Lotus and drove off to the church. The priest was busy saying Mass when I arrived, so I lined up to take Holy Communion. I knelt at the altar rail and he came along the short line and gave me the host and the blood of Christ.

After the service had ended, I went round to the sacristy and knocked at the door. He answered still wearing his gold-embroidered garments.

'Hello, my dear, how can I help you?'

'I'm from the *News of the World*.'

'Do come in.'

I went into the small sacristy. It smelt of incense and had candles everywhere.

I got to the point. 'I understand that you've been using sex chat lines.'

'There is no way I would do anything like that.'

In Bed with the *News of the World*

'Kinky Kicks, Teenage Bondage and Big Boobs Are Us. Here's the evidence.' I placed his phone bill down on the table in front of him and he visibly crumpled as he looked at it.

'The woman who helps you out in the parish office gave it to us. She also told us you were fornicating with a member of your congregation, and you know that's not allowed.'

He looked up at me and started to cry.

'Please don't ruin my life. I'm much needed here.'

I stood watching him coldly for a few moments, then said, 'All these activities will be in this week's *News of the World*. Any comment?' I pulled out my silver mini recorder that I usually kept running whilst hidden in my handbag.

I noticed that his green and gold cloak was open at the neck and stared at the glinting gold crucifix embroidered on the front of his garments.

He said, 'I'm not guilty.'

I said, 'Oh, but you are and now the whole world will read all about it.'

As I left the church, I could hear their folk group practising 'He's Got the Whole World in His Hands'.

I never knew what became of this priest after he appeared as a page three and four spread. I would imagine that, as usual, he would have been moved to another area to carry on regardless.

In order to be at the forefront of the action, we had staff from the most exclusive London nightclubs on our payroll. They would tip us off if there were celebrities in who were up to no good with regard to drugs or extra-marital affairs.

I once went to a nightclub with orders to follow Victoria Beckham into the loo and ask her whether she was going to split up with David. I couldn't find her in the club so spent the night chatting to Teddy Sheringham.

During these times, I filmed drug-taking I witnessed with a secret camera hidden in my handbag. Often I would wear a wire strapped to my bra with recording equipment under my designer evening dress. I was regularly handed thousands of pounds in cash to put in my diamanté clutch bag to spend in the club. I used to go to Harrods first to buy a new dress to wear, then some Manolos in Harvey Nicks and maybe some Fendi perfume in order to smell loaded. Then I would have champagne and dinner on their fifth floor with whoever I was working with before we headed on to the club.

In for the Kill

If we were able to get hold of what we suspected to be drugs but may not have been, we used to post what was left through the door of a GP in west London for him to analyse. He would get another envelope with cash put through his letterbox for doing the job.

Since the paper came out on Sunday, Saturday was a work day and we had Mondays off. On Tuesday morning, all journalists then had to have three stories ready for conference, which was usually run by Clive Goodman, the paper's royal editor and a quiet, kind man with a penchant for colourful waistcoats. Conference was held in a boardroom in the corridor along from *The Sun*. The *News of the World* was bracketed off from them by a large sign that said: 'You are now entering *The Sun* country'.

We were meant to find the three new stories on our two days off. I found this really hard, but Clive once reassured me that I was vital to the paper. He called my investigative abilities, the 'Christine Hart magic'. Because of his appreciation, I used to smile disarmingly at him during conference and say that I was working on a few special projects and that I wasn't free to think about new stories. The truth was that I found it virtually impossible to do this.

Clive went around the table in order and would sometimes tell a journalist that their ideas weren't going to make it. There were about ten of us on the news desk at that time and there were usually a lot of worried faces.

Ricky Sutton, a perky blond, always had his three ideas, and one that sticks in my mind was about doing a feature on the stray dogs that were running round the streets in war zones. He seemed to have a lot of interest in stories about animal cruelty. Other journalists would come up with tales about celebrities that they had heard from contacts and run them past Clive.

The paper mainly ran on 'ring-ins', where people called in with stories that were followed up. We got a lot of calls from MPs' secretaries who would be wined and dined by the paper and then put on the payroll. They would be paid in cash so there was no paper trail. They were often beautiful women or young graduates who were infatuated by the world of newspapers and the media. We learned all about the secret movements and the love lives of several MPs courtesy of these women. There was a lot of infidelity going on at Westminster and this kind of information could be really useful as leverage.

In Bed with the *News of the World*

After the meeting, we would all leave to pursue our various assignments, which usually meant spending an hour on the phone in the office and then heading out on the road. The offices seemed to be empty most of the time.

When another newspaper, usually the *Mail on Sunday* or the *Daily Mail*, had got hold of someone that the *News of the World* was looking for, war was declared. This type of saga would usually start by us being leaked the information that another paper had someone and was keeping them incommunicado in order to do an exclusive on them. If we had any interest in the same story, we would make plans to do what we cheerfully nicknamed 'kidnapping'.

First, we would find out which journalist on the rival paper was doing the story. This was quite easy, as someone would pretend to have info about the story and ring up their news desk. They would always give us the name of the journalist on the story. The staff at the *Mail* were all very jolly hockey sticks and polite, making them easy meat for us as we were so aggressive.

The next step would be to ring the newspaper's travel company, pretending to be that journalist, and ask them to book us an extra night in the room they had already arranged. Then we would pretend we were out and about and had forgotten the actual name of the hotel where we were staying. The travel company would always oblige.

On arriving at the hotel, we would call the journalist down to the bar using some pretext involving the hotel management. Once they were in the bar, we would slip up to their room, thump on the door and 'persuade' the subject of the story to come with us. We were very dominant in our approach.

We would stand there eyeing them coolly and expect them to comply as soon as they heard who we were. They would usually say something like, 'Where's the person who was looking after me?'

We would tell them that they had pulled out, that all the newspapers were on their way and so to save them we were offering them the opportunity to come with us and secure a more lucrative contract. We would then race them and their suitcases down the emergency staircase and out into the car and back to the office.

If the *Daily Mail* editor or whoever it was we had raided ever rang and complained when they saw their story in our paper that Sunday, Greg would put down the phone without saying anything.

In for the Kill

We ruled Fleet Street and we did it through aggression. The other newspapers knew it and backed off.

The *News of the World* also kept close tabs on their staff and on occasion I would be asked to use one of James's army guys and sit outside the office gates to watch and then tail a reporter who wasn't up to scratch to see what they did after work.

Journalists who didn't match up to the job were given the worst stories until they took the hint and left. Total dedication was expected. If you wanted to work only a fifty-hour week, then you were considered lazy and on the way out. On one occasion I remember a journalist complaining about the effect that the long hours were having on his family life. While the immediate response he received was sympathetic, it was clear that his days on the paper were numbered.

At the beginning of my time at the paper, I felt sick with guilt about what I was doing. At confession, I would sit with my favourite priest, Father Phil, and say through the grille, 'Father, I have sinned again this week and it is six weeks since my last confession.'

When I told him what I had been doing in my work, he said, 'It's clear that within your workplace there are evil people infecting the company. How can you carry on there?'

I knew it was wrong. I had suffered in the same way as the people I was now exposing. I told myself if I only earned enough money to pay the rent with no luxuries and didn't buy any property with the money and did voluntary work at the same time, my soul would stay unblemished. So I taught young offenders in Feltham Borstal how to read and write, and I stayed in my rented apartment and didn't buy a house so I wouldn't profit, but I still felt grubby and guilty.

On the other hand, however, I was addicted to the taste of blood. I swooped on my prey and ripped them apart, and our quarry – the rich, the famous, the powerful – all bled; they bled profusely all over the pages of Sunday's first editions. The feeling of power was a high like no other. In some ways I felt like I was getting revenge for all my thwarted dreams. Why should these people be allowed to be rich, successful and happy when I felt like my life was such a failure? I was angry and resentful, and exposing their very privileged private lives was a powerful way of venting these emotions.

In Bed with the *News of the World*

Back in my apartment with Greg, I stroked his soft, dark hair and studied him after we had made love, late one Friday night.

Greg and I had grown close after I began working at the *News of the World*. Following his divorce, he came round to my flat a lot. He used to call at my apartment and either come up or I would go to have long, relaxing lunches with him in a nearby restaurant on the Thames called the Pont de la Tour. He would seek my advice on just about every story on the paper and ask 'How do we prove this is happening?'

So many people called in to the paper with stories and we had to be able to back them up before printing them. This was where my investigative skills came into play. If a story couldn't be verified from three sources, then it wasn't run. I often wondered what Greg saw in me, so I constantly gave him free advice on investigations.

After a lot of flirting, our relationship had started in the back of a cab on the way home after a Christmas party – how original! I thought Greg was devastatingly good looking with his silky dark hair pushed back in an Elvis-style quiff. He had intense dark eyes that made him look like Al Pacino in his role as Tony Montana in *Scarface*. His moody good looks had drawn me to him, and I felt completely protected in his company. I was coming to realise that I liked hard men, as I felt like I needed protection, which is apparently common for those who have been abused or bullied during childhood.

Greg had had a very hard life and I could tell that his past had affected him. Now he was giving his all to a newspaper for no apparent reason – a lot of news editors didn't work half as hard as he did. I wished that I could mother him to heal his pain but I didn't know how.

I often got the feeling that Greg was angry at the world. He told me how when he came to England from the Ukraine he had to change his name from Ihor, as no one could pronounce it and he found it difficult to get job interviews.

'I had to change my name, Chris, so I could make my way over here. It always rankled. I never forgot or forgave. Imagine how I felt having to give up my own name.'

'Yes, they did that to me,' I said. I remembered how I had suffered when I went through this trauma as a child, so I understood Greg's pain.

Armed with his intellectual genius and highly dominant

personality, he made inroads into Fleet Street and eventually worked his way up to the position of news editor. Socialising meant little to Greg; he would never talk about anything unless it was linked to the job. His one exception was his beautiful daughter, whom he adored.

One thing that cheered Greg up was his close friendship with Alex Marunchak, his buddy editor running the news desk. Alex was also Ukrainian and *Private Eye* often called Greg and Alex 'the Rottweilers', which amused them. It was an apt description. They often reminded me of two Serbian warlords. Greg barked instructions at people and woe betide anyone who didn't listen.

Most of the men around the office seemed wary of Greg, but all of them seemed to fear Alex. Alex was in his 50s, an austere, classy, fit-looking man who was a hardened Fleet Street hack. He had made his way up from a cub reporter.

It only took a few glasses of wine for Alex to tell everyone what he thought of them, and this would involve winding people up. Despite this, I adored Alex and would enjoy long wintry evenings with him over a few bottles of Cabernet. He was a perfect gentleman, making sure we had constant plates of nibbles, complimenting me on my intellect and making me feel like a woman.

Outside the office, Alex's closest friend was a former Flying Squad detective whom I met and spent time with. On one occasion, he and Alex invited me to the gold-themed Rivoli cocktail bar at The Ritz. It was in this James Bond setting that I was introduced to an American that the Flying Squad officer told me was CIA. When the grey-haired Yank and I got chatting at the glossy glass bar, I found out that the guy was indeed a senior member of the CIA. I had deliberately been invited along to meet him and it led to a later attempt at recruitment by the CIA, who asked me to train up young Muslims to go undercover in mosques in London.

Alex stood sipping his bourbon as we stood in the Rivoli bar. 'Chris has been trained up by the spooks – she's our top girl.'

His Flying Squad friend told me, 'Watch Alex. When he's had a few drinks and in the right mood, a red mist drops and he gets very sarcastic. He'll start cutting everyone down to size. Beware – he can make grown men cry.'

I got my experience of this when, at a *News of the World* executive dinner party – along with Les Hinton and Tom Crone and all the other gods – during a lull in the conversation Alex announced to everyone, 'Chris once met the Moors Murderer when she was a schoolgirl, didn't you, Chris?'

I blushed and stammered while Alex smiled and threw his arm around my neck. He pulled me to him and whispered in my ear, 'Come on, show you're a real woman. Stand up to it and explain that you were halfway between a needy orphan and Inspector Clouseau.'

Staff parties with the rest of the factory-floor journalists were less lavish. Male journalists would disappear with female journalists into the toilets for sex or furious groping in a cubicle. The rest of us would stand around discussing who had made some poor soul commit suicide that week.

We partied hard, with dancing and champagne, until dawn. In the early hours, the inner circle would move on to an elite private members' club in Mayfair, where there would be cocaine on the bar and beautiful young girls to perform private dances. Turned on by their tight bodies, I would go back with Greg to my place where we would consume each other on my double bed. My normal frigidity seemed to be melted by all things Miskiw.

There was a problem in our relationship, however, and this was the fact that Greg wouldn't give me a byline on my stories. He wanted to keep me his Fleet Street secret, but by doing that he was hampering my career and my progress. He didn't care about this, however; he cared about himself. I tested this theory when I asked him outright one night in The Old Rose, 'Greg, do you mind if I go up to *The People* and do a shift this Saturday? The editor rang me today and asked me.'

Greg let his bottom lip curl as he looked at me, his dark eyes ablaze. He picked up his highball whisky glass and slammed it hard against the wall. The whole pub turned and looked at us, then slowly turned away. The glass had smashed and golden liquid was trickling down the white wall. But I had worked with hard men most of my life. They would fight in front of me and play Russian roulette. A glass of whisky smashed behind me didn't upset me.

'I own you – don't forget that. I've taught you everything you know,' he snarled at me.

I blinked hard. He had taught me nothing.

Of course I said no to Jimmy. Perhaps Greg did own me. I was often told that by men. James had also told me that he owned me.

In for the Kill

I wondered why that was. *Did other women get the same thing?* I wondered. I was Greg's flunky.

I worked long hours for Greg and was remunerated so badly I had to work secretly for other newspapers as well as freelance for companies like Michael Oatley's Ciex in order to keep up rent payments on my expensive penthouse apartment.

That night of the tossed whisky glass, Greg and I returned to my flat and there was still no apology. That night in bed we made love and it seemed like we were cooling off. Afterwards I asked him again. 'Will you let me do pure writing work in the office? I loathe undercover investigations. I've been doing it my whole life – I'm sick of it. I want to write.'

'You're far too old to be a journalist,' he said as he dressed, put on his raincoat and went out into the night.

I lay awake and stared at the ceiling. I was 32 years of age, how could I be too old to be a writer? I felt like he wanted to keep me down.

Ten

The Fake Sheik and Me

Your power exists to serve me. And it is mine to control. If and when the time comes I decide you are to lose it, I myself will take it away.

Kananga to Solitaire, *Live and Let Die*

Not long after this incident, Greg pulled me into one of the side offices at work, sat on the desk and said with a grin, 'I want you to meet Mazher Mahmood, get to know him and how he works, and then work with him. He usually refuses to work with anyone else and he hardly ever comes into the office, but he's shown curiosity about you and agreed to pair up. I think if I put you two heavy hitters together, then the sky's the limit.'

I had never met the enigma that was Mazher Mahmood but I had read most of his explosive weekly investigations for the *News of the World*. He was our extremely highly paid investigations editor and yet never came into the office. He apparently looked down on the office journalists and had a massive budget all to himself. He had a crew of freelance surveillance experts who worked with him, doing observations and electronic surveillance, as well as a gutsy ex-army bodyguard. Maz had famously dressed up as a Fake Sheik and conned a long list of well-known faces. There was a contract out on his life from the gangland underworld. He was a ghost.

One unseasonably hot afternoon in April, my porter Alan called me. 'There's a car waiting outside for you.'

I knew Mazher was coming to pick me up to take me to work on a job with him in Hertfordshire and I had put on a long red silk Dior dress and sky-high red Louboutins. I put on some deep scarlet lipstick in front of the mirror then thought again and wiped it off with a tissue. 'The Host of Seraphim' was playing on my CD player.

I went down in the lift from my apartment and out to the car. It was a green Merc, a new one. I got in the back and settled myself, waiting to make small talk with the man who was driving.

He turned and looked at me as he drove off.

'Wow, you look hot, Jackie!'

I looked back at him, worried. 'I'm sorry? I'm not Jackie!'

'Not Jackie? I've come to pick you up to take you to the party?'

'Oh, no. Oh, shit. Look, I'm so sorry – shit.' I turned round and looked behind me as my apartment block got smaller and smaller. 'Please – look, can you take me back home? I'd love to be Jackie and come with you to your party but I'm waiting to be picked up by someone to go to work. Can you take me back?'

He looked at me. 'Christine, Christine, calm down, it's me, Mazher. God, you're gullible.'

He laughed as he drove. Mazher Mahmood – the *News of the World*'s secret weapon.

As we drove fast with the windows wound down and a breeze cooling our faces, I looked at this legend. He had an aquiline nose, beautifully contoured lips and well-shaped hands with tapered fingers. But the remarkable thing about Mazher was his eyes: they were amber and they actually glowed. When you looked in his eyes, you believed all that he said – he was hypnotic. He also had a regal air about him, so no wonder his Fake Sheik blag worked. I remember thinking, *So that's your secret weapon – your beauty*.

We were off to a five-star spa and hotel in Hertfordshire to entrap a creepy sixty-year-old paedophile who was luring thirteen-year-old girls to pose naked in his house for him with money and promises of fame and fortune.

As we drove, Maz ignored me. He did it in such a way as to make it feel like it would be beneath him to even speak to me. I was so used to being disrespected that it didn't bother me at all.

After arriving at the hotel in the countryside, we got settled into our luxurious rooms. Maz always got the best. While other journalists had to stay in three-star, he was five-star all the way. Later, we ate a candlelit dinner of fricassee together, washed down with a cherry Malbec as we looked out over a moonlit clipped lawn.

The Fake Sheik and Me

My suite had a connecting door to Mazher's and after dinner Mazher lay on his kingsize bed with his shirt off and I lay on the settee. I couldn't help but secretly run my eyes all over his body. He was so lovely, but he was something one only looked at rather than thought of devouring; he was too exquisite.

All of a sudden a cache of photos fell out of his file – hundreds of photos of young girls with their genitalia exposed and legs akimbo. This was the evidence he had collected to back up the story about the paedophile.

'Oh, Christ.' They were completely disgusting.

'Oh, sorry about that.' He cleared them up with a superior grin.

I felt sick and retired to my room. I knew Mazher saw stuff like that all the time. Cops did too but they were fit for it; I wasn't sure Maz was. Heinous photographs like that can seep into the mind and eradicate the innocence that we all need to cling to.

The next morning he banged on my door early and we went down to a breakfast of porridge, scrambled egg and a pot of coffee, and made our plans to kill. Our job was to approach the sleazy pensioner to try to buy the offending photographs from him.

We drove to his house, sat outside for a few hours and then followed him to his bowling green. I ended up telling him I was from the local newspaper, doing a feature on bowling, and asked if he would help us out. I played bowls with him so we could get a good shot of him for the paper. Then someone else from Maz's crew did the deal with him about the photos, while we went back to the hotel and directed the rest of the operation from there. The job ended up as a middle-page spread and the file was passed to the cops. But I didn't get my name on it; Greg forbade it. Hatred for Greg was growing in my heart.

Maz and I quickly established that he was top dog and then we worked together frequently. We both attended Sylvester Stallone's wedding in The Dorchester on London's Park Lane in May 1997. When I arrived at his luxury suite, which was a floor below Stallone's, Maz answered the door in his gold silk dressing gown, sipping a glass of milk. He looked me up and down. I was wearing a leopard-print dress and a leopard-skin hat. Maz stared at me and said, 'You look ridiculous.'

'What do you mean?'

'That leopard-skin shit.'

'I'm your wife – you're an Arab.'

'You really have no idea, do you? Get it off.'

I had to get a cab over to Harvey Nicks to pick up a beige pinstripe Nicole Farhi suit. I picked up a hair fascinator on the ground floor.

When we were tipped off that Stallone was in the bar, I held Maz's hand as we descended in the lift, to make out I was his wife. I felt a strong sexual thrill as I did so. He turned to me.

'You're getting off on this, aren't you? There really is no need to hold my hand, Chris, to get your jollies.'

I let his warm hand slip. He enjoyed mocking me.

Mazher had on his full Arab prince robes that were white and flowing with a headband in white. He had an entourage of six black-suited guys. One of his men walked up to Stallone and asked him if he would allow the Arab prince a few minutes to talk with him, as His Majesty was a big fan. Sylvester grinned and was only too happy to agree. He told us he was honoured to meet us both, and was charming.

We sat with the delightful Sly Stallone and he spoke about how happy he was to be marrying his beautiful bride. Mazher got his quotes.

The next day we all woke up late. I had my own room downstairs but we had to meet up in Maz's room, so when me, Maz and the photographer Steve Grayson had all been holed up for a while waiting for orders I slipped into his cavernous bathroom to have a bath. His suite was amazing! I had a long hot bubble bath with the Burberry toiletries and then I slipped on a thick white towelling robe and looked down from the window at the world's press who were gathered outside the hotel. It really was a sight to behold. As I leaned out of the window, the cameras all turned upwards and flashed at once. I felt like Marilyn Monroe, so I waved and the cameras flashed again. It was great fun.

Maz shouted at me.

'The wedding's nearly over. They're marrying on the roof. Quickly – what are you doing in there?'

He grabbed my hand and we both ran up a hundred stairs of the emergency exit as fast as we could and climbed out onto the roof of The Dorchester.

Mazher held on to my towelling robe at the back as I leaned out over the roof to try to get a view of the next roof where Stallone was marrying. It was tricky but I hung over the edge and shouted back to Maz, describing what the bridesmaids were wearing and what the bride, Jennifer Flavin, looked like while he dictated this over his mobile to the copy-takers back at the office.

After this drama, I got dressed back in the room and we went down in the lift and outside to the waiting limousine, which one of Mazher's guys was driving. As we came out of The Dorchester, the world's press was waiting outside for Stallone and his bride. There was a clatter of flash bulbs as we ducked into our limousine and sped off along the M4 to Oxford and the reception.

After failing to gatecrash the reception, Maz and I ended up with the rest of the press in a countryside pub in Woodstock. On the way back to The Dorchester, giddy from Budweiser, I was giggling in the back of the car – it was the stress of the day coming out. Mazher sat taking photos of me and made remarks about my hat that had miraculously stayed put on my head all day. Steve was enthusing about an episode of *The Sweeney* that was being repeated on TV that night and how he was dying to get home to watch it.

Back in The Dorchester in the suite, I wanted to have some champagne with the boys to debrief. Mazher slumped on the bed said, 'Undo my tie, would you?'

I obliged. Then he said, 'You can stay and have a drink if you and I can go to bed together tonight. If not, 'fraid you have to leave now.'

'I'm leaving,' I said as I walked towards the door. I went home and felt lonely. I had no one to go and cool off from the day's stresses with.

The next day was Sunday and it lifted my spirits immensely to see the photos of Stallone with us blanked out and my descriptions of the dresses I had seen from the roof. I had described the bridesmaids as wearing lemon chiffon and this was reported all over the world. But I knew I had got it wrong – hanging over the edge of a roof wasn't conducive to thinking straight about material. When I confided this to Greg when I was next relaxing with him at mine, he suddenly turned nasty.

'Chris, if you didn't know what material it was, why say it was fucking lemon chiffon? That's the problem all round: we get it wrong, then we get accused of making things up.'

I sat and burned with shame. Lemon chiffon! It was hardly the end of the world. I looked at him and realised just how much I had come to hate what we did.

In for the Kill

Greg finished off the last of my brandy as he ranted on about how useless I was and how most of the staff in the office were greedy and worthless and sickened him. Then we made love and he got dressed, picked up his coat and left.

A few months later, the evening before Princess Diana's funeral, the paper had rented out a room at The Tower Hotel and we sat around drinking Bollinger and swapping stories about Diana. Alex Marunchak was there, as was Neville Thurlbeck. Tall and shy, Neville reminded me of a cop because he was always spouting the law. Phil Hall and Ian Edmondson were also there with Greg and me. A few of the reporters got maudlin and sobbed into their canapés. I looked around and thought, *What a thing. We have been vilified for chasing Diana to her death, but here we all are, acting as if she was our family*.

Greg and I got drunk on bourbon in a quiet corner and he said, 'Well, want to come up to my room?'

We went up towards the lift and all of our photographers dived after us. As the lift went up, they banged us off with flash bulbs popping and shutters clattering. Greg covered his face to avoid the flashlights. They pasted the photos of us going upstairs in the lift all over the office the next day and I kept two of them.

Up in his suite I had a ham sandwich, and I looked at him then back at the sandwich.

'I don't know what to eat first, you or the sandwich.'

He laughed. 'Finish your sandwich, then come to bed and eat me in that wild way you have.'

After we made love deeply and passionately, we lay in each other's arms and fell asleep. I woke in the night and looked out the window to the Thames and the view of Tower Bridge. I had the same view from my apartment. I got dressed in his white shirt, rolled up my black-sequinned Katharine Hamnett dress under my arm and strolled back across the bridge at 3 a.m. in the summer dawn. I enjoyed the stroll across the ornate bridge. London felt like it belonged to me, yet I wondered where I was going. My work was making me hate myself and I wanted to do something worthwhile or important.

The next morning, the office rang early about a story. I was still tired and wearing Greg's shirt in bed. The call was about a very famous person.

'We're pretty sure he has a love child and he's supporting him at an exclusive private school in London. We've been tipped off about the first name but we have no idea of the mother's name or the kid's surname. Get to the school and find out the name. Then we find out who he's been shagging.'

'OK.' I was still in bed and I rolled over to look at the clock. I winced; it was seven in the morning.

'Get up and get over to the school to see the Head and find out who the kid is.'

'OK.'

'Get up and do it fucking now. We need this by ten o'clock.'

I sipped a coffee as I got dressed, shoved a bit of burnt toast in my mouth and ran out past the porter's desk to my Lotus in the underground car park. As I drove across London with the roof down, I realised that I didn't like the idea of interfering in the life of a child, so I made a plan to not bother to do the job but to say that I had failed. I sat in my car round the corner from the school and ate a Mars bar, thinking about how sleazy the paper was. Just as I got stuck into reading the *Daily Mail* and a front-page story I had covered for them about a man dying of cancer on TV, my mobile rang.

'Where the fuck are you?'

'Right outside the school,' I lied.

'Listen, it's nuts for you to try to do this. We're calling in the SAS,' he growled dramatically.

We sometimes used ex-SAS guys for surveillance ops. I had been trained by ex-spooks myself to carry out surveillance and counter-surveillance, but nothing beats the SAS. They really are ghosts.

'He's going to meet you outside the school. Do what he says, Chris, and follow his lead. Say nothing to him about our business. He won't want to talk to you anyway.'

I hung up and felt angry. Now I would have to go round to the school. I made a promise to myself to not go inside.

As I walked around to the school, through the leafy squares of Kensington, I entertained myself by wondering what the SAS guy would do. Would he abseil through the window, like in the Libyan embassy siege, and grab the child and then ask him his name? Rumour had it these guys had been trained to kill with their bare hands. *This will be interesting*, I thought to myself.

A well-built dark-haired guy came swaggering up the street. He glanced at me but didn't bother asking who I was. He said quietly, 'Follow me. Keep schtum.'

In for the Kill

I thought, 'Oh, OK, he's going to speak to the Head.' I followed him down the dimly lit school corridor. He marched towards the Head's office, then, to my horror, he lifted one arm towards the lists of children at the school and proceeded to rip them off the wall. Sheet after sheet, class after class. I saw some women standing watching him in shock.

He then stuffed the lists down his shirt and walked out purposefully, as if daring anyone to stop him. They wouldn't have been able to. Twenty people couldn't have stopped him.

I followed him like a little lap dog, saying nothing. By the time I got out of the door and into the street it was empty. I looked up and down – there was not even the rustle of a leaf.

I rang the office as I sat in my car.

'Mission abort. Forget it, Chris, and get back here.'

As I drove through Knightsbridge with the top down, I felt disgusted; those lists were needed, it was horrible. I needed the money but I wanted to leave.

In the paper the following Sunday, there was no mention of the story.

As a child I had enjoyed a TV series on Saturday nights called *Enemy at the Door*. It starred Simon Cadell, who brilliantly portrayed the part of an SS officer called Hauptsturmführer Klaus Reinicke. Whenever Reinicke came on screen he generated dread and the SS were whispered about and much feared. It seemed to me that the *News of the World* was, at that time, like the German SS. I often felt that the investigative side of the paper was formed in a similar way to how the SS must have been formed, with those who showed certain personality traits – craving for power, aggression and ruthlessness – being moved into an elite group.

Reinicke was a twisted psychopath, willing to do anything to keep his hold on power. Power was the drug. I once asked one of my colleagues about how power came into play on the newspaper.

'When we appear at their door and say we're the *News of the World*, they're terrified. Major politicians, the rich and famous all quake in their boots. They know that their life's over. That's the moment – that's the kill. And killing's a high like no other – nothing is more seductive than having power over life and death. It makes us elite – like gods.'

We were behaving like Nazis to experience a power high or a buzz that inflated the ego. This was also the reason why Satan spat in the face of God.

The Fake Sheik and Me

I was feeling worn out and sick of the evil I was mired in, and when I talked again to my priest about what was going on, he told me to leave the paper. But I was also a hypocrite. I had ambitions to write a book and I didn't want to burn any boats. And if I'm honest, being part of the front-page news in the morning was a heady experience, as was knowing all the unpublished squalid secrets of the incredibly rich and politically powerful.

I went downstairs to the gym in my apartment building. It was a delight at the end of the day to walk across reception in my long, pink silk dressing gown, heading for the heated blue-lit marble swimming pool, and afterwards have a candlelit jacuzzi with a glass of champagne. It was how I relaxed. Greg joined me in the pool at lunchtime the next day and we stripped off, kissed and then made love furiously in the bubbling-hot jacuzzi. Our lovemaking was often a Hall of Fame event. After letting off steam from the job, we lay back and chatted about the news that day as we sipped Bollinger from the bottle in a silver bucket. An MP had been caught by us seeing a rent boy and it was set for the front page. Greg was laughing about it as the man was married, and after lunch we were going to go round and doorstep his middle-class, much-sheltered, blue-stockinged wife and tell her the good news.

'Who's going to do the kill?' I asked curiously, as I climbed on top of him again.

'I don't know yet, I'll decide after lunch.' I kissed him passionately as he pushed himself inside me.

We had a lazy lunch beside the pool, with more lovemaking, fillet steak and tossed green salad. Afterwards, Greg dived expertly into the pool and swam 50 lengths as I watched him admiringly from the edge, spooning raspberry pavlova into my mouth. I stayed on after he went back to the office and swam hard, and when I got back up to my apartment the phone was flashing with messages. The open French doors to my balcony were swaying in the breeze and it seemed very hot. I was tired and I went to sink onto the bed, planning a bath and to relax. I had really exerted myself. But then the phone rang and, stupidly, I picked it up. It was Greg.

'Get on the fucking phone and find out what the Ripper's wife Sonia Sutcliffe is up to. She's getting married today and she's in a hairdresser's. Find out what she's had done – a colour or a cut – then find out where she's going afterwards.'

I hung up and felt a bit odd. I had pins and needles all down my left arm and my jaw started to ache. The phone rang straight away as I put it down. It was Greg again and this time he shouted, 'GET ON THE PHONE! SHE'S LEFT THE HAIRDRESSER – FIND OUT WHERE SHE'S GONE NOW!'

I lay on the bed and listened to my heart beat like a drum. Something odd appeared to be happening. I felt the room fade to black. I don't know. Was it the way he had spoken to me? I picked up the phone and rang my porter. I managed to get out 'I'm having a heart attack' before I blacked out.

I woke up in the London Bridge Hospital on Tooley Street. I seemed to be strapped to different heart monitors. The white cubicle curtains were drawn around me and all of a sudden they twitched and a familiar face appeared between them. It was Greg.

The heart monitor began to beep and the doctor came and fixed it.

'Are you OK?'

I could barely breathe and my throat felt constricted. I started to weep.

Greg sat down on the bed and reached out for my hand. I felt as if he was the Devil and I wanted to beg him to piss off. Somehow, however, I realised I was acting like a child – it was only Greg, and at this moment he seemed to be very caring and loving.

'I couldn't get you. I was going crazy. I rang your porter, Alan. He told me he'd rung an ambulance for you. I jumped in a cab and got round here as quickly as possible.'

I turned my head away. He looked so concerned about me and I cared about him too. But I wished he hadn't come.

It turned out that I'd had a massive panic attack. Greg laughed when the doctor told me. He helped me to dress and I started to cry weakly. He put his arm round me and we went to a local pub near London Bridge. We sat at the bar and I felt as if we were two lonely people pretending to be friends, but we weren't. I had strong feelings for him but I wasn't sure if I hadn't confused love and pity. Greg seemed to struggle with life somehow; he was a loner, like me, and didn't mix well.

We sat enjoying the quiet of the pub until I said, 'I can't do it, Greg. I just can't do it any more. We're evil.'

'Don't talk shit. What will you do for money?'

'I'll write a book.'

'About what? This pipe dream of yours to write a bestseller – very, very few people can do that. You're a brilliant journalist; the paper couldn't run without you. Forget the silly daydream of being a bestselling writer – you've got nothing to say.'

'I can't carry on working. I've just had a heart attack.'

He started to laugh. 'I was there when he told you it was a panic attack, you bimbo.'

'Yes, but next time it will be the real deal. I'm afraid.'

'Look, let's get you back home. There's still time to nail Sutcliffe. Let's just find out where she's getting married and then get you an early night.'

I felt my chest tighten and I started to cry. Greg looked stressed out. I wished that he would get angry with me but instead he sat and looked sad and rather pathetic. I felt desperately sorry for him; I knew he wouldn't cope without me advising on investigations. He didn't have a clue, so I went home and found out for him where Sonia Sutcliffe was getting married and then went to bed, but my heart was still beating too fast to allow sleep and I sat up half the night fearing it would happen again and crying with fear.

The next night I was due to meet a good friend, Karl Van Riebeeck, for drinks. I had met Karl through James when I was about 19, and he was a London-based corporate investigator of the highest order. He owned a very successful company that was up there when it came to the private spy industry and was incredibly well respected in the ex-intelligence corps world. He was a true James Bond-style spy.

Karl was a very attractive man with liquid brown eyes and a sensitive mouth. He had a public-schoolboy accent and was cultured, well read. He drove a dark green top-of-the-range Range Rover, had his own yacht moored in St Tropez and property in Mauritius. He went skiing four times a year in St Moritz, spent his Christmas in Mustique, and his client list contained well-known celebrities and those on the *Sunday Times* rich list.

Karl worked for a lot of top lawyers as an adviser. He also was well used and incredibly well respected by the ex-MI6 clique. In his plush offices, full of high-tech spying equipment, he kept a large white Persian cat and he used to like to sit with it on his knee, stroking it as he interviewed his rich clients. He was not a man that many would have crossed, as his contacts were so powerful and he was so liked by them.

In for the Kill

I had called Karl one night of the blue, looking for some intellectual companionship. I was now thinking that it might have been a mistake and felt uncomfortable as he carefully watched me during the cab ride along the Embankment to the OXO Tower.

As we sat at a candlelit table eating oysters and drinking champagne, Karl told me about some of the clients he was working with and then said, 'You've done very well for yourself without James – living around here, your upmarket flat. How are you earning your money?'

I told him about my new career in journalism and he seemed impressed. I basked in his admiration, as Karl was someone I had always looked up to. I also began to wonder if my connection with him might help me to get out of the trap I now felt I was in at work.

Back at my flat, I looked out of the window at Tower Bridge and the lights on the Thames. I felt I had to do something drastic with my life. I felt like I was in a moral sewer.

I believed that I could get by on little money and then concentrate on becoming a writer. I needed to escape but I also needed to make a plan. It would be risky. I was just about to engineer the collision of the world of espionage with the *News of the World*.

I sipped my milkshake and admired the dark rippling Thames. I had often thought of putting Karl Van Riebeeck and Greg Miskiw together. They were similar men – dark-haired, good-looking, both incredibly ambitious and both dominant personalities.

I rang Greg the next day from bed. 'I want to get into more serious journalism, Greg, but I know a man who can take over from me supervising undercover ops.'

'Tell me more.'

'He's called Van Riebeeck. He's a big shot, but bona fide.'

'Introduce me – I'm free tomorrow night.'

He was too eager. It should have rung alarm bells that my days were numbered, that I might be entirely replaced, but it didn't. I also realised that I knew little about Van Riebeeck. I was only attracted to him because of his dazzling Dirk Bogarde good looks.

That Friday night, the three of us met in The Wolseley in London. We sat round a large dining table with a white tablecloth, sipping champagne aperitifs. These were two powerful men from two very different yet intoxicating worlds. The media used low-grade private eyes for legitimate investigations, but never before had they forged a link to the highest level of professional espionage.

Greg was excited about meeting Karl; he had dressed up in a navy Savile Row suit. I was wearing a creased black dress from the Prada sale and high black Manolos, with my blonde hair pulled back in a diamanté slide. Karl was in a dressy black dinner jacket, white shirt and black shiny brogues on my left and Greg was on my right. It was interesting to see their chemistry. Greg was on top form and oozing charm – Mr Bountiful, insisting on more Bollinger and Beluga caviar as he was covering the bill. Karl was laid back, oozing power.

As I we sat chatting, I pictured myself settling down to a more sedate life. Naively I thought that Greg would now only give me intelligent and complex investigations to carry out. What a fool I was.

I watched the two dark heads bent over the dining table together, enjoying their coffee and brandy. I suddenly realised the real reason I had got them together was to imagine them both with me sexually in a *ménage à trois*. I imagined being in between them, Karl kissing one side of my neck, Greg other the other, then pushing them both downwards to dine on me. But we dined on tender steak and both men ordered a succulent rib eye with a bloody Merlot to wash it down. I was superfluous and I felt angry. The last thing I wanted to do was truly help Greg get on in life. Yet the two had a very real chemistry. I began to feel a bit of a stupid tart for introducing them. Neither had ever done me any favours and there was something about them both meeting that gave me a feeling of dread.

After dinner, Greg and I stood outside underneath a lamppost that cast a yellow glow over our faces. We watched as Karl, collar up against the rain, walked down a nearby dark alleyway, climbed into his parked Range Rover and with splash of muddy puddle was gone. There was a cold light rain. I shivered and Greg pulled me towards him. I got a bad feeling as I looked up at his happy rain-soaked face as it descended to mine for a lingering kiss. Dislike throbbed through me. He took his coat off and put it around my shoulders to keep me dry.

He turned to look at me. 'I'll put you in a cab – I want to go home to my place tonight and think about all this.' He held me close and I could smell the garlic and tobacco on his breath.

In for the Kill

Our kiss outside The Wolseley was our last. When I went into the office the following Tuesday, Greg called me into his office and explained that concerns had been raised about my former career as a private investigator. It was felt that this might attract negative publicity to the paper and so he felt it was better that I leave. I was welcome, he said, to bring in stories but I would no longer be needed to work on them.

'You need me to advise on investigations as well as journalise!'

'Look, Chris, why not go and write that bestseller you've always wanted to write?'

'Will I see you later back at my place?'

He smiled at me gently. 'No.'

It is a hard thing to be dropped out of such a powerful organisation; there is a huge bump when you hit the ground. Walking back to my apartment over Tower Bridge it felt as if I had been cast out to civilian life. I was sobbing badly. I couldn't believe that I would never go there again; the paper was like my family.

Whatever the real reason was for my sudden departure I'll never know, but it was all too late to stop fate. I had already introduced the news editor of the *News of the World* to one of the key players in the elite world of espionage.

Eleven

The Torture House

If you ever return to Ireland, you'll be arrested and then your genitals will be wired up to an old radio transmitter in a barn in Dundalk until you let us in on what your agenda is.

Senior republican commander to the author

I sat contentedly in my first-class seat on the flight to Ireland. Ron Wood from The Rolling Stones sat down next to me and when I told him I was afraid at take-off and touchdown he insisted on holding my hand through it all.

'I know what women are like. My wife's exactly the same. Here's my hand. Go on – hold it.'

I held Ron's strong hand and looked out of the window. I could see the khaki-coloured Irish Sea dotted with boats and liners. I held my breath at a sudden flood of sentiment – Ireland.

A sign as the plane landed read 'Welcome to Belfast'. Ron gave me his home phone number and invited me to the house to meet his family when I could get there. I hugged him goodbye and went to collect my bag. Then I bought a cup of hot tea from the takeaway stand and stood shivering in the cold, clutching the polystyrene cup with raw, red fingers, watching the taxis pull up.

As my taxi reached the city, I looked out of the window at the dark and poverty-stricken place. I felt a painful pang of loneliness. Sometimes having no family made me feel rootless and flimsy – as if I could just blow away and no one would cry or care.

I was still welcome to write for the *News of the World*. I just wasn't welcome in the office any more or to do any investigations for them, as Greg had told me that the paper no longer did any investigations all of a sudden. I was allowed to find my own investigative stories to work on and would then put them forward and either be rejected or commissioned on a case-by-case basis. I had put forward a story and Greg had commissioned me to find out what was going on between the factions of the Ulster Defence Association (UDA). They were busy blowing each other up and the news of the bloodshed had reached the mainland.

'Hit the ground running,' he had told me, which meant no dossing in the hotel or sightseeing, I was just to get straight into the investigation as soon as the plane touched down.

I had asked the hard-working librarians at the newspaper to send me as much info as possible on the UDA, which I'd downloaded to my laptop. I read it all during the flight and by touchdown I felt much better informed.

I had booked into the Clinton suite at the Europa Hotel. It was the best room in the hotel, paid for by the *News of the World*. I ordered a juicy fillet steak from room service, with a green side-salad and a large glass of strawberry milk. The steak was so good I rang down for half a bottle of Barolo to do it justice. When I had finished, I followed it up with a phone call for half a bottle of dessert wine. It was all covered by the paper, so I made the most of it.

Steam rose from the bath in white billows. My body felt relaxed in the hot water. I sipped the dessert wine and let the alcohol dull the pain of loneliness. The room was cosy: a home from home.

At eleven, wrapped in a thick towelling robe and lying on the bed, I tucked into a packet of cheese and onion crisps from the room's mini bar, then I opened a bottle of fine cognac and mixed it with Coca-Cola. It tasted good. I then searched around in the fridge and found a family-size bar of fruit-and-nut chocolate and broke off a chunk. This was the life! And it was all on the house. I knew I was eating too much food but I was trying to stuff down the feelings of loneliness and boredom with junk.

My mobile rang.

Greg's voice sounded stroppy and I could hear the clink of glasses and pub noises in the background.

'Are you there – you sound odd?'

'I'm eating – what's up?'

'Chris! News has just come in about Kim Basinger currently buying a holiday home in a village in the mountains near Donegal.'

He sounded excited. 'Since you're out there, get yourself across there and interview her about living in Ireland and that fracas she had with Alec Baldwin before you cover the UDA story – OK?'

'OK. Fine. Fluff first. That's what I like about the *News of the World*, it knows what really matters in life.'

'Chris, how the fucking hell would you know what makes a top fucking story?'

'Sorry.'

'Just get on with it.'

'OK – sorry.'

I put the phone down, sipped the Coke and cognac and tried to feel better, but I was angry. Donegal was buried deep in the west of Ireland. The idea of a long drive across country did not appeal.

I got up early the next day and drank a large coffee to ease my cognac hangover. Then, to make myself feel better, I hired a sports car. The sun was up and I drove with the roof down, letting the wind rasp through my hair. The road leading to the west of Ireland was somehow foreboding and claustrophobic – like approaching the ends of the earth. I felt as if someone had wandered over my grave. I travelled through Dungannon, then Ballygawley, past secluded farmhouses and on into Donegal.

I shivered. It all seemed so backward and shut off from the rest of the world. Why would Kim Basinger consider living here? *This is like the film Deliverance*, I thought grimly, driving as fast as I could.

Once settled in a hotel in town, I was met by a photographer, Abraham. He had dark hair, blue eyes and a friendly, flirty smile.

'I'll drive you around later, if you like? Have your lunch and I'll pick you up around three and we can go and get some pictures of Kim's new home.'

He returned at three on the dot. 'Do you like scenery? We have some of the most spectacular around here – really delightful. I could show you, Chris. It's a lot prettier than London. But it depends what turns you on,' he leered at me good-naturedly.

I smiled at him. 'OK, lead the way. I'm into greenery!'

We got into his blue Peugeot and he drove around Donegal and out along the road towards what he said were 'the mountains'. 'Has no one showed you the mountains? They're spectacular. Spooky too. You'll see. They say they're haunted. There's a legend around them.

'Yes,' he paused. 'There's also an amazing empty old house around here. It's built in the middle of a forest. It's a total gothic monstrosity. The owner says it's haunted. He's let it go to rack and ruin, and some say the IRA use it to torture people and leave their bones in the basement.'

'I've time to see the mountains but no time for torture chambers. That's not my thing at all!' I felt a little afraid. This was IRA territory.

Nothing had prepared me for the beauty of the scenery we were driving through – the rich, red earth that climbed and dipped in sensual, brown curves, the rolling hills and waterfalls.

'Chris, look, this is the mountain itself – they say it's the home of demon spirits. No one likes to go there after dark.' He smiled. 'Legend has it that the spirits judge a couple on whether there's true love there or not. If they feel the couple is in love, they bless their lovemaking by giving them a child. But they have to bathe in the green algae lake. It's this emerald lake that has dead bodies at the bottom of it. Well, that's what they say.'

I laughed. 'Great story. Typical Irish-legend crap, though, isn't it?' I said, wrinkling my nose.

He smiled at my cynicism. 'Yes, we're a bunch of fucking old women, aren't we, us Irish? Spectacular to look at, though – wait till you see it.'

We parked the car and walked in silence for half an hour through the woods until we reached a clearing.

We were looking up at the huge forest that spread before us in a rolling, verdant glen. An arrogant grey sky hung above it, claiming the silver-tinted mountains as its own. At the centre of the beauty, lying like a jewel, was a perfectly round emerald lake covered by light green algae.

'Quite something, isn't it? Oh God, you do like it, don't you? You OK?'

Tears were streaming down my face.

'Shit – sorry – it's made me feel weird. I don't know why – free or something. Weird. It's romantic as hell, isn't it? I can see why a Hollywood star like Kim Basinger would want to live here now! I can taste something supernatural here. It's making me want it.'

He looked me up and down.

'I'd love to fuck a girl's brains out here and check out that legend. Still, I'm not ready for a child yet – even if it were the Son of God.' He laughed.

The Torture House

I turned to him and smiled dismissively. Even though he'd been ribbing me, he walked on with his head down like a rejected schoolboy.

I swigged back a can of warm Coke and let it fizz down my throat. The near-flat drink had a pleasant taste. I breathed in the sweet mixed scent of honeysuckle and bluebells seeping from the woods.

Abraham now went on, 'About 50 years ago a young girl was found dead in the lake. They say someone killed her as a sacrifice to the demons for the life-giving properties of the lake. Creepy, huh? Must be a nut who dreamed that one up.'

'No shit!' I felt sick. Why had he saved that morsel till now? 'Right, let's go – beautiful or not, I told you I didn't want to see that haunted house. Now there's a spooky life-sucking, emerald lake and a dead girl thrown into the mix!'

'The girl had been missing for weeks. Her mother said she had gone for a date with a new boyfriend but no one knew who he was. Not even her close friends. There was nothing in her diary except a fascination for a local lad. They dredged her up and they only found half her face.'

I watched him out of the corner of my eye; he was clearly enjoying himself telling me the local horror stories.

'Hey, you're really freaking me out!'

I walked back to the car ahead of him. The ridiculous story of a young girl being murdered in that remote spot upset me; it was what Brady would have done. To be reminded of horror made me feel sick. Brady's crimes came floating into view.

What had I been doing, talking to a monster like Brady?

There seemed to be an answer just eluding me. Brady had told a journalist that he'd made sacrifices of his victims to a face of death he had first met at the age of 17. Sacrifices to invisible creatures! It was like the made-up killer of the girl in the green-algae lake. Other-worldly influences to murder.

Back at the hotel, I made enquiring pretext phone calls to local estate agents to find out the location of Kim Basinger's holiday home. Abraham lay sprawled on the bed, watching me admiringly as he smoked a cigarette. Then he made a sharp intake of breath. 'There's a big IRA convention tonight. We could shimmy on along there. Might be good for you to see the boys? Any interest in the IRA, Blondie-locks? I could show you all the main players, then we could go for a drink after?' He picked at his teeth and feigned nonchalance.

In for the Kill

I thought of the jaded stories I worked on for the paper that always seemed the same, then compared them to the marks that James had asked me to investigate. Meeting the IRA was James's territory. Despite all his promises of us fighting evil together, nothing had ever materialised. My heart leapt. Here was a chance to walk in James's mysterious world, one I had been told that I could not enter, one of great evil.

'Yes, I'll go with you. If I don't, I'll only sit on my own watching rubbish on television.' I smiled at him and felt excited.

He laughed as he ushered me into the car then issued me with instructions: 'We wait outside – not in. Just ask questions as they come out. I'll point out the big boys, if there's any here tonight. Should be.'

My stomach started to flutter. The IRA scared me.

We drove for miles into the dusky countryside until we came to a narrow country lane. A group of journalists waited outside a picturesque old stone-walled pub. A yellowy light shone from a lattice window into the growing dark. One by one, as midnight neared, tall figures began to emerge.

I held my breath. Abraham was nudging me excitedly.

'See him, it's John O'Neil [not his real name]. Real hard man. Responsible for all the bombs in London in the '70s.'

The heavy-set male looked as if all humanity had somehow been squeezed out of him.

'God, he looks dangerous!'

'He's the head of the Hydra then?'

'Sure. Hey, that's very army-speak!'

I gave him a fake smile and eyed O'Neil. If I could become a confidante of a man like that, I would be invaluable as a journalist. The ambitious side of me was coming to the fore and overriding my fear.

'Can we meet him? Any chance?'

'Don't be so silly! He's an unreachable. They have to protect themselves against spooks.'

'Who?'

'Spooks, ghouls, gooks: the secret services, Chris. Mind you, if one went near them they'd cut them into pieces.'

'Yes, I have heard.'

I swallowed hard. 'Introduce me to someone in charge here!'

'I don't know the any of the IRA leaders personally. Christ! You lot from London are real hard-arse, aren't you? You can't meet him – no way! None of us ever have.'

'I'm going to give it a try!'

I stepped forward purposefully. It was midnight now. A full moon hung low in the sky. Owls and squirrels were noisy in nearby trees. As I walked up to the group outside the pub, a raincoated man immediately stepped in front of me, barring my way. He was devastatingly good looking with cold, grey, almond-shaped eyes. I stared back at him, feeling a mixture of curiosity and annoyance at not reaching O'Neil. I held his gaze for a few moments, then he looked me up and down, staring like a schoolboy at my breasts, before moving back to my face. I felt heat spread up like a hot flame under his intense stare that seemed to reach inside me.

'Stand back.' He reached out and gave me a vicious shove that toppled me backwards in the darkness with a light scream.

Abraham came running over. He scolded me as he helped me out of the ditch. 'This isn't London! You're not interviewing MPs and their simpering wives.'

I picked myself up and wiped the wet mud off my ruined clothes.

'Do you know who you just smacked into? He's one of the IRA's top guys. Lucky for you he seemed distracted. Anyone else might have been dragged into that pub and given a beating!'

'What's his name?'

'Sean Flynn [not his real name].'

Flynn! My heart began to throb, making me dizzy. Wasn't he the sadistic psychopath that James had told me about? The rising star tipped for the very top and one to watch? I looked over at the backs of the group of men. This was a splinter republican group who were opposed to the peace process and wedded to the armed struggle. They had disagreed with the main body of the Provisional IRA, so maybe now Flynn would lead the new split-off faction. I could feel his menace in the pure country air.

An owl hooted. I shivered and realised it was a Sunday. Sundays had always scared me with their dullness and the fact that they were such a family day. A day in which I had always felt awkward and out of place – until now. Today, I was making the moves. Today, I had met Sean Flynn – the major terrorist threat to the Crown.

I would investigate him, get close to him and then bring him home – like dragging a stuck pig behind me with a rope. It would make me a somebody – I would become a renowned terrorist hunter.

I drove back to Belfast the next day and rang a cop who was the friend of a guy who had once sent me his CV to do surveillance work. I was in luck – he was available for lunch. He gave me the name and phone number of a UDA man, whom I rang and arranged to meet in a nearby bar. He told me a story about what had been going on with the UDA, but it didn't ring true.

I went back to the hotel, where I lay on the bed and felt like a failure. How was I supposed to do an investigation when I had no contacts here, no ears to the ground? Maybe I could go round and charm them to get them to cough?

I poured myself another cognac and Coke and wondered what to order from room service for dinner, all the time thinking about what I should tell Greg. My mobile rang as I was in the bath. It was the UDA man. 'I've got the info you wanted. It was a consignment of guns that came in. Someone grassed on us and the guns got taken. We thought it was A company that did it, so we offed one of them.'

I got out of the bath as he talked. What he had given me wasn't enough. I might be being used for propaganda, so I would have to check it with my cop. I rang the cop and arranged another candlelit dinner for two in the most expensive restaurant in town. I plied him with ice-cold Bollinger and caviar – the paper easily ran to it and with cops we were told to spare no expense. The champagne flowed and he confirmed all the information.

After returning to the hotel, woozy from the champagne, I got into my robe and wrote the story up on my laptop before filing it over to the news desk.

I got back to London late on Saturday night and then on Sunday morning went to buy the paper at my local newsagents on the corner. There it was – a middle-page spread, my story, my investigation, with the byline James Fitzpatrick emblazoned across it. I was crying as I made my way back to my apartment. Perhaps it was childish to cry but it was the pettiness of it that got me. Fitzpatrick was a made-up name and Greg had put it on my story. I rang him at his home.

'Why are you ringing me at home on a Sunday?'

'I fucking hate your fucking guts.'

'Are you mad?'

'My byline – my bloody story!'

'You told me that the UDA were dangerous. I was trying to protect you.'

'The UDA know who I am as I told them.'

I hung up and sobbed into my pillow. Then after an hour I remembered something. I rang the newspaper library. 'Give me all you have on a man called Sean Flynn – pictures, words, all of it.'

'OK, Chris, but I need a clue. What is he? Crime or what?'

'He's IRA.'

The stuff later came spewing out of my porter's fax machine and he came up in his grey peaked porter's cap to push it under my door. I got up out of bed, my face still tear-stained, to get it. I glanced at the words but concentrated on the photos. Flynn. There he was with his stone-grey eyes and that tight mouth. All of a sudden I felt full of purpose. I stuck his photo to my corkboard pinned up over my computer.

Was he evil? He felt like evil. I chewed my lip. The IRA. Yes, people said they were evil, and Flynn was a Godfather. I went to sleep happy. I wanted to dive into Flynn, find the evil and finally know it.

Twelve
Deadly Desire

Electra, I could've given you the world.

James Bond, *The World is Not Enough*

I sat in my silver open-top Lotus and chatted to Greg on my mobile. He was busy telling me about all the office politics. Apparently Alex was being reassigned to cover Belfast. I was glad as I liked Alex, and military defence and terrorism was quickly becoming my bag.

A leather-clad figure astride a 750cc bike sweltering in the London heat nodded at me and then zoomed off along Whitehall weaving in and out of the traffic. I watched him as I said my goodbyes to Greg and hung up.

It was like an oven in the car and smelt of my Youth Dew. I opened the window to clear the stuffiness and wiped away a crease of sweat clinging to my forehead. I then switched on the radio to hear news that a pub in London's West End had had a nail-bomb blast; 13 people had been badly injured. I turned off the radio. It was the third pub bombing in a month.

After I pulled over, the photographer I was using for the story I was currently working on, a solidly built man, climbed into the car clutching an oversize long-lens Nikon camera.

'Has Carter not come out yet, for fuck sake?' His cursing was low and deep in an accent from somewhere just south of Newcastle.

I cleared my throat.

'No. Our orders from Greg are to sit and wait for him – then go on to the Real IRA's secret meeting in Kilburn.' I eyed the freelance photographer. 'We're to infiltrate the private IRA meeting. We've to go undercover as Real IRA supporters and try to find out why they're in London when all these pub bombings are going on. It's very cheeky!'

The man with the Geordie accent stared back at me. 'Did they give you a photo ID of the terrorists?'

'Yes – we've got the British intelligence files from Greg's former MI5 contacts.'

I showed him the photos.

'These are the ones that will be attending the meeting on our patch. Patrick Gracey [not his real name] and the other one Flynn and ...' I searched through the three buff-coloured British intelligence files. Four sticky Mars wrappers and two empty packets of chocolate buttons tumbled out of the glove compartment as I searched for my notebook. I felt ashamed. I had tried to stuff my loneliness with endless confectionery.

'Flynn is their military leader.' I pored over the grainy photograph and thought of how dangerous Flynn was. He would be under surveillance as soon as he stepped onto English soil. The idea excited me. I hoped that it would somehow bring James out of the shadows and into my arms.

'David Morton [another photographer] has gone after what he thinks is him just arrived at Heathrow.'

I looked again at the black-and-white photograph of a man of about 45: dark brown hair, a savagely angelic face. He looked the same as when I'd first met him that dark night in the countryside of the west of Ireland when he had pushed me into a ditch: glinting grey-eyed and contemptuous.

'These men are here to try and raise funds for the Real IRA. They're not low graders.'

Rain covered the car's windscreen and I felt a familiar surge of claustrophobia.

'He's a psychopath, you know, the Real IRA leader!' I said, to break the uncomfortable silence in the car. The photographer was looking out of the window and appeared not to be listening. 'Amusing, isn't it?'

'S'pose so,' he managed to answer without opening his lips. I felt irritated by his surly presence. *What's the matter, baby? Want to be with the wife instead of carrying out surveillance of the Real IRA?*

The mood lifted a bit with the arrival of Ralph Carter. Carter had light red hair and an Eton background. He was friendly, we had often worked together and I was looking forward to our usual repartee.

'What exciting things have you roped me in on now, Chris?' he asked as he clambered into the car, bringing with him the smell of cologne and Havana cigars.

'Greg has sent us to cover this secret Real IRA meeting in Kilburn. Flynn's going to be there. He wants us to go undercover as supporters.' I smiled at Carter and broke into a laugh when I saw his face crumble.

'Great fun!' he said. 'I just feel like getting tortured by dangerous terrorists!'

The air was balmy; the rain had cleared, giving way to a blue sky and a weak white sunshine. The photographer had got out and was trying to flag down a black cab. There wasn't room for us all in my two-seater car, so he was going to make his own way to the meeting and catch up with us there.

'That snapper was a real wuss.'

'Why?'

'*I want to be with my wife, not meeting the Real IRA. It's dangerous. We don't get paid enough,*' I whined in contemptuous imitation.

'Grass him up immediately, Chris, and he'll get the sack. You know how they hate anyone who isn't a workaholic.'

'I won't, but he should think about a different career. This job is twenty-four seven.'

'It's us who should get our heads tested. Come on, let's go. By the way, I'm meeting up with MI5 before we go inside. They'll give us a bit of a low-down on these characters. Flynn's one of the splinter group's current leaders. He's lethal – have you shot soon as look at you, or rather give the order to . . .' Carter paused, seemingly deep in thought. 'My guess is they'll advise us to play it straight with high-ranking terrorists like that around – tell them we're Press and ask them outright what the hell they are doing in London.'

But while we were on our way to Kilburn, we got a call from one of the staff on the newsdesk to say that the meeting was now set for the following night. Carter had been trying to read the intelligence files on his knee but he now made me pull up in a side street in the middle of nowhere and got out. He looked over at me before he strode off. 'These guys never turn up to first meetings. You know that by now, don't you, Chris?'

I rang my contact to check out the IRA meeting. He confirmed it had been changed to the following night. Flynn had come in from Ireland, though, and we now had him plotted up at the address where he was staying. A lot of newspaper work was spent in cars sitting outside places, waiting for people who never showed up.

I glanced out the window as I drove home. The rain had made the leaves on the trees glisten. Water dripped from them onto the busy streets below, shining in the strong summer sunlight. After stopping the car, I leaned my head back against the leather headrest and glanced at myself in the wing mirror. I was still feeling the effects of the adrenalin that had started to build in anticipation of confronting Flynn again. It was April 1999 and I was 32 years old. I wondered how I had ended up becoming embroiled in the world of terrorism.

After my introduction to the Troubles in Northern Ireland, with the story on the UDA, I had gone on to cover the terrible events of the Omagh bombing for the paper. It had affected me so badly that I had suffered panic attacks that made it difficult to do my job. I wondered whether other journalists were similarly affected after covering such atrocities. 'Post Traumatic Stress Disorder,' a psychiatrist had called it after the paper had sent me to see him.

'Bad childhood?' Dr Pike had said, looking at me questioningly. 'You say you never knew your real parents. An orphan. Now you're single with no family of your own – husband – children? You're in your 30s? Why's there no man? Are you a lesbian, Chris?'

I felt a boil of shame. 'No, I'm not bloody gay!'

He looked at me kindly. 'This terrible bomb, working on it, attending the inquest, it seems to have triggered things from your own childhood. It's best all out, Chris.'

He paused and looked sympathetically at my pale, worried face. 'Forget your spying and go and relax.' The doctor's face was sincere and caring. 'Sometimes if we've had a bad childhood – sexual abuse or beatings, that kind of thing – we keep people at arm's length and find nourishment in our work. We become workaholics, addicted to food, drink – anything.'

I thought of my interest in evil – Brady, now Sean Flynn. I had even made it my job; I had become an investigative reporter to study evil.

'When work fails to nourish us, we can have a breakdown because we have nowhere else to turn – no connection to life except for our addiction.' He looked at me all too intently. The wind blew noisily outside the window. I stared out as if trying to escape his words in the rain.

'It's a terrible waste of a life for an attractive, intelligent woman like you, Chris. Avoiding intimacy by addiction means these people will never have a wedding day. They usually never have children.'

Children. I yearned for a child. Oh God. I leapt up, tore out of the office and down the corridor.

'Chris!'

I could hear Colin Pike shouting after me as I ran, my heels clattering down the steep steel staircase as I headed for the reception area and then out into the rainy courtyard. I sat in my car crying, sobbing, trying to catch my breath. I wept for an hour, clinging tightly to the steering wheel for dear life as I tried to fight off the terror of the idea of never having a child.

My mobile now woke me from this grim recollection. It was Ralph Carter.

'MI5 says the Real IRA meeting is set for tomorrow afternoon. I'll pick you up tomorrow at around twelve. Be ready.'

The next morning was a warm April day. We drove from leafy central London and my glossy penthouse apartment into the more downmarket area of west London, turned and parked outside a Catholic church hall.

'Off you go,' ordered Carter in a dry voice.

'Oh! Thanks! I go while you sit here in the getaway car in safety?' I queried mockingly.

I got out of the car and made my way into the hall, trying to swallow down a throat-blocking panic attack. The sun was high at one o'clock. I bit my lip and pulled at my flowery dress, which kept riding up. As I entered the hall, several heads turned and looked at me.

'Is there a meeting in here?' I asked, looking around a dreary room that stank of beer.

An old woman I took to be the caretaker said, 'No, but there's a party on in our back room, love.' The slightly built Irish woman then held open a curtain to reveal a large gathering of men in dark suits who looked deep in conversation.

I craned my neck at the gathering and spotted Flynn. My chest tightened as I caught sight of his face from the side with his clearly defined features in profile.

I bit my lip, made my way outside back to the car and scratched my head nervously. 'It's them. Flynn . . .' I swallowed hard. 'Flynn's there. Oh God. What the fuck is he doing in London? He knows the place will be swarming with security.'

I marvelled for a minute at his daring. 'Oh, hang on! That's what everyone's supposed to think – what a great recruitment drive. He's showing off. He'll probably recruit hundreds out of it. What a leader.'

Carter looked at me. 'Does that impress you?'

'No, it disgusts me. But I do want to know why he's evil.'

Carter smiled. 'Chris, come on – let's be brave. MI5 have them in their sights.'

I looked at his face as he pulled on his coat. Why did civilians always see MI5 as all-powerful when in fact they were usually to be found frantically flapping about in desperation against the tide of terrorism? Flynn was a major force to be reckoned with.

The family meeting had broken up in the back room and the care-worn woman was handing round plates of sandwiches. Again I caught sight of the man who had pushed me into a muddy ditch in Ireland.

Oh God. I have to stay away from him – keep away. He makes me feel weird – like he's whisky and I'm an alcoholic.

I felt I was going to hyperventilate. *Will he remember me? No, course not.*

I felt in my handbag for the brown paper bag I'd been told to carry for my panic attacks. 'Breathe into it slowly and calm yourself,' the psychiatrist had told me. Just hearing it rustle reassured me – I wasn't going to be able to bring it out in this setting.

A man with white hair approached me – Pat Blair [not his real name]. I could hardly wait to spill the words, 'We're Press.' As soon as I'd said it, I felt relieved. The paper could not now force me to go undercover as a Real IRA supporter.

'Follow us over and come up to the attic, where you can meet our leaders.'

I looked into his cold, blue eyes. *Why a hidden attic room?* I wondered to myself.

Noise spilled out when we opened the door to the pub. Irish folk music was blaring out from the jukebox. As soon as the men from the meeting showed their faces at the door, they were led up the stairs. I whispered to Carter. 'Shit, the bloody Real IRA. I'm afraid.'

Deadly Desire

My mind ran over the book I'd been reading about the Troubles, *The Dirty War* by Martin Dillon. The methods of torture the IRA used on spies when they caught them were horrifying: knee-capping, electrocution. I swallowed hard.

A thick throaty Irish accent behind us said, 'Up the stairs, woman! Keep going up till you can't go any further.'

I kept my eyes straight ahead. Maybe they were going to showboat and bump off two journalists. Al-Qaeda didn't seem to mind beheading us. A quick slideshow of horror played in my head until I felt completely paranoid.

The room in the attic was dank. At the back hung a large tricolour flag, taking up all of the wall space. Behind me stood a tall man with an acne-scarred face. There was no way out. No way out if I found I couldn't breathe. In my briefcase, the four private buff-coloured files from the anti- terrorist police seemed to burn a hole through the leather.

Outside in the street there was shouting. The far right had gathered in a tiny crowd. I knew it would be the BNP. How had they found out about this? The details would have been leaked by the media to create a story around the pub bombings, I guessed. If the far right got themselves too worked up, something burning would be hurled through the window.

At the back of the room stood Flynn, his dark-brown hair greying at the temples. He was incredibly good looking with his narrowed flinty grey eyes and flawless skin, well-shaped hands and sharp, polished nails.

He radiates power, I thought curiously. *It's affecting me. It's his air of omnipotence.* I could feel my eyes flicker over him. I shuffled my feet nervously, dug my nails into the palms of my hands and tried to concentrate on what the speaker was saying about the English illegally occupying their country.

Two journalists from the broadsheets turned up. I recognised one of them from *The Times*. Their presence made me feel more secure; I knew they would hardly bump off the four of us. The sound of the shouting outside got more and more agitated, however. Scuffles with the police had broken out as a ring had been formed around the entrance to the pub.

A voice reached me. It was Carter whispering in my ear. 'Speak, speak. Come on, Chris. Ask the scumbags a few questions. I feel like I'm on my own here!' He looked at me intently. 'Chris, you're miles away. This isn't like you! CHRIS.'

I stared back and focused on the angry flabby face.

'Shit, sorry, Carter.'

I turned towards the Real IRA terrorist making the speech and cleared my throat.

'I can't,' I whispered to Carter.

Something inside me was reacting to Flynn. I could feel it bomb the pit of my stomach and then rise like a tight bubble up my torso into my throat, choking me, preventing me from asking questions. Carter's face was peering into mine and he was whispering at me again.

'Chris, what's up with you? You're fucking miles away! Usually you have the story in the bag after the first few minutes.'

He studied my white face in surprise.

'Sorry, Chris. I didn't know you were feeling unwell. Must be all the fag smoke in this filthy attic.'

We went downstairs into the clearer air of the bar. I looked up. Flynn descended the stairs slowly, like an emperor, looking at me with his direct stare as he reached the bottom. We held each other's gaze. I spoke, knowing I had to find out why he was making me feel so attracted to him.

'Join the press for a drink, Mr Flynn?'

'I don't drink.'

He looked back at me, his face stony with disgust at my arrogance in communicating with him. I leaned back against the bar. If I let him out the door, I would never see him ever again. We would get some moron from their political wing giving us the bum's rush over the phone. I had to act quickly.

One of his guards came up to me and aggressively lit my cigarette. I reached up and kept my eyes on Flynn as he stood near the door.

Speak. Speak! Go on, do it, I urged myself.

'I would like a contact phone number for Mr Flynn, please. I may need to interview him.'

The Irishman walked over to Flynn. I heard murmured conversation followed by laughter. He returned and pulled out a roll of paper from his pocket and a biro, scrawled a mobile number on it and handed it to me with a grin on his face. Flynn watched the whole thing from the door, unsmiling. I knew if he looked back before he left, I had him. I kept my eyes on him. He left without a backward glance.

Oh, so it's going to be like that, is it?

Back in the car I found it hard to swallow the McDonald's Carter had fetched. I sipped at an ice-cold Coke. Carter was excited.

'Flynn made my blood run cold – he controlled the whole room. He's extremely dominant and an intellectual – what a powerful mix! Did you notice the way the other top Real IRA men grovelled around him as if he was God himself?'

'No. Yes. Did they? I didn't notice,' I murmured.

Didn't notice! I feel like I've just been infected by some kind of virus.

Carter bit his hamburger and sipped his drink through a stripy straw. He started to chew, tomato sauce covering his lips. 'The military can't get near him. He can just walk down a London street and we can't touch him. He's the single major danger to safety we have in London along with al-Qaeda.'

'Carter, stop talking – please.'

Carter paused and looked across at me, seeing my face screwed up tightly in pain.

'Hey, Chris – you all right?' He looked at me with affection. 'You're tired. Come on, let's get you home.'

'Yes, I need something. I've an awfully bad migraine. It's making me feel sick.'

Holding my throbbing head, I couldn't stop thinking about the effect Flynn's presence had had on me. It had been like catching flu. Now I felt sick with it – whatever it was.

I pulled myself together and stared out of the car window at London's nightlife. 'Remember we investigated that satanic ritual-killing cult last year, up in Birmingham, and the leader was highly charismatic?' I knew this would sound strange to Carter, who was busy licking his salty fingers. 'He had that messianic air of omnipotence?'

'No, but go ahead.'

'Well, the Real IRA almost seems like them somehow – know what I mean? Not one bit like the old Provisional IRA. They seem to have formed a cult around Flynn. Oh, I don't know.'

I bit my lip.

'It's like – messianic. Can you feel it in him? I can, I can sense . . . I don't know. Some kind of quality that I'm drawn to, in a kind of a religious way. It's like a power that is coming from somewhere else, that he's harnessing. Cults, you know, they always have these leaders with that kind of power.'

I fell silent and stared out of the window thinking I'd probably said too much.

In for the Kill

Carter called the newsdesk.

'We're coming in now – to write something up. Meeting up with MI5 first in a bar in Shepherd Market.'

I glanced at him. The one question I had managed to put to Flynn had not given us enough for a good political-interest story.

'I'm sorry about not being myself in the meeting, Ralph. You must have felt pretty much on your own.'

'Forget it. You were OK,' he said, smiling at me good-naturedly.

Later that night, tucked up in bed, I found the day and Flynn's effect hard to shake off.

What's wrong with me? I have a good life. Yet I feel completely numb and desperate, and convinced that something terrible is going to happen all the time.

Thoughts of Flynn crawled over me like ants. I tossed around in bed. He was so dominant and had exuded such power that I found him erotic. I thought of him and me naked, intertwined and grabbing at each other madly and passionately – verses, chapters and then a conclusion. I got out of bed feeling like I was going mad – he was forbidden fruit. *Flynn! The biggest threat to national security there was at the present time.*

Downstairs, I turned on the light, poured a glass of cold milk and mixed in three spoonfuls of strawberry Nesquik. I drank it back and felt better immediately. I knew we were all being watched today. James and the rest of MI5 and MI6 would show themselves soon. I could sense their presence in the company of the Real IRA commanders. They had haunted the meeting like ghosts – spooks.

I fetched Flynn's mugshots from my briefcase, sticking them on my corkboard to join the other photos of him I had been sent from our library. I stared at them. *Hmm, quite something, aren't you?*

I finished the milkshake and retrieved the screwed-up roll of paper from my handbag. Flynn's mobile number.

I dialled it and a gruff voice answered. I held it silently to see if I could hear anything useful in the background, then hung up soundlessly. It wasn't Flynn's number. As if it would be. Bet it was one of his lackeys. I took the silent phone back up to bed with me.

Thoughts of Flynn came to me incessantly like a moth fluttering around a naked light bulb. I sat up in bed and lit a cigarette, stared at the ceiling and felt anxiety wash over me. I would not get near Flynn. Not with my MI6-influenced background. He would kill me.

Thirteen
Taken Prisoner

When the Real IRA get hold of you, no one will be
able to hear your screams.

Senior republican to author

The Real IRA had attacked London relentlessly the previous
summer. MI6 had been struck with a mortar grenade and
before that the Hammersmith Bridge had been bombed. Now, in
March 2001, it had been the turn of the BBC and everyone was
wondering who would be next. I knew that Flynn must be part of
the group involved. I could feel him somehow – all that hate.

I went out and walked across the blue and white Tower Bridge,
buying a toffee apple from the vendor halfway across, and watched
the luxurious speedboats run underneath it as I chewed. They
had filmed the action scenes of many top British thrillers here.

It was a beautiful warm spring day and American tourists were
in evidence around the Tower of London. I imagined the IRA
making their getaway after shooting at the MI6 building and
wondered about the mind that had planned it. It was Flynn. I
knew it – I could smell his mind and its ambition.

My mobile rang just as I was cleaning my fingers of sticky
toffee.

'Those evil bastards, Chris,' Greg started forcefully.

'Who?'

'The Real IRA. Sean Flynn.'

I jumped at the sound of the name.

Greg went on, 'You're one of the few who has met Sean Flynn.
I want you to go off to Dundalk and interview him for us – sound

him out! I want to know what he's really like. Is he really the
leader of the Real IRA? Why is he attacking London? Make him
open up to you! Then do what you've always wanted to do for us
– write – and I'll add your byline this time. You get me some
exclusive material. Hole up there for a few weeks. I'll cover the
expenses. Do whatever you have to do, Chris.'

'OK.'

I tried to sound light-hearted, but the idea of being face to face
with Flynn again made my stomach churn.

I telephoned a republican contact I had made through another
journalist. 'Can you fix it for me?' I asked him. I tried to take a
breath of calm. Flynn would be impossible to reach. There was
no way a man like him would grant me an interview.'Unreachable,'
James had called them.

'Wait a while then ring me back. I'll put it to one of Flynn's
boys.'

'Tell him I'm the one he pushed into a ditch.'

I was remembering the way he had stared at my breasts and
hoped this would jog his memory. I was using my looks, but didn't
everyone? I also knew it would fail. Looks wouldn't penetrate the
thick wall that surrounded a killer like Sean Flynn.

I waited ten minutes, polished off the toffee apple, and then
called my contact again, expecting the refusal that I hoped for.

'Eight o'clock next Thursday evening. Come alone to a place
just outside Dundalk village. We'll make contact and let you know
where nearer the time,' the deep voice advised me. I sipped from
a can of Coke and felt sick to my stomach.

'I didn't think Mr Flynn gave interviews?'

'You must have a really big pair of tits.' I could hear him silently
smirking down the phone.

'Tell him I'll be there.'

I hung up, my heart beating fast. They would be unkind to me;
I knew it. Make me sweat for information. They were inviting me
to come and play nasty because I was English. I felt afraid.

Dalkey was the haunt of moneyed celebrities. Most of them had
built their homes on the cliffs overlooking the sea. I pulled my
soft pink cardigan around my shoulders and shivered, then stood
and stared forlornly out of the wet hotel window across the bay.

My boyfriend, Paul, was thundering out self-composed
masterpieces on the hotel's baby grand piano. His fingers weaved

over the keys expertly and the patrons in the bar smiled happily at his playing. I wished he'd stop showing off and give me some attention. I'd been seeing Paul for about six months after meeting him at an exhibition in London. He'd recently proposed to me and I had brought him with me for company, but now I was beginning to regret it.

Shit, I'm lonely. Cold rose inside me. *Please make it better – someone, something, make me feel at home in the world. Stop making each day a cold, grey, airless ordeal.*

Out of the window I could see a wintry sun fluttering honey light onto the sea, which surged toward the land and rippled onto the shore. It was cold outside and you could feel it in the air even indoors. Damp, salty Irish weather. As the window was slightly open, I could smell the seaweed and see long-tailed rats that were clambering amongst the rocks leading down to the sandy beach.

I took a deep breath and spoke loudly. 'Paul, stop playing, will you?'

His audience glared at me and I looked downwards, not trusting myself entirely.

Paul came over. He sat down and smiled at me indulgently, but the smile didn't melt my irritation.

'I hate Ireland. It's all grey, salty and tragic,' I finished over-loudly, trying to vent my hatred at the people in the bar who I felt had unfairly judged me.

'You should have stayed at home, Chris, and not fancied yourself as Lois Lane, the intrepid investigative reporter!' Paul looked around, grinning at the people who had been admiring his playing. I hated him for enjoying playing the part of the martyr to my harridan girlfriend.

Later, full of well-cooked fresh salmon and white wine, we left the hotel and caught the train to Dublin, then crossed the city streets on a bus, heading to Dundalk and my rendezvous with Flynn.

I hung out of the window of the bus and pulled on a cigarette, lost in daydreams. The twilight over the countryside was breathtaking, the smell of damp hedgerows intoxicating. Paul slept beside me, only to wake up as we pulled into Dundalk.

We ate chicken burgers at midnight and chatted to the person who worked in the fish bar. He made us two plates of salty fries covered in warm mayonnaise. We picked at the fries and flicked through the County Louth Yellow Pages in search of a cheap B&B. I was still in a dreamy mood. I fiddled with a dirty teaspoon on the long bar and let it make tiny splatters with my milky tea. Paul ordered some homemade fruit cake from the counter and I bit into it hungrily.

Flynn's world was a hidden and dangerous one. I had no idea where to get a smell of it or a feel for it. *Oh God – why am I here? It's stupid – scary and stupid.*

At 2 a.m., we still hadn't found a B&B. Tired and fed up, we booked into an expensive hotel – The Fairways.

'Why are you upset?' Paul started, as he lay in the gloriously comfortable bed. 'You'll get a good story. I don't know why you don't believe in yourself a bit more. You'll be fine with Flynn and get all his secrets out of him. Don't allow yourself to be alone with him, though, Chris! Keep it all above board and safe.'

He leaned over and caressed my face. 'Let's order up some hot chocolate and some biscuits and see if we can't find a good old black-and-white movie?'

'Mm, yes – and some cold beer.'

The next morning Paul sprang out of bed, showered, dressed, and then went outside to wait for me. When I emerged half an hour later, he was sitting on a wooden fence across from the entrance to the hotel, chewing on an egg sandwich he had taken from the breakfast buffet table. Cars streamed past. The air smelt wet, earthy. I thought it must have rained heavily in the night.

A bus ride took us back into Dundalk and then we took another bus to our final destination, one that, as we approached, seemed cut off from civilisation.

When we disembarked, a marine-coloured sky was holding the heat of the fine spring day. Puffs of white cloud hung heavy over the mountains. I felt overfed and heavy from too much chocolate.

'It's a bit chilly,' Paul shivered in his thin T-shirt.

'I know – chilly is right. I wish we hadn't come here. All my instincts are telling me I shouldn't have.'

'Yes. We're strangers, Chris. They won't like them round here. They'll assume they're spies – this is a no-go area.'

'Oh, Paul, stop going on so. Be quiet and let me think,' I snapped, pulling up the collar of my leather jacket.

'Chris, let's just go. I know we've travelled for miles, but I've got a bad feeling. Let's just treat it like a mini-break. We've had a really nice time, haven't we, babe?'

'Kind of. Actually no, not really. It's not a bloody holiday, Paul. I'm here to interview Flynn, a Real IRA commander.'

He looked around wildly, as if waiting to be approached by some invisible stranger.

'They're just wary of strangers, relax yourself.' I fingered my press pass in my pocket and tried to feel confident.

'Let's get the next bus out. It feels like a trap!'

I brooded on the strangeness of Flynn's kingdom – the way it seemed like it was set back in time. 'Let's go and have a quick drink in the local bar or we'll look suspicious to anyone who might be watching.' I looked up at the sky. The air was awash with the smell of wood-rose that came from the fields surrounding the 1930s-style houses.

'One drink then and we're off, OK? God knows why you would ever want to come here, Chris! It's like the end of the earth.'

'It's my job to check out the ends of the earth. Journalists are the most curious people alive.'

The bar smelled of stale stout and the walls were peeling peach paint. We sat opposite a large cabinet of stuffed wild birds and I felt afraid. A long corridor of old, dusty lino passed the unhygienic toilets. Paul sighed and looked down at his pint. The Guinness had steamed up the edges of the glass. It tasted thick and creamy, though, and we both began to loosen up a bit.

I leant my head into my hands and watched Paul admiringly. He really was very handsome and I felt bad about the way I treated him sometimes.

He smiled at me indulgently, the beer foam lining his upper lip, but then my attention was distracted by three men who had come in, avoided looking at the pair of us as if we were invisible and then taken their place at some tall red stools at the bar.

I felt a familiar sense of dread as I contemplated the view of their backs. I knew they were there because I was. As Paul got up to go to the toilet, they stood up in unison. One got up and covered the door. Another put his arm around my shoulders and grinned into my face menacingly. The third, short and wiry with ginger hair, went after Paul in the bathroom and I heard him kicking the metallic door of the toilet cubicle open.

I'm going to pass out in fear, I thought, feeling light-headed.

The heaviest one spoke. 'The boy has to fuck off. You're here because you've been invited. If all's OK, Flynn will give you an audience, just you and him.'

In for the Kill

I looked numbly over at Paul as he returned, struggling to free himself from the hold of the red-haired man. 'Chris, Chris, I'll get the police! Don't worry! Chris. Chris?'

I stared at him, caught in the grasp of the dark-haired man.

'Take it easy, arsehole. If it checks out that she's not a spy for the British, you'll be all right. But, Sonny Jim, if the cops are called for your girlfriend, say goodbye to ever setting eyes on her again. This is our land you're on now.'

I knew I had to try to be brave and calm the erratic Paul. 'Paul, wait for me at the airport. I'll join you there by this evening. There's a hotel in Balbriggan – Balbriggan Court. Wait for me there. Don't call the cops, Paul! Wait however long it takes. I'll come back.'

The dark-haired man spoke while pulling on my arm roughly. 'Don't be so fucking sure.'

My eyes met Paul's and as we were both dragged out of the pub I saw real concern in his white face. I looked around at the Irish countryside and felt my body numb out as I recognised the overwhelming stupidity of being here.

The tallest of the men took me along to a terraced house close to the pub. In the front room were quaint ornaments of green leprechauns and the Virgin Mary. These and the bumpy wallpaper reminded me of the trips to Liam's relatives when I was a child. I shivered; the room was freezing.

A nondescript woman in jeans and jumper with straggly hair sat on the sofa and reached out, gesturing for me to hand over my handbag. I gave it uncertainly and reluctantly. I had no choice. The thorough search of my Gucci handbag eventually revealed some wages slips from a company called Ciex Ltd.

The woman's hard hazel eyes met mine and she spoke in the harsh Irish accent of the mountains. 'What are they?'

I looked back at her and tried to muster some courage that I did not feel.

'I don't remember.' I felt sick. I had done some recent surveillance work for Michael Oatley and he was also former MI6, like James's father.

The woman asked again – this time louder, 'Who the fuck is this?'

I knew it was useless to lie. How had those wage slips found their way into my bag? What kind of a sick joke of a highly trained operative was I? Where was my basic preparation? I couldn't even conduct a complete search and check of my own handbag.

The tallest of the men from the pub with a pockmarked face came towards me and jabbed at my face with his lit cigarette. I screamed. Another came up behind me and pushed his flies into my bottom and started to feign sex.

'Undress the cunt and let's all take turns.'

I felt my bowels soften.

The woman with the blonde hair and hazel eyes looked at me evenly – something about her made me respect her.

'Listen, woman, it's best you tell us who you are.'

The man with the pockmarked face spoke up. 'Tell us the truth or I'll put you in the oven and turn it on and roast you. I fucking love roast British whore.'

The other men laughed and dragged me towards the oven. With what seemed like prior practice, they folded my limbs in a coldly logical way and pushed my head inside it. I smelled the stink of gas as they turned it on and off again.

'Gas her, gas her!' they chanted now.

They dragged me out and laid me flat on the floor with their feet on my hands and ankles and their leather boots pressing on me until I told them.

'It's a private firm owned by Michael Oatley. It means "cie", which is French for "company", and the x means company "X",' I whispered, hearing how stupid it sounded as I mouthed the words.

'Oatley was a top MI6 agent who liaised with us,' said one of the men.

'I know. But I truly am just a journalist. I only used to be a private spy and this is a coincidence.' I started to retch from the gas fumes and my head pounded.

'A private spy? Are you fucking joking with us?'

A voice piped up. 'We've got one of the dirty bastards – she's another Nairac. Let's take her outside and slit her neck.' (Robert Nairac was an SAS man who had come to a no-go area in Ireland undercover as a friendly passer-by and had been killed as a spy by the IRA. It is said that his remains were ground up and fed to the pigs, and he was tortured so badly his gum and three teeth were found under Drumintee Bridge.)

I felt my face numb over and my eyes fill with tears. They dragged me up and into a cream-painted parlour with a naked bulb and no furniture.

In for the Kill

These men are killers! Killers! Why did I come here? It was Flynn. I wanted to meet him again. It was being drawn to Flynn that brought me here.

I started to bang on the badly painted wooden door and scream. The scream brought more fear and soon I couldn't breathe. The doorknob just rattled in its round white plastic frame.

They had scraped in the dirt and found the Intelligence Corps, who they absolutely loathed.

Oh God. I hope they do kill me. I have no home to hurry back to anyway. No husband, no child, no family.

I screamed and rattled the doorknob again. The man with the pockmarked face opened the door and came marching up to me. He put his pitted face very close to mine and said, 'If you don't stop this journalist lie, I'll hack your tits off.'

He marched out and locked the door. I stood staring at it, hardly able to move or breathe. I sat on the floor and thought about my life. I knew I had no future and I had an ugly past. I didn't get on with women and could not open up to men. I lived on a planet that I had not been welcome on since birth. I was still an outsider here and because of that I had grown to loathe it.

For the next four hours, I sat alone in that empty room. Painful and tortured sleep came fitfully, riddled with dreams of being dragged into a fire, screaming in agony as flames engulfed me. I woke wet, sweltering and sobbing, feeling death was imminent. I stood up when I heard footsteps approaching the door. He was there with his pockmarked face. He spoke on a mobile in front of me and laughed.

Three young boys dressed in green combats and army boots stuffed me into the footwell of the back seat of a stale-smelling, rusty car and drove for half an hour or so before pushing me out into the freezing night. 'Fuck off, Brit Army cunt!'

The door slammed shut and they were gone. I listened as the sound of the rattling engine got fainter and fainter.

I still had my handbag with me and I had money in it. The folded notes added up to three hundred pounds. They must have seen it but they hadn't touched it. These men had left the world of petty crime behind long ago. I set off stumbling in the dark along the unlit country lane, hoping the moon would light up the ghostly larch.

As I walked, my mind was filled with memories of childhood holidays in Ireland. Hot summer days swimming in the Dublin

Liffey with no knickers on and Liam Hart, the man I called 'Daddy', making me swim harder. I could see his face as I looked up from the cold brown water. He was always so very angry that I never became as good a swimmer as the other children.

Maybe an hour later I realised I'd reached a dirt track that led up to a village. It was the same village I had started from. I could see the pub where earlier I had sat with Paul. My instinct was to run but I needed sustenance, warmth. I headed away from the previous pub, though, and veered towards the warm comforting yellowy lights of one round the corner. When the blonde barmaid asked me what I wanted, I ordered a large brandy and sipped at it to take away the shock.

The pub had an old-fashioned jukebox, there were pictures of men hurling on the wall and a fire that burned in the grate. The smells made me relax – beer and cigarettes. But the light-heartedness of that afternoon with Paul seemed years away. A local who I had seen before, the old one with tears in cornflower-blue eyes, smiled at me. And then, as if in slow motion, the same dark-haired man who had held me already that day came into the bar and said to the old man, 'We'll look after her now, Mick. Thanks.'

Mick looked away with his cornflower eyes. The dark-haired Irishman grabbed me by the shoulders.

Oh no! No! No! NOT BACK TO THAT STINKING ROOM!

The idea of escaping had been uppermost in my mind. Now I knew the worst. Flynn would want to see me. How stupid I had been to think that I would be getting away. This was their turf, their kingdom.

The man led me outside again, into the cold, black, country air, which now had a real bite to it. I breathed in the night. The tall pine trees were solid and reassuring but I was too wrapped up in my own dread. God seemed like a voyeuristic sadist, enjoying each moment.

I was walked up the street to the shabby terrace house, and this time the front door opened onto a room full of men. There was the smell of cigarettes and alcohol. I felt I was going to retch. Retch up all the madness that had made me come seeking Flynn's world.

The faces before me blurred. I kept my head down. I did not want to see them. I smelled their sweat and I could smell something else. Hatred. Their racism was blatant. Men gathered in their hatred of the English. Why did they hate the English so very much? Part of them wanted to rip my Englishness to pieces. The fact that I was a woman made no difference to them. One with a higher-pitched voice than the others began to shout, 'I'm going to get this English cunt and put a live rat up her spying hairy cunt.'

He lunged at me, grabbed my hair and shook me viciously. I screamed what I felt was my very last scream as he swung me by the hair to the floor.

I clawed furiously, pointlessly trying to stop him. The other men were cheering abuse now as I struggled and they took turns helping to bind my hands behind my back with tape and hold me down. Round and round went the yellow duct tape.

They led me outside and put me into the back of a car. The engine started and the car began to move. When it stopped, they took me out and put me in an upstairs bedroom, with my hands still tied behind my back with duct tape.

I lay on an unmade bed, reduced to an animal. There was dripping condensation on the misty window. Liam Hart would always wipe the windows when I was in bed as a twelve year old before sex. He would ogle my body in my thin white nightie, making out he was cleaning condensation off the window. My sexuality is so damaged because of all that he did. Too much sex as a child rots the brain.

In the bedroom was the man with the pockmarked face again and he was grinning. Sean Hogan [not his real name], I'd heard the other men call him. If it was him, he was fresh from prison in England. He had pale blue eyes in keeping with his pale face. I was afraid of him and his coldly indifferent eyes. I knew that if I showed my fear, he would hate me for it.

'Are you a friend of Flynn?' As soon as it was out, I wished that I had not spoken.

'Aye – why? What's it to you?' He leant up against the white wall with his yellow T-shirt on, watching me with his muscled arms folded.

'He hates me, doesn't he? He hates me because I'm English.'

'He just wants to know what he is meeting before you're taken to him is all. We'll keep you until then. Just relax!'

'Why is he so suspicious of me?'

'Because you're an Intelligence woman.'

'I only came here because I was invited. I'm a journalist.'

'We'll see. We're making enquiries. You'll be surprised how high up our contacts and sympathisers reach.'

Outside the condensation-covered window, the rain now beat

a drumbeat of ridicule against the pane in a rat-a-tat-tat.

'If Flynn thinks you're up to no good, there'll be one bullet right there.' He pointed to the middle of his forehead. My eyes met his and I saw he was assessing my fear. He stared at me for a long time. Then he came over and lay down on the bed next to me, his cratered face very close to mine. We lay fully dressed on his metal-framed bed. His breath smelled like oranges. It was icy and dark outside the window. In here, just the two of us in the silence, it was warm and humid.

A knock at the door reverberated through the house.

Men came up the stairs, through the door and into the bedroom. I could hear what sounded like dozens of pairs of hobnailed boots clattering on the stairs. It sounded as if the whole village was on its way up.

I'll be sick and choke myself! It would be a way out.

'May's waiting for her.' The accent was very deep and the words growled out.

Sean stood up. 'Orders are to take her to the house. He'll decide what's to be done with her. Not you. She belongs to our brigade.'

Sean smiled slyly. Muttering and defeated, the others left and Hogan held out a pill and a glass of tap water. 'Better you sleep through what's going to go on next.'

My eyes met his. Some part of me didn't want to leave him. I was somehow bonded with him now he'd saved me from probable death and was offering me an anaesthetic for the next stage of my dissection. I looked at the grey capsule; it was going to affect me and make me lose control. If I didn't take it, he could force-feed it to me anyway.

Hogan sipped from a brown hip flask and wiped his mouth with the back of his hand. His face was devoid of expression. I stared at him as I swallowed the pill – it tasted bitter. I began to feel dizzy and I focused on his grinning mouth. Car doors banged and Sean seemed to be carrying me into one. There were strong arms under my armpits and I felt like a sack of potatoes. Down on the floor of the car, through heavy eyelids I glimpsed a pool of dark liquid. It stank and my stockinged feet slid across it as I slipped around in the back of the car. A large foot on my head pushed my face hard into the mess. I felt the cold splatter, smelt a metallic smell, and then . . . sleep.

Fourteen

Naked in the Emerald Forest

Xenia Onatopp: You don't need the gun, Commander.
James Bond: Well, that depends on your definition
of safe sex.

Goldeneye

A dawn chorus started gently, then became louder and louder.
I stirred and blinked my crusty eyes open. My throat felt like
sandpaper, dry and sore. My head throbbed violently. *How could I
have fallen asleep?* I sat up disorientated in an icy bed. Another
strange bedroom. *Oh God – where am I now?*

I rubbed my head and eventually remembered the drug Sean
Hogan had given me. I felt a stabbing pain in the pit of my
stomach – its side effects. *Oh no, where am I? What are they going
to do with me? Murder me – after questioning?* Would they stick to
the rules and not kill a journalist? I was sick with fear and dread.
They didn't believe that I was a journalist; they thought that was
my cover.

The empty house was silent. I got up and stumbled to the
window. Outside there was the darkest wood. I walked around
tentatively. There was no sound as I went to the bedroom door
and down a long flight of oak stairs, my bare feet padding silently
on the steps. In the kitchen were half drunk glasses of red wine
and crumbs on plates.

I took a stale sandwich and stuffed it down, finishing off the
dregs of red wine from the dirty glasses in an attempt to calm
my fear. I looked out of the kitchen window as my head pounded;
it had been raining heavily in the night. Some of the windows

were covered with French-style shutters, painted a light pea-green.

My mind began to spin. Instinctively I knew where I was. The house in the wood. The beautiful, remote house near the lake. A dead body flashed into my mind – a girl with half a face, floating in algae.

I heard car doors slamming outside and men's voices. Dread surged through me – it was too late to run. I darted back upstairs and instinctively crouched down at the bedroom window, my heart pounding in my chest. I looked over the sill, pure fear choking me. He's there. It's Flynn. I could just make out his voice saying, 'Going to be a long, hot night tonight, lads.'

I heard someone coming up the stairs and Flynn appeared at the door. His bottom lip curled as he stared at me, his face taking on a sadistic sneer. My heart skipped a beat and thumped fear into my dry mouth.

He ushered me down to the kitchen. Over by the gas cooker, one of the other men unloaded a shopping bag and started to cook breakfast. The sausages sizzled in the pan, giving off a mouth-watering smell. It made me feel hungry and sick at the same time.

The sky was a cold grey outside the kitchen window. Furious whirlpools of comet-like light twisted around the lowering grey clouds, darker and darker – it congregated in a scowling throb suspended over the dripping, rain-soaked forest.

Some of Flynn's men seemed to be going into the woods to off-load equipment. Weapons? Were they the hidden Sam-7s that the Brits had been pulling this coarse-looking countryside apart trying to retrieve over the last few months, assuming the dissident IRA had got hold of them?

Flynn kept laughing while he sat at the rough-hewn kitchen table. He was eating the burned pork sausages and fried eggs that he'd mashed together so they resembled nursery food.

I let my eyes slide over that sculpted face, the straight nose and the defiant grey eyes of the Real IRA commander. He was so very hard to fathom. He displayed nothing. Everything was hidden. His MI6 profile would contain exactly what he wanted it to.

From somewhere, an old memory came back to me. It was of Liam. I was so much smaller. 'I've cleaned up for you, Daddy. I've painted a picture for you, Daddy.' There would be no answer. The silence ran through me and I felt utterly desperate. Desperate and afraid. I thought of the times when Liam would pull back my bedcovers and I would be trapped by fear as he ran his hard, strong hands over my warm, childish skin. I remember, strangely without the usual guilt, thinking that I had ruined my parents' marriage by being a temptation.

Out of the silence, finally Flynn spoke. 'You're here to smell us out.'

'No.'

'Who asked you to speak?'

He sounded like evil personified. I could feel it coming from him. There was thick dark treacle in his voice, which sounded vicious.

Why? How did he come to be as he is?

Something forbidden and dangerous ran through me like a newly burst dam. He gave me a long sideways stare and our eyes met. Flynn could smell my fear. He could also sense my attraction to him.

'Let's get moving before the light fades,' said Flynn. 'We're going to take you into the woods near the Mountains to show you where Nairac was buried, right next to one of our arms dumps.' He laughed and winked at one of the men. 'You'll look at what's there, then tell your country that we have control of all IRA weapons. The governments know that, but they're busy trying to keep it out of the media. They came to us – begged us – but we ignored them. We're in control – not the yellow-belly Provos.'

His grey eyes narrowed and I could see how arrogant he was.

Outside, the woods were wet and water dripped from the budding trees. I walked, freezing in a thin blouse and skirt, following the men, and thought about how they were a 'lost boy' army. Boy soldiers, now grown into men, who could not give up their war games. The Real IRA was addicted to conflict and only death would ever halt them.

A weak sun filtered through the tops of the trees, the leaves forming a blanket against a now duck-egg-blue sky. We tramped for miles and I could feel my feet cold and wet inside my shoes. A stream bubbled near our path. The fuzzy mauve rockiness of the mountains was over to my right, the air smelling of green moss and purple lichen.

After an hour walking into the deep woodlands, I feared that we were lost. I glanced at Flynn and saw he had been watching me. My face was cold and ruddy, my eyes watering. The smoke he exhaled from his cigarette was visible in puffs of cloudy white wisps. We stopped in a clearing. Sean Hogan had gone on to the arms dump that was apparently full of the automatic weapons that this 'lost boy' army favoured.

It began to rain, a light hail hitting us both in the face. I could hardly see. I looked at Flynn and his glossy dark hair. The rain was soaking us with its fine mist. The chill had started to sink in now, in that wet, vile way that a virus spreads into the blood and the bones. The floor of the dark wood was covered in wild bluebells, which gave off a heavenly scent. Trains sounded their horns in the distance as they raced through remote Irish country stations.

Flynn stood in front of me. He walked up close, pushed my hair back off my face and kissed me hard.

'I think you're here for me – is that true?'

'Maybe.'

'Lay you on down then and you'll get what you've come for.'

I complied. But the Real IRA commander liked it rough.

Sea-green ivy vines ran along the icy-cold, wet ground of the forest. Flowers sprouted all around us in pinks and marmalade yellows. His skin felt smooth and cold. He pulled at my knickers and tore them from my legs. He took off his trousers and pulled off his underpants. He broke down the boundaries of my body; his bones crushed into mine.

All around, the trees seemed to close in on us, voyeurs, leaning and swaying – amused and cruel. The lake was still there somewhere, something watching from the algae-covered water. I moved my head back to look at things upside down. The oak tree near where we lay had a powdery bark and smelt of damp sawmills. Rainwater lay like crushed diamonds over overgrown grass, damp underneath us.

It started to rain again, turning into a swift, merciless spattering of white stones as another hailstorm opened itself over the wood and we were pelted as we lay naked on the forest bed amongst nature, wet and sore. Then the hailstones ceased and sunlight flooded gold through the trees. A rainbow appeared in the sky. Flynn jumped up and looked down at me.

'Get dressed! You'll go back and tell MI6 and the British public that we want the British off our land and DO NOT consent to power sharing!' His voice was curt, commanding and back to business as he told me that they were planning a huge campaign of violence in Ireland and Britain. 'We won't rest until we have sent every English soldier back home in a coffin.'

'Yes, yes, I understand.' I put my clothes back on, eager to cover myself.

We walked on again in silence for another 20 minutes, until we came to another large clearing. Sean Hogan stood watching my face carefully, his breath making little puffs of smoke in the cold forest air.

'What kept youse? Right, bitch, dig there with your hands until you find bones.'

'No, no, I can't.'

'Do it.'

I fell to my knees and grovelled in the cold hard soil until my hand hit something hard. I started to scream, thinking it might be a skull.

'What the fuck is the British arsehole doing?' said Flynn.

'Fucked if I know.'

'Digging for her friend Nairac.'

'She misses him, that'll be it.'

'Sure, she'll have some dig. He got made into cans of McGrath's dog food about 20 year ago.' They both started to laugh.

I struggled to my feet and wiped my face with the back of my hand. They led me on until we came to an underground hideaway. It was opened by lifting hidden chains. They both jumped down and then helped me down. It was an arms dump in the floor of the forest, covered up with dirty beige tarpaulin, and neither of them seemed to want to draw it back.

'Where's the Sam-7s?' I asked.

Sean answered. 'Don't go getting all smartarse on me, Army Woman, or I'll lock you up down here and leave you to the worms.'

I looked over at Flynn for protection.

Flynn spoke. 'Leave this journalist arsehole to me.' He leaned forward and pushed me hard. I toppled forward, banged my head on something hard and landed with a thump on the floor of the dump. The crisp leaves against my pale cheek where I fell smelled like a childhood walk to school in my favourite red wellington boots.

Sean Hogan was walking about eating a bread roll. My joints ached from the endless hours of walking in the cold that I'd just survived. Flynn had disappeared and there had been no goodbyes from my new lover.

Hogan took me to his dirty white Fiat, allowing me to sit in a seat this time, and we made the long drive along the high-bushed lanes into Dundalk village. He then put me on a bus. I was too exhausted to speak. I took one long last glance at the man with the pockmarked face whom I had shared a bed with. It was a fragile sunny day steeped in silence, gold grass everywhere. All I could hear was my own rapid heartbeat and the panic inside my head. I tried not to remember the whole experience as I sat and silently screamed.

The sun was just coming up, bright white even at seven in the morning. A sheep stood silhouetted, an opaque shadow on a mountaintop. There was the peculiar tranquillity of a day that had not yet fully woken. I cleaned my face with a bottle of Evian water and some tissues from my bag. I stared out of the window and thought about what had happened. I had acted terribly unprofessionally on an assignment for the paper. I saw my face reflected in the bus window. I had got the exclusive interview the paper wanted. I was good at my job but I was also going to get killed if I continued to wander lost amongst the devils, still searching for pure evil.

Fifteen

The Spymaster

We've never had anybody this close to the top of these murdering bastards in the Real IRA.

Spymaster to author

P aul watched me intently as he took a cup of coffee with milk from the air hostess.

'What about a glass of brandy? You look so pale, sweetheart! Are you sure you're OK? I'm raging. I'll kill them, Chris, if I ever get my fucking hands on them for taking you like that. It's not on. They should respect journalists.'

'It's par for the course with these new boys. They didn't hurt me. Nothing happened to me. I just need to relax and I'll be fine.'

I smiled at him wearily then turned and stared out of the blurred window of the plane until the clouds got thicker and the whole landscape was blocked from view.

Paul nibbled on a digestive biscuit, took off his shoes and wriggled his feet. I shivered and pulled down a blanket to wrap round my shoulders. I felt a shot of fear as the plane's descent was announced and sipped some Rescue Remedy, trying to forget that I had been frolicking about the countryside with the Real IRA. I brought out my laptop and wrote up an interview for the *News of the World* and called it 'We Get Inside the Real IRA'. I wrote down all the information Flynn had come out with while we lay together, naked on the floor of the forest, and filed it to Neville.

I thought of our lovemaking as I wrote but it already seemed so unreal that I then tried to blot it out, to forget it in case it destroyed me. His hard body, his groaning, the intimacy of it. The way I had burned. For a moment I felt my body thrill with want for him again. I turned to look at Paul. His kind green eyes were worried.

'You OK?' he asked again.

'Yes, I'm fine, thank you.' I smiled at him.

His skin was covered with a light spattering of brown freckles that somehow emphasised his innocence.

'I love you, my dear fiancé,' I whispered in a voice that masked the guilt I was feeling at my enjoyment of Flynn's body.

'I love you too, Chris. Chris, I'm so afraid of being alone.'

'I know you're afraid of life – don't worry, I'll never leave you!'

I leaned over and squeezed his hand. I felt glad he was so afraid. It lessened my fear of losing him and my own fear of life and the horrors it had to offer.

'Paul, I can't talk much. I feel sick, overwhelmed with anxiety, you know my panic attacks.'

I stood up and went to the toilet in the cabin. My knickers were stained. I took them off and pushed them into the sanitary towel dispenser. The plane bumped and jogged around and I clung on to the edge of the sink. The seatbelt sign pinged on. I felt sick from the antiseptic tang of the cramped toilet cubicle. I looked at myself in the mirror and tried to powder my face with a trembling hand as the plane rocked and jumped. I put the cotton wool into the sanitary dispenser, sat down on the closed toilet lid and wept.

When I returned to my seat, I was ashen-faced. Paul held my hand tightly as the plane began its noisy descent into the safety of London with its little rows of suburban houses where people were living normal, healthy lives. I looked out of the window and felt again that I was about to confront something horrendous I had, until then, managed to avoid – my own inner demons, the box in the attic.

For some reason I thought of James, the spymaster, and I felt frightened.

Sixteen

Orders to Spy

Andrea Anders: He is a monster – I hate him.
James Bond: Then leave him.
Andrea Anders: You don't walk out on Scaramanga.

The Man with the Golden Gun

James stood smiling at me as Paul and I reached the entrance to my apartment. He was holding a copy of the previous week's *News of the World* with my exclusive interview with Flynn. Greg had called me 'our girl' and it had made the front page and a spread. I soon found out that Greg had been off duty when I filed copy and it was Neville who had fairly put my byline in place on my story, something that hadn't happened in many years of writing top-of-the-mark front pages for News Corp.

'I love this.' James brandished it. 'You *are* getting stuck in to this Lois Lane lark, aren't you? But do the snowy white *News of the World* editors know how close you got to him to pull this one out of the bag?'

I smiled at him. 'How could I have thought that you weren't watching my every move, James? Sudan too hot for you?'

Paul was looking upset.

'May we speak in private?' James said, gesturing with his hand towards a car waiting outside the doors. 'I'll not take up too much of your time. Do excuse us both,' he said, smiling at Paul.

Paul narrowed his eyes as he asked, 'Will you be OK, babe?'

'Yes, wait for me, Paul. It's just a debriefing about Ireland.'

I sat with James in the back seat of the heated limousine.

'I'll cut to the chase. We need to know what's going on with the

In for the Kill

Real IRA. They're galloping all over South America, training Farc rebels and God knows what other terrorist groups. They're still out in Eastern Europe, stockpiling weapons. Your new pal Flynn is a close friend of Don Gunning [not his real name], the multi-millionaire who owns the IRA – all the factions of the IRA. No one can get near him. We can, of course, but only with your help. You just wandered in there and met Mr Big Shot, all by pure chance.' He blew out a plume of blue smoke slowly and watched my face muscles twitching with fear.

'Mr Big Shot? Pure chance?' I asked, as I let my tongue explore the front side of my teeth. I had gone for Flynn deliberately.

James pulled out a silver Dictaphone and switched it on. I could hear the dark, measured West Irish accent of Flynn and another man with a Dublin accent. It was a recording of a conversation in a pub between Flynn and a close friend. Flynn's voice was distinctive and nasal.

'We could use a sympathetic journalist. I'll draw her in.'

'She's had dealings with 6.'

'So what? She won't be one of them. She's not their type.'

'All journalists are in with the spooks.'

There was a pause and the sound of the bar in the background.

'We can start by giving her a few tales – see how she handles them. We don't need to trust her. She just needs someone to liaise with. That someone can only be me.'

The other man agreed. The tape went dead and I looked at James.

'You're to be trusted, Chris.' He sucked on the short cigar like an oil magnate who had just struck an abundant new source, then he began to laugh. I looked him squarely in the eyes.

He re-lit the cigar. The aroma reminded me of Christmas with the Harts, and the Hamlet cigars my adopted father would light after the plates were cleared away. James blew out a thin stream of blue haze between the two of us.

'Flynn will try to find out what you want most in the world. When he discovers your deepest desire, he'll try to fulfil it. He'll get close and then he'll show you behind his veil. Behind the veil is evil, and evil close up is not nice. If he gets into your cracks, he'll place Semtex there and you must let him. After that, just get as close to him and the Real IRA as you possibly can.'

'Why is your father's company so interested in the Real IRA? There's no money there.'

'On the contrary. The government is handing out wads of it to anyone who can bring back intelligence on these scumbags who are calling themselves the Real IRA. My father was very close to Gaddafi, though Gaddafi once threw him into prison, you know, on a whim.'

Again I felt a tightening in my chest. The recent strain had affected my heart. It was beating strangely and the ache made it impossible to swallow.

Years ago, when James had rescued me, I had not really been aware of who he and his father were; it had all seemed like a lark. Now they had decided it was time to cash in their investment.

'I'll end up down a hole. I can't believe I'm still alive as it is. It would be suicide to return to Flynn.' I swallowed hard and felt like a victim, a victim of Flynn, a victim of James and his pathetic need to match up to his spymaster father.

James pulled out a packet of gum and, without offering me one, took a piece and began to chew it.

'You were a big temptation to him, Chris. And since he's already had you, another few times of lying back and thinking of England won't matter.'

I almost expected him to laugh, while deep inside myself I wanted to cry. He smiled tightly and ignored the long slow tear that ran down my pale cheek as he chewed casually.

'Meet me in the morning at my office. I'll send a driver for you.' He studied my eyes to see my reaction. 'You'll be briefed on the whole history of Flynn as we know it and the significant members of this amalgamation calling itself the Real IRA. Then you'll go back to Ireland and spy for us on the Real IRA.'

'I could refuse you.'

'"No" isn't an option. You can't go and hang out with one of the most senior and dangerous terrorists of all time and then go home and settle back to watching *Coronation Street*.' His voice sounded cold. 'Of course you would be paid well for anything you bring back to us.'

'And I would be a marked woman for the rest of my days. You must really care about me, James.'

Fear spread out from my solar plexus in a warm glow. It was so intense it was almost pleasurable. I had learned all there was to know about spying through my work with James's father's company, but I had never actually seen any action, not with terrorists anyway, not with a man like Flynn.

A part of me wanted to freak out, to scream, so he would think me crazy and not want to use me. Rage shot though me and I had an urge to tear at his face with my fingernails, but I fought all of it. I decided to tell him that I would go back and see Flynn for him, but merely get what I wanted from Flynn to satisfy my own desire to study evil.

'You'll meet me tomorrow. I'll send a car for you, as I said. After that, we'll send you and your boyfriend on holiday. Wherever you like – Bahamas, Mauritius, St Lucia. Have a rest for a few weeks on a white sandy beach. You deserve it.'

He took a long drag on a freshly lit cigar. 'You'll stay on holiday, relaxing on the sunniest beach of your choice, until the Real IRA makes contact with you. Don't worry, they will. I've a mountain of books for you to read on the IRA and its history. Read them all carefully – become an expert. Study all the splinter groups – the INLA, Saor Éire; study the Officials and the roots of the organisation. Imagine you're cramming for your finals.'

He admired his freshly manicured nails and then looked deep into my eyes.

'I don't need a holiday, James. You keep your money and your gifts of designer clothes and your friendship.'

I wanted to run and run into my fiancé's arms and have him rescue me. But where would it get me? James would only take it out on him and the agency knew enough boot boys ready to off people for a few bob. Besides, how could I marry Paul now? Rope him in to this dirty game? I knew from my own experience that spies were the loneliest people on the planet; they floated around, reported back. Spies were the nobodies, the people with no face and no name – and that was all I had ever been.

Seventeen
Intimate with the IRA

When the time is right he will be killed . . . I shall kill him.

Fiona Volpe to Emilio Largo, *Thunderball*

It was late summer 2001. Shortly after my meeting with James Stratford-Barrett the Real IRA had made contact with me, just as he had predicted. I was invited as a journalist to interview Sean Flynn in an unprecedented interview at his home.

I squinted my eyes tightly and looked up at the Irish mountains. I had booked into a local B&B to freshen up for the so-called interview with Flynn the next day. I had a beachfront room and I could smell the salt and hear the shingle on the beach out of my window. It was the end of August and a pink and orange sunset hung over the high tide. It had been a hot, memorable summer and it was not yet over.

The next morning I was off early in my navy-blue hired Saab convertible. The road became more rural with each mile. Ireland looked like a mythical fairyland in the books I had read as a child. An old country of ancient kings, wicked queens and dark legend – Rapunzel territory.

After 70 miles, I was lost in the countryside and my stomach was rumbling with hunger. The weather outside was hot and the wheels of the car were churning up yellow dust on the dry road. The landscape was mountainous and seemed utterly devoid of houses, people and all signs of human life. I turned the radio on, closed the electronic roof and tried to enjoy the scenery. I put on sunglasses to see the road map more clearly. Loneliness stabbed.

I would have done anything at that moment to have a girlfriend to phone.

The Saab seemed to stick in third gear, so I started to worry about the steep dry-mud valleys and winding roads. I knew I had more wilderness to drive through to get to Flynn's secluded home. I squeezed the wheel tighter and thought about Flynn, about the way he and I had made love in the forest. James had told me to spy on him but what did Flynn want from me?

I lit a black Sobranie cigarette with a gold filter from a pack I had bought in Duty Free for a joke and exhaled the smoke. My mobile buzzed. It was James.

'Hello! Chris?' James was still saying this as I went through a deep mountain pass and the lack of signal began to make his words unintelligible.

'Chris? Chris? Chris, can you hear me?'

I looked at my mobile. It had cut off. I turned up the car radio and put the mobile away in the glove compartment. I wanted to be alone. I didn't need James, he was both a weakling and a coward.

I pushed my foot down on the accelerator. The memory of Flynn deep inside my body made me feel as if I was going to faint. I was nearly overwhelmed by fear that shot through me like a bolt, making me breathless with panic.

Flynn's two-storey house had white flowers and white vases in the windows, with a neatly mown lawn outside. Cotton curtains and a woman's touch were visible in small wooden giraffes and plaster cats on the windowsills. It was miles from any main road – a long drive down a dirt track with such high bushes it was impossible to see anything on either side. I locked the car, put the keys in my pocket and felt safe as I held on to them.

I crunched over the gravel, up to the front door and knocked on it, fighting a rising panic attack.

'Come on in,' Flynn said after opening the white oak front door with a slow smile. It felt odd to see him again and my stomach flipped with arousal.

'Hope you're hungry. I've done you steak au poivre. It's my specialty,' he grinned at me.

I stepped through his front door. Books lined the walls and paintings hung on expensively papered walls. He took off my coat in the hallway, leaned forward and kissed my cheek. I stepped away, feeling ill at ease. I could smell onions frying in a pan. The house was hot and I felt nervous and hungry at the same time.

After eating the steak and baby roast potatoes, we drank a weighty red wine and sat talking in front of his open fire. It burned bright and I felt my face heating to a rosy glow. Flynn sat in front of it and stared at me like he was a cat with a mouse he had managed to trap.

'So! I wanted to meet up with a journalist I could trust and give them some political stories.' He fingered the stem of his glass as he spoke.

I nodded. 'Great.'

He stood up. 'You must be tired, though. Let me show you to the spare room.'

I was glad. I wanted him to be nice to me to calm the fear of him that was beginning to rise, hard and terrifying, inside me. We were miles from anywhere. The reality of the dangerous situation I had walked into again was just beginning to hit. I stood up.

'I won't go near you.' He laughed at me, took a deep breath and looked serious. 'I've not had feelings as strong as this about anyone.' He came up close and looked at me as if he hated me for making him want me so badly.

'Oh.'

'What about you?'

His skin looked so white. I cringed, yet something about him seemed so familiar and oddly comfortable.

'I don't know. No idea.' I had felt drawn to him like a moth to a flame ever since I had set eyes on him, yet to say so would be ridiculous.

He seemed to compose himself again. His grey eyes sometimes looked lethal, his thick bottom lip curled in arrogance and contempt, and yet it was all hidden behind a thin veneer of politeness.

I retired to my bedroom and looked at myself in the mirror. I wasn't sure why he had invited me to his home, but time would tell. I knew it was frowned upon by his people to mix with journalists, but who would tell Flynn what to do when he was at the top?

In the bathroom there was a wedding photo of Flynn and his wife, from whom I understood he was separated. In the picture they were holding hands over a wedding cake, looking very much in love. I felt such a strong draw for the dark-haired Flynn that it scared me. Here was what I wanted with someone – a white wedding – but it was not Paul that I wanted to experience it with.

I slipped off my diamond engagement ring, putting it into my pocket, and sprayed on some Chanel, rubbing it over my breasts and throat. Then I straightened the red lace bra I had purchased to lure Flynn into being my puppet.

Flynn knocked at the door of the bathroom so hard it made me jump. I could hear his voice clearly. I knew he would have his face pressed up to the door. I turned on the tap to feign activity.

'I thought we could go out the back and sit on the veranda. There's a river runs across the back and you can see for miles.'

He spoke as if imparting a well-kept secret.

A ceiling of stars was spread like silver foil over the secluded house. Flynn read my mind, pulled open a cold bottle of Budweiser from the freezer and handed it to me. I swigged back some of the ice-cold drink. It gave me a lovely, warm, muzzy glow. The bottle was wet and ice-cold between my fingers. I felt relaxed in a demure flowery blouse and a modest green skirt that I had felt sure he would like.

I could smell his skin and the distinctive aftershave that he wore. There was the sound of insects and the air was warm. I looked at him, remembering our violent coupling in the wood. I was afraid of Flynn yet I was intent on digging around and trying to pull out his evil, so I could examine it, feel its texture, taste its consistency, then dissect it like a surgeon to find out what he was capable of.

The breeze blew up from the cool of the river. He opened another bottle of beer with a smart click, brought it out to me and stood beside me sipping his own. The air was so still and the night so silent – it was an eerie wait where you could have heard a pin drop. I thought of a poem I had once written. 'Here I sit in the cold stone dread. The ashes in the fireplace, the cold ice of my heart. This is an empty house – this house is a house of waiting . . .'

I drank more beer and glanced over at Flynn. In the deathly silence and the clear half-light, I caught him looking at me – a penetrating stare. He began to smile so much it turned into a laugh. And something else – he was almost blushing and coy.

I have power, power, over the same kind of man. What is it about me that evil men seem to trust and like?

He came over to me and picked up my hand. I pulled away

from him and looked around. A grey mist had fallen fast and wrapped itself around the garden.

'I can't. I can't. I don't let other people come near.' I got up and walked towards the river. Something inside me wanted to walk and walk forever into its cold depths.

'Chris, come back. The river's got a very slippery bank. You'll fall.'

The mist came down thicker over the garden – a foggy film of grey – and down too came rain. The lights to the side of the garden had gone out, plunging us into darkness. A cool night breeze began to blow.

'Can't. I can't. I can't.' It reverberated and the wind flapped the tarpaulin on the edge of a boat moored on the river. I could see my reflection in the black of the window of the boat and it shocked me with its age.

'You made me,' I turned and yelled.

I held my breath, startled at what I was shouting at him.

Flynn came up behind me. 'You need to see it like that so you won't feel guilty about enjoying it.' He put his hand around my neck from behind. 'I saw it in you the first time I laid eyes on you – shame. You have such a deep need to let go of the shame and live, Chris. I do just what I fucking like – you sense it and it draws you!'

The darkness in the garden seemed to get blacker. The flowers had already curled into tight balls.

'You're a killer, the whole world knows it.'

'No, no, no, I'm no killer – no. The English put that out as propaganda – you must know that.'

'Then what are you?'

He took my hand in his. 'Chris, Chris.' He stroked my face. 'I've never killed anyone.'

I was wet with the cold night downpour. He lifted my virginal skirt and went down on me. I tore roughly at his drenched brown hair with wet fingers and moaned against the force of the rainy wind. He was my safe haven. Mum and Dad could reach me no longer. I had the Devil to protect me in the darkness. He came up to look me in the eyes and spoke against the force of the rain cutting into his mouth. 'I'll give you what you want, Chris, and you'll never leave me!'

I felt protected by his evil. I could sense and smell it, and I slid inside where I felt safe and hidden, where no one would dare hurt me. I was inside the cage with the scary killer. He would kill my mum and dad. I would be safe now.

'You want me, don't you? You so, so want me.' Flynn's voice interrupted my thoughts in a voice that seemed like a whisper. 'You've fallen in love with me, Chris. I bet you don't even know why!'

The black rain fell heavier until it blinded everything from view.

He clenched onto my arse cheeks, hiking me up so much that I was astride him as he entered me. We clasped each other's nakedness hungrily with loud slaps and screams in his back garden. From a distance, our naked, joined bones must have resembled a mad ballerina, tumbling and prancing across a stage, out of control in a performance of lunacy in the wet mud of his back garden.

'Say it, you fucking bastard!' he urged in a loud whisper.

'This is great. So, so good,' I mumbled, inexperienced and gauche.

'This is lovemaking, you spying ENGLISH BITCH. SAY IT,' he shouted.

'I love you.'

He grinned. 'You fell in love with me at first sight, didn't you? I saw you. I saw you being turned on by me. Then you couldn't stop yourself, could you? You couldn't stop until we're here like this. Ha! The little English snoop.' His eyes looked vicious, mad and alarming so close to mine. 'You didn't care. You didn't care what they said about me.'

He moved me up against his garden wall roughly. 'And you didn't care they say I assassinate with my favourite 45. All lies of course. I have no 45.' He pressed my body against the wall and began to laugh deeper and deeper, biting at my neck.

'It draws you and you had to reach me. Do you know why, Chris? Do you fucking know why?'

He was evil; it was shining out of him. I could feel its power. Yet it was subservient to me. It somehow needed me just to exist. And this was what I needed. To be its Lord and Master. All at once, I was a ringmaster in a circus, lashing a whip as an orange tiger paced the ring. As I struck the whip, it jumped through a large wooden hoop. It ran along the edge of the ring, faster now – all at my command. The packed audience offered thunderous applause. I turned. I held the whip high above my head and then bowed a deep long bow. The applause exhilarated me. The auditorium was packed. I raised my head. I stared in horror. Everyone in the audience was the same. Thousands upon thousands of my father and mother: Liam and Georgie Hart. They were speaking to each other.

Georgie: 'What's she doing, Liam darling?'

Liam: 'Nothing. She's doing nothing. Don't worry – she'll make nothing of her life.' He looked at Georgie like a child wanting to please its mother. *'She thinks she's controlling evil.'*

'Evil?'

'Yes – yes . . . it's . . . she thinks . . .' He smirked and then laughed heartily. *'She thinks if she does that then you won't lock her in a cupboard and beat her every day, and me – I won't steal her sexuality and rape her every night.'*

Georgie: 'I don't understand.'

She turned and watched me as I began to make the tiger leap through the hoops at my command again.

Liam: 'If she controls evil, life won't have destroyed her. She can make us into decent people – good people who won't have broken her.' His voice was cocky. *'Because she's the one who has control, see?'*

He began to rock with laughter at the absurdity of my life and the way I wasted it, locked in some kind of prison, trying to change the past.

I was stuck inside a prison cell with the caged tiger, trying desperately to tame evil.

His joyous laughter got louder and was joined by Georgie's. I looked up and wondered why the audience was laughing. The loudness of the laughing increased until I came to. I was intimate with another killer. I could feel his juices running down my leg; my whole body was drenched with tiger cum. I was a collector of the most evil men on the planet and Flynn was a new addition. I had worked hard all of my life to hunt them down, get as close as I could and then move in for the kill. I looked up at the harvest moon over the mountains. It seemed to be watching me.

'When you go back to England, ring me and say things like, "Your cock doesn't satisfy me, because it's not big enough."' He began to laugh.

'Why?'

'Because those whores are listening in.'

'Who?'

'The Provos, I mean, not just the Brits.'

135

'Oh.'

'Let's give the girls something to gossip about – me and the English spy. Do you know, if one of them was caught with a bitch like you they would get court-martialled for it? Want to know why?'

'Why?'

'The Provos are a gaggle of little girls with pissy pants is why.'

'How do you mean?'

'We aren't afraid of bitches like you.'

Down in the water that ran along the end of his back garden, the small boat moored to a wooden gate dipped about noisily. Flynn led me back into the warm house and ran me a bath that he surrounded by scented candles. I sat in it until I glowed and my wet golden hair clung to my pink cheeks. After he had been gone for a while, he returned and dried me with a warm blue towel. He rubbed hard at my skin, and then softly at my wet hair. Down in the kitchen he sat me down and made us some homemade broth with barley, carrots and cabbage and small squares of buttered white bread, the crusts cut off carefully.

'Are you warm enough?'

He was tender with me, as if I was a child. A special and much loved child, dressed in his oversized green dressing gown. The kitchen was warm and smelled homely. It felt like the safest place in the world. He was tall, slim and graceful in his movements. He fluttered around the kitchen, taking care of me in a homely way that made me weak to him.

'The soup is lovely, thank you.' I followed him around the kitchen with my eyes as I sipped it. He had taken my trainers that had been covered in mud and stood washing them carefully at the sink before hanging them on a wrought-iron hook over the Aga. I sipped at the broth; it had chunks of fresh chopped vegetables in it.

Flynn looked at me wrapped in his gown. I knew I looked beautiful. I looked at the lonely black of the night in the garden outside his cosy kitchen window, then I turned to stare at his back as he stood at the sink.

'Why so much violence, Sean?'

'It's a war.'

'Hitting civilians isn't war.'

'Oh, I'm not a party to anything like that. I'd like to see top targets taken out.'

Intimate with the IRA

I sipped at the salty broth and chewed the white squares of bread and butter. 'You're going to take some of them out? But who could do close-quarter apart from you? It's so specialised.' I took a spoonful of soup. 'You've got someone? The *Sunday Times* asked me to check out a guy a few weeks ago – they thought there was some guy from Meath who was hot. Is he on side?'

He looked at me with a smirk. I put my spoon down and looked at him with rising anxiety. He wasn't so slow.

'Don't you like your soup, Chris? I love making soup – it's my thing,' he smirked. 'Now stop the investigative-journalist bullshit and eat up.' He stroked my wet blonde hair. 'Poor lonely Chris, it's been cold in the wastelands, hasn't it? See, you told me all your secrets, Chris, out there in the darkness.' He twisted my blonde hair tighter around his fingers. I pulled my head away from him.

'You're prying,' I said.

'You confessed.' He reached over and ran his fingers over my breast. 'I'll tie you up and drip honey over you. How about it? Or if you like, I'll tie you up and do other things to you – things that hurt you.'

'No thanks, not into it, buddy.'

He was scaring me but I pressed it down. If I showed it, I would be finished and his paranoia would escalate until my death.

'OK, you hurt me.'

'Maybe later, if you're lucky.'

Flynn dressed me slowly and carefully in a pair of his pyjamas, only stopping to tenderly touch my nipple with the ball of his thumb and then move down with his mouth. He watched me in a strange, perverse way. He turned his head slowly, his eyes slanting sideways. He hid all that he was, like my father leering through the crack in the door. Then he led me into the spare room where I climbed into bed exhausted and he closed the door and retired to his own room.

I lay awake thinking, *God, here I am in one of the founders of the Real IRA's homes at three o'clock in the morning.* I couldn't sleep, so I turned back the duvet and let my toes dig into the short-pile carpet. I was freezing. I took the dressing gown from the hook on the door and pulled it on, tying the belt tightly. I opened the bedroom door quietly. I could hear Flynn snoring as I crept along the landing.

It was even colder in the hallway, which was lit by the moon. I

137

went down the stairs, into the kitchen. I ran my hands along the wooden table. I could not see his computer anywhere, yet he had told me this was where he worked. I opened the door to the garage and looked around frantically. It was even icier and I cursed. My bare feet were freezing on the concrete floor.

To one side there was a door. I pulled it open. A smell of beer rose to my nostrils. There seemed to be a storeroom attached to his garage. It was pitch black as I went down the stairs. I felt around the cold stone walls and stumbled against something hard and metallic. I felt a round switch with my fingers and flicked it down. The single light had a yellow bare bulb with a moth fluttering around it. I looked around. On one side there was a large wooden wine rack full of bottles. A dial nearby had a temperature-control. The gauge was set at five degrees centigrade. Then I spotted it. There was a computer on a makeshift desk and I booted it up. I went straight to Flynn's emails. Nothing. I opened his Word files. They were boring attempts at public speeches by his men.

I shivered as I spotted a chest of drawers. Inside was a pile of papers. To my amazement he had a whole pile of magazines on submarines. *How mad*, I thought to myself. *What did they think they were going to do, fight the English underwater? Maybe it wasn't crazy. This lot were that ambitious. What is he up to?* I wondered.

I turned off the computer, switched off the light and ran up the stairs in my bare feet. On the kitchen table, Flynn's mobile was recharging. The telephone contacts list was as I had expected – empty.

Behind me, I heard a rustle. I instinctively ducked down, heart thumping. Flynn must have heard me and had woken up.

I held my breath and crouched low, my heart pumping in terror, but there were no footsteps. I turned and saw a tiny canary fluttering in a cage. I stared at it for a while until I heard my own breathing. Beside the cage, something caught my eye – it was a brush with long strands of female hair in it. I put it back down next to the cage. My father Liam seemed to be inside my head. I could see his face clearly and he was laughing. I listened in the hallway for a minute and then crept out of the kitchen.

Back up the stairs I crept into his bedroom and stood over the sleeping Flynn in the shadowy silence. A moth thumped softly against the windowpane. The white net curtain billowed in the breeze of a slightly opened window. The clock on his bedside table clicked over to 4.20 a.m. The light of the moon shone in. I could smell his sweat. I went over and lay down next to him. He opened his grey eyes and they looked amused.

'Find anything interesting?'

'Nothing.'

'That would be because men like us are raided by the cops every couple of weeks, Chris. Don't you know that?'

'No.'

'Well, now you've learned that little bit of information it's made you a better spy for the future.' He laughed as he rolled on top of me. I let him push his body inside me as his conceited eyes met mine.

I went back to the spare bedroom after he fell asleep. My feet were so cold they were like lumps of ice but I fell asleep eventually, thinking that James wouldn't ever believe that I had found this man's den only to discover his plans to fight England underwater.

He had to be crazy. But you never knew – Goethe always said boldness had magic and power in it.

Eighteen
Pillow Talk

If you come back here, do you know what will happen? You'll be arrested and then tortured until you tell us what your agenda is.

Senior republican to author

The morning sun shone cruelly through the window. I opened my eyes and remembered where I was. I opened the window and craned my neck out at the Irish countryside. It smelt like a holiday haven. The freshness of the air was intoxicating. Downstairs I could smell eggs and bacon cooking and hear the sizzling from the hob. There was a strong smell of fruity soap and toothpaste in the bathroom. On the shelves were deodorants, aftershaves and some pills in amber-coloured bottles.

In the main bedroom, behind a closed door, I found Flynn's bed with pale primrose-yellow sheets. It was still impregnated with the warmth of his body and his sweat had dampened the yellow cotton. I went downstairs and Sean appeared, bringing out a hot cooked breakfast. Soft fried eggs and toast and baked beans. Strongly brewed hot tea in thick green mugs. We sat silently chewing at the table.

Later, after breakfast, we drove along low country roads. Sean often slowed down the car to lean over and kiss me. It was another motionless day of late summer, hazy and honey-coloured with huge pine trees meeting the aqua blue of a silent sky. He looked at me seriously as he held my hand and rubbed at it with his thumb in the heavy sunlight coming through the open window of the car. 'There's a lot of this in our relationship, isn't there?'

'Touching? Yes.'

He pulled the car over and went into a garage shop to buy us choc-ices. I opened my door and followed him into the old-fashioned shop next to the garage, with its sacks of potatoes outside and postcards of the local Irish villages in wire stands. I marvelled at the strange things they had for sale – old-fashioned sweets in huge glass jars and dusty children's books.

'Here's a Magnum – like 'em?'

'Thanks.'

I stared out of the window as I ate the choc-ice. The countryside passing outside the car window was reminiscent of Tuscany – old houses, poppy fields. Flynn had gone silent.

An hour later, we pulled in along a wide country road. An archway of trees led down to a house, a large old house at the end of a twisting driveway. I blinked as we drove slowly down the private drive that was lined with cup-like yellow flowers and large weeping willows. The Georgian windows had pea-green shutters. I took a deep breath. It was the Gothic-looking house the IRA had brought me to and kept me in while waiting for Flynn to arrive.

'It's beautiful from the outside.' The magnificent house near the algae lake loomed large in front of us – a handsome, old-fashioned structure built of grey stone. The grounds were alight with purple forget-me-nots

'This is where I always went as a child,' said Flynn dreamily. 'The owner won't sell it. Weird really. It's all open, so the boys and I make use of it.'

'You brought me here when you interrogated me. It's not far from the green algae pool.'

'Oh no, you aren't one of those fools who believe in the legend, are you? Come on, Chris.'

'No, I don't . . . I didn't believe it.'

Two iron lions guarded the entrance to the house. It had a heavy black front door covered in dust with a faded brass doorknocker shaped as a lion's face. Inside I could see the wallpaper and imagined how its inhabitants had once lived.

Back in the car I looked out of the window. I could see myself in the wing mirror. My make-up was smudged and it was a hot day. The sun made my eyes ache and I thought I looked old. An old princess, still hoping to marry. I used to dream of a prince who would kiss me and then wake me from my sleep so that I could come alive. But I had long since given up that dream.

Pillow Talk

I put on some mascara from my make-up bag and blinked at myself in the wing mirror. Flynn thought it looked good – I could tell. I looked at him as he drove down the narrow lane. He seemed quiet and pale.

'Are you OK, Sean? You look white.'

He replied without meeting my eyes. 'Yes, I'm fine.'

Long, low stone walls curved over the thin country roads. The car went over bumps and holes. I took off my cardigan and stared out of the window, enjoying the sight of cows and sheep and horses in the passing fields. He drove on in silence then said, 'Do you believe, Chris, that we all have different sides?'

'Yes, I suppose so.'

'I'm myself when I'm with you. It's a side of me that's more powerful.'

'How do you mean, Sean?'

'I'm talking about being in contact with a deeper, more powerful part of myself. One that knows more – sees deeper – what lies beneath. Relax, Chris, you're awfully tense.'

Ten minutes later we came to a lake. As we walked down to the wood we passed a magnificent waterfall. Past the gushing falls set in the side of a mountain there was a lovers' seat. Sean sat down and smiled.

'The waterfall looks gold to me. Does it to you?' He looked at me carefully, as if it mattered how I replied.

The cold, frothing waterfall thundered in front of us as we sat beneath it on the lovers' bench, listening to the crash as the water hit the bottom. It was deafening.

'Yes. Er . . . yes, it looks gold to me too. It's the sun shining on it.' I could barely hear my own voice, drowned out as it was by the waterfall.

Flynn took a deep breath. 'Chris, I've never felt as strong as this about any other woman. I want to marry you.'

I looked up at the blue summer sky.

He spoke again softly.

'Don't leave me and I'll never leave you. You're my guardian angel, you know that?'

It was a hot day on the edge of the green algae lake.

'I think it's what you need, Chris, really need – a family.'

I looked up at the sky. 'According to the doctors, I'm infertile.'

He smiled. 'What would you call our child?'

He looked at me, his face serious and thoughtful.

'Cloud,' I said, still looking up at the blue sky with white cotton puffs drifting past.

He laughed. 'You know, I think you would. Go and bathe in the lake, Chris, it cures infertility. Go ahead.'

I walked naked into the emerald lake, then came out and lay next to him, feeling totally relaxed. He turned over onto his front. I lay on top of him and brushed my mouth against the skin on his sun-warmed back to dry myself. I could hear the waterfall gushing down loudly. The heat bore down even more heavily. Tiny grey rabbits hopped delicately through the forest behind us. Tall larches towered over us, high against the sky, forming a pattern like black lace. The water running in the stream near where we lay sounded like rain. He turned round and made love to me.

'My wife and I are over. Come here and live with me.'

'Maybe.'

He went down on me in the heat. The wood smelled of mint and pine, the breeze was soft, warm and summer-fragrant. Facing demons was easy when you joined forces and flew in the sky with them. Flynn still looked deathly pale. His skin was whiter than chalk, whiter than marble. A tiny stream of blood poured out of me onto the blanket.

Flynn sat up. 'You're bleeding? Is it . . .?'

'Oh God. I should have got dressed. Oh God, it's so embarrassing. I'm sorry, Sean. It's my period.'

'Don't worry. Doesn't matter. It's natural.'

The sky had gone a delicious slate grey; the water lay still, and now there was not even the flicker of a breeze. Flynn bathed me tenderly with water from the stream. He gently pressed wet tissue into the folds of my body to soak up the blood loss, cleaning me repeatedly with the cool stream water. Shadowy fish slid through the gloom of the stream. The dry weeds stood motionless. I watched curiously as he went back and forth to the stream. The sky was turning heavy with the threat of rain over the forest. A breeze came from the larches.

I sat up and lit a cigarette. 'I didn't know you smoked,' he said to me, surprised.

'I don't much.' I blew out a long stream of blue smoke and smiled at him.

I had hunted him down and he lay weakly in my lap. I stroked his hair; he was another trophy for my collection.

Nineteen
Dial a Dirty Number

You English are cold, ruthless, despicable bastards.
You'd do anything.

A republican activist to the author

Evening was drawing in, Flynn told me that he was going out to get us a bottle of red wine and so I started to cook dinner. I looked in the fridge and pulled out a fresh chicken to make a casserole. I chopped some mushrooms and onions, then found some herbs in his back garden and mixed in rosemary and lemon thyme.

His mobile lay on the table. I reached for it and started to comb through it, into the saved messages this time. I found a message from someone called May, saying she was coming round. I was curious and wondered if it was his sister or his mother, and what time she would be round. I rang the number. I stayed silent and I could hear a woman asking was it Sean. Stupid – she had caller ID. I recognised her voice as the woman who had interrogated me.

Half an hour later, the kitchen was quiet and still, the chicken casserole simmering slowly. I got up and went upstairs to lie down but after a while I thought I could hear noises coming from downstairs. It seemed to have been a long time since he had gone out. I felt fearful and I couldn't work out why. Was Flynn here? I could feel something watching me.

Back down in the living room the clock ticked out from the mantelpiece into the silence. Family photos in silver frames stood on the shelves next to small ornaments. I fingered each of them.

In for the Kill

There were long shadows over the blue settee and the television set. I crept out into the pitch-black hallway, my heart beating hard and fast. I looked at myself in the hall mirror. There were lines round my eyes, the start of the lines of middle age. Yet I felt like a young girl whose life had not yet started. What stared back from the dressing table mirror was Georgie but when I blinked again I saw it was the face of another middle-aged woman. This one had never married.

I went to check on the casserole but as I walked into the kitchen I saw a woman's face at the black kitchen window.

My heart beat painfully inside my chest.

'Who is it?' I called.

She stood silently. Fear paralysed me. I stood with my heart thumping in the dark kitchen, looking at her. I stepped back – was she friend or foe?

'Who are you?' I called again.

'May – but who the fuck are you?'

'I'm a journalist.' I looked over at the cooker. What kind of journalist cooked dinner for Real IRA commanders? I unlocked the back door. She pushed past me and I got a strong waft of Opium perfume. She had on a short skirt and looked ten years younger than me. It wasn't his wife, so she must have been his mistress.

'What the hell are you doing, sniffing around? Up to no good, no doubt. He may think he can control you and play with you but I see what an ambitious bitch you are.'

She ran up the stairs and I could hear her bursting into the various bedrooms. She came clattering downstairs in her high heels, clutching my white cotton underwear.

'Come on, this is unbelievable,' she shouted, waving them under my nose. 'You English are cold, ruthless, despicable bastards. You'd do anything to spy on our people.'

I walked to the front door and yet I wanted to run. I grabbed at my handbag and my coat. I struggled with the lock on the door. It clicked but would not open.

She leapt at me like a demonic cat. I screamed. She tore at my hair. The latch slipped up. She raised her fist and brought it down again. I held on tight to my coat but she wrestled me to the floor, where I fought her off. My lip started to bleed and she pulled out a knife. I got up and backed up to the door, blood from my lip spurting down my front.

Dial a Dirty Number

I ran out of the house and into the heavy rain. I skidded the car away just as Flynn appeared in his. He got out, shouted and watched me drive away, grinding through the gravel. He came running after me but I drove at top speed down the thin country lanes, skidding along the dark unlit roads, swerving and nearly crashing into bushes. I had no idea how to get out of the maze I had found myself in, so I drove around to get some distance and then pulled over. I put my head in my hands and sobbed. *What am I doing? What am I doing? Oh God!* I lit the leftover butt of a cigarette in the ashtray with shaking fingers, wiped the blood off my face with my clothes and pressed it to my split lip.

The woman could have stabbed me. I had hated being their prisoner before, yet I had come back and walked into that same sinister world. I was searching desperately for something. But what was it? I had no idea. I was the girl who wore a false face and I had a hollow centre, hunting a connection to a higher power. I sought evil to find that spiritual connection I hungered for. Flynn wasn't what I was looking for. As far as he was concerned, he was fighting a war. Like all commanders of armies all over the world, he killed as they killed. I had just been badly beaten up by one of his women. I wanted to move on, to forget Sean Flynn and Ireland and its dogs of war.

Twenty
MI6 v. *News of the World*

A man comes. He travels quickly. He has purpose.
He comes over water. He travels with others. He will
oppose. He brings violence and destruction.

Solitaire foresees Bond's arrival, *Live and Let Die*

The flight back to London was bumpy and I felt riddled with
shame. I arrived back at Heathrow just before midnight and
was glad to be out of Ireland.

The next day, after a few phone calls, I arranged to meet James.
He had a hold over me but it was time for me to break it and take
the consequences.

It was a grey afternoon when I arrived at his office. James
glared at me as he lit a cigar, keeping his angry blue eyes on my
pale, tired face.

'Whoever tried to attack you was a lover of Flynn's. He's a real
ladies' man and those Irish republican women are very feisty.
One of them took exception to a flashy English blonde being in
his bed. You could've fought back. What was the big deal? Why
didn't you keep in fucking contact?'

He re-lit the cigar and blew the smoke towards me. 'You have
to go back, have to, Chris! You were on the verge of entering the
inner sanctum – a place no one else has ever been before, let
alone a British spy. The inner ranks of the Real IRA.'

'I can never go back.' I said. 'Oh God, I should have known he
had a girlfriend. I saw her stuff in his bathroom. Why didn't I
think? I feel guilty. That's his woman and I . . .'

'You fucked him royally!' James smirked. 'No one told you to get so dirty! You were there to do a job.' He smiled at me. 'Good will come of this, Chris. You will use your skills that we gave you to get close to the Real IRA and get to Don Gunning – understand?' He looked uncomfortable for a moment and then regained his composure with a pull on his cigar.

'Oh, James.' I felt my eyes water with the prickle of self-pity.

'You're a real-life Electra – a woman wanting to get power over her evil all-powerful daddy – but you're also a very talented close-ops spy, Chris. Get it? A spy is a spy is a spy. You actually hunt these nasty bastards to try to fuck them over – literally. You're like a huntress of evil with a long black flowing cape in a cartoon. It's amusing and very useful to us.'

'I'm sick of it. It doesn't even pay. Look at me. I'm in my 30s. I didn't have time to buy a house because I was so busy working, and now all the prices have trebled. I'll never afford one now. This life of mine is bullshit. I've no family. I sure as hell have no friends, no home, no community and I'm getting older. I don't even know who I am. You've just used me. I've wasted years. You've fucked up my life. Now you want me to spy on the Real IRA, something that will mark me for the rest of my days. I won't do it, I tell you.'

'Oh, but you will. And you've fucked up your own life. You were going nowhere, on the scrapheap when I picked you up.'

'I could have got some kind of a job. I'd probably have been married by now with children.'

'You'd find civilian life as dull as ditchwater. You know, Chris, I've been supporting you for years – all the private work you had knocking at your door.'

'What private work?'

'The Israeli Intelligence – remember the nice man who took you to the Ritz for dinner? Then the Arab businessman who gave you that surveillance job? All contacts of my father, all fed to you to keep you afloat.'

'They came to me from my advert in Yellow Pages as a surveillance specialist.'

He laughed hard. 'Are you that green? Chris, if you continue to show this independent side of your nature, I will pull the tit clean out of your mouth.'

'James, I did the work and I did good jobs. How much looking after have I had?'

'We have made sure you got on well in the newspaper business. God knows you're not one of them.'

I put my head in my hands. 'I don't know who I am.'

'So many people long to be spies and you've done it – why not just enjoy getting on with it?'

'I'm a woman who has no idea who she is. I could be evil, but I don't know. I could be a bitch, but I just don't know. I'm a stranger to myself, James. Do you know how terrible it is to just be a ghost?'

'I don't bother much with others either.'

'But I want to be a person – a regular person with friends, a home and a child.'

'What do you know about that kind of world?'

'It scares me but I want to try. I want to have a child – be a mother.'

He ignored me and sounded excited. 'We've never had anybody this close to the top of these murdering bastards in the Real IRA. They're sinister, they're dangerous and they aren't ever going to give up. They'll change their name over and over to fox us but it'll be the same crew.'

I felt angry at his indifference. 'Get someone else. Get your wife to do it.'

He ignored this as well, and carried on, saying, 'Chris, we have intelligence that Flynn and Sean Hogan are having a barbecue at Don Gunning's at the end of next month. Turn up! Tell him you got scared of your feelings for him and ran. Now you're ready to give him your all. Tell him you believe in a United Ireland. Let him convert you to membership of the Real IRA.'

'I, I can't, James. I don't want to spy on an army commander and his woman . . .'

'His woman nothing – nothing.'

I stared out of the window at the grey, lightless sky.

'I can't. I'm sorry.'

'Go back to Ireland. Turn up at Gunning's. It's a private function for the IRA and their families. Get in and go and confront Flynn. And, Chris, when you're there, see what and who's there and get near Don Gunning. You'll be allowed in. Flynn had a big mouth when it came to you.'

'I can't go, James. They're clever.'

James looked earnest.

'The Real IRA won't smell us. They have no idea how much up their arse we are.'

'Oh, but you're not. That's what you want me for. Do you think

I don't know that you're nowhere near them? It's an intelligence black spot. Even the Yanks can't get to them.'

He hid his anger, pulled on his cigar and then stubbed it out in the delicate china saucer.

'You'll fucking do it, Chris. You have no choice.'

'Get stuffed.'

'You can't run now, they'd chase you anyway. It's the Real IRA, Chris. Who do you think you're dealing with?'

'I'm not going to run.'

'You might have to if we spread black propaganda that you gave us information that helped put one of them away.' James's face looked twisted and ugly as it caught the late-afternoon light that was filtering through the tall lattice windows.

'Chris, if you get Flynn for us, we will put millions into your bank account and you'll have property and prestige. You can't go back to the world of civilians and live amongst them as a pauper. Make some money first by helping me.'

'I'm going.'

'Where to?'

'Civilian life!' I wrapped my coat around my shoulders and stood up.

'Go and hide yourself. Be a tin-pot reporter somewhere in the suburbs. One day the Real IRA will find out all about you and then they'll come for you and it'll be messy.'

'I've not spied on them.'

'That's not what I'll put about.'

'Bullshit!'

'Flynn will suck it up. You've hurt him already, so he'll want to save face by leaving you by the side of the road like roadkill with a bullet in your bonce.'

I drove back home and began to think about how my life had reached a dead end. But I was still only in my 30s. I would start again and I would forge a life for myself. I would find a quiet little village in England and hide myself away and try to be like a normal suburban woman.

I met Greg for dinner. The girl I eventually found out he had dumped me for was pregnant and he was madly in love with her. I didn't care. I saw it for what it had been – we had been fuck buddies. Because I didn't feel hurt by him any more, I felt as if we were still friends.

'She's cute!'

'Who?'

'The blonde!'

He grinned. I knew he was cockahoop that he had scored a young girl. I was pleased for him. I also knew that with his addictive attitude to work it would never last.

Greg also told me about his new investigator called Glenn Mulcaire, whom he seemed happy with. This was not good news for me. I was flat broke and it didn't look as if I would be getting any more investigative work.

I felt rather angry and depressed. As soon as I got home I rang Karl Van Riebeeck.

'Long time no see.'

'What's doing with the *News of the World*? I've heard they have some guy called Glenn Mulcaire working for them,

To my surprise, he laughed – long and hard. This was when I discovered that Mulcaire had previously worked for Karl and that Greg had poached Mulcaire from him. I had inadvertently told Karl, who hadn't a clue Mulcaire was working for Greg. It was soon after this that the news broke of Mulcaire's illegal activities, something I was never aware of, as I left before he arrived. I was shocked to see that Clive Goodman fell with Mulcaire. I winced when I watched the news unfold on television. Clive had been an excellent editor. I had a feeling that it was only the start of the bloodbath. The *News of the World* was now a dead dog, it would just take a while to die.

Twenty-one
Shootout with the UDA

His death didn't mean much to me. I carried on watching *Casablanca*.

John White, UDA commander

I moved on from the murky, dangerous world of investigative journalism for a hard-hitting tabloid and I was glad of it. I wrote my own, more intellectual, investigative pieces for different papers like the *Daily Mail*, the *Sunday Express* and the *Sunday Times*. Now and again I got a call from the *Mail* or *The Times* to borrow 'my genius', as they put it.

I knew that my phone was being tapped by the spooks. An ex-Flying Squad boss told editors that I knew in Fleet Street that my home was also bugged. That made me feel hemmed in but it didn't stop me flying back to Belfast to try to cover the UDA civil war that had broken out for the *Sunday Times*.

The city was in a state of siege as in-fighting and bloodshed continued between various loyalist factions. The news of the war had reached the mainland. The man I wanted to speak to was John White, a leading loyalist figure who had been imprisoned back in the 1970s for a double murder. White had savagely knifed a Catholic couple to death as they had been kissing in a car and served over a decade in Long Kesh for it. The loyalist factions in Ireland were just as deadly as the hardline republicans and I had always wanted to get close enough to study their evil machinations. White was a widely feared leader of the UDA. Was he evil? I had to get really close to smell him.

After arriving in Belfast, I rang White to arrange an interview but he wasn't having any of it. A frustrating text conversation ensued, which ended with me saying: 'I'm NOT going to take NO for AN ANSWER, I HAVE FLOWN OVER FOR A INTERVIEW, JOHN.' I got no reply.

The next day I got a taxi to drive me over to the Shankhill Road, a lawless loyalist stronghold and especially risky for a Catholic like me. There were men with sawn-off shotguns hanging out of the windows as we drove into the estate and as soon as we got to the fortified house I was looking for, a group of thuggish men burst out of the front door, pulled the driver out of the car and violently slung him over the roof of his taxi.

I got out of the cab. Just as I did, a yellow minivan drew up. From where I stood I could see John White crouched down in the back of it wearing a donkey jacket, his face covered in camouflage cream. I strode over there.

I had interviewed John before in a cafe and got a front page for the *News of the World* out of him with my byline. The splash was: 'UDA ARE READY TO TALK PEACE'.

After the recent assassination of another loyalist called John Gregg, all the media were looking for John White, as well as assassins for the other side. I couldn't believe I was looking at him in the back of the van.

I leaned in the window. 'Hey, my pretty!'

Just as I did so, a burly figure pulled me back.

John spoke up, 'She's OK – let her talk.'

I seized my chance. 'Beautiful, I really need to interview you for the *Sunday Times*. Let's sort out all this talk about the assassination, bring a halt to it.'

'I'm not giving interviews. You see how it is.'

I put my hand on his arm. I knew the value of touch. I let my breast rub against his arm and our eyes met. I knew I had him as soon as I saw the arousal in their green depths.

'I'm not a journalist to you. I'm a friend, John.'

'Come with me then,' he grinned.

'Gotcha,' I thought as I climbed in the back of the filthy van.

The back of the van was tiny. John lifted up an oily tarpaulin and said, 'Lie under here with me.'

I thought for a split second about how he hated Catholics so much, and the memory of how he had cut the breasts off his female victim made me hesitate, but getting a good story and finding out the reason behind their civil war pushed me forward.

Shootout with the UDA

'OK.'

We lay under the tarpaulin as the van moved off. We drove for what felt like ten minutes, then it came – RAT-A-TAT-TAT-TAT-TAT-TAT. I screamed. I knew that I was going to die. It sounded like gunfire was hitting us.

'Lie flat, as flat as you can.'

He manoeuvred himself on top of me. I heard more rattling against the side of the van and screamed again. The driver shouted and the van skidded. I squashed myself tight to the bottom of the van as it wiggled and jumped along the road. I could feel it was going at a breakneck speed.

John was lying on top of me and suddenly I could hear something else: it was him laughing. I had nearly soiled myself.

'That was a close call. How did those coked-up arseholes place me?' said White in his strong Belfast accent. My whole body felt numb. It felt odd to have him lying on top of me but I was glad of the protection.

We drove and drove for what seemed like ages. When the van finally stopped, I could see that we had arrived at a big house. Inside, it was expensively decorated, there were a lot of antiques and a lot of security cameras. In the luxurious living room, with a leather chesterfield as centrepiece, calfskin rugs and a glass coffee table, White lit a large warm fire and we both relaxed as he told me about the night of the killing of John Gregg. I took notes, curled up on his settee with my legs underneath me, as he paced around in front of me wearing an open shirt and grey trousers, clutching a glass of Noilly Prat that he sipped from.

'I was watching *Casablanca* the night John Gregg fell and when he fell, he fell badly. It just got to the bit where Bogey was saying goodbye to the girl. The phone rang and someone told me that Gregg had been taken down.'

I remembered the scene of carnage on the news – Gregg slumped forward dead in his car, his skull riddled with bullets and the windscreen cracked and plastered with blood. It had been a bloody assassination ordered by a pro.

John was still talking. 'Someone said, "The cunt's dead." I replaced the phone. His death didn't mean much to me. I carried on watching *Casablanca*.' He smiled at me as he finished, then asked, 'You OK? That shootout was pretty hairy. They nearly had us, you know that, don't you? We were nearly mincemeat. I've about 200 assassins out looking for me as we speak and that was only a few of them.'

'I'm OK.' But I wasn't. I felt as if I was in a dream. John's good-looking face seemed to fade out. I felt weird.

'You may go into shock.'

'I think . . . Oh God . . .'

Water flowed down my face and I realised that I was crying.

'Oh, come on, where are my manners?'

He sat down beside me and put his arms around me. I got the rest of my exclusive interview with White cradled in his arms.

'Where do you live, Chris?' he whispered to me.

'Richmond.'

'I'm going to have to get out of town and lie low for a few years. Richmond – that sounds as good a place as any. Is it quiet and decent there?'

'Mick Jagger and Richard Attenborough seem to think so.'

'Then Richmond it is.'

Our eyes met.

'What's evil, John?'

'Evil?'

'Yes, you know – they call you an evil gangland mafia boss, don't they?'

'I'm not sure what it is. I don't think I am evil. I earn by these hands and this mind. I don't feel evil.'

I stared at him. If he hurt others, then he was evil, and yet he exuded an air of wolfish charm. I began to see that it was what the Catholic Church had deemed demonic evil that I wanted to hunt down – the real, low-down enemy of the High Church. White wasn't it, though he was dangerous enough.

My exclusive interview with John White featured in the *Sunday Times* under the headline 'MAD DOG'S MEN QUIT BELFAST FOR SURREY'. Bankers and stockbrokers in their Richmond mansions no doubt choked over their coffee and croissants as they contemplated their arrival.

The following week I wrote the *Sunday Times* Focus piece – 'WE UNCOVER THE GANGSTERS' – about the UDA gang wars and the many vicious assassinations.

After I returned to London, John rang me late one Saturday night.

'Chris, I'm no longer with my wife. I thought . . . well . . . I thought perhaps me and you? We're good together. I need a strong woman.'

I was tempted to say yes in a way. For a woman who had been

bullied as a child, it seemed like a way to feel safe in life. But I felt bad about his victims. I heard through my journalistic sources that John moved to Manchester and became the reverend of a church.

I rang Flynn the same night White called me. His mobile rang three times then to my horror a gruff Irish voice I didn't recognise answered.

'So! I've been waiting for this. The little bitch that comes fluttering on back to him to get more information. Flynn would be court-martialled if it was ever found out about you and him. Do you know how bad that is – him and a British journalist? But it's worse, isn't it? It's you. Do you know it's a well-known fact in Ireland that you're a very senior MI6 officer?'

'What, you think I'm Stella Rimington?'

'Senior on the ground.'

'How come I'm dirt poor if I'm such a hotshot?'

'You're in deep cover,' he replied gruffly.

I kept silent.

'If you come back here, do you know what will happen?'

'No.'

'You'll be arrested and then your genitals will be wired up to an old radio transmitter in a barn in Dundalk until you let us in on what your agenda is.'

He was serious.

'Did Sean say anything about me?'

'You'll never set eyes on him again, are you clear about that?'

'Yes.'

I put down the phone. They made me sick. I realised that I would never again be able to visit Ireland and I felt furious.

Back in London, I was lonely and wondered if I could make it in the normal world – could I love a normal man like other women? I felt like I had never even tried. I had long since called off my engagement to Paul, who had moved on and was living with someone else. So I met a normal man from the normal world. Nick was a wine dealer in his 40s, dark haired and handsome. We first met in his local wine shop and bonded over our passion for Argentinean Malbec. The relationship quickly evolved into regular dinner dating. He was a widower and he was kind. He had intense blue eyes and was very muscular and attractive.

It felt strange to be living in the sedate civilian world after so long in the field of undercover work, but gradually I started to have feelings for Nick. He had less experience of life than me but I told myself he was a good man. After about eight months we started to talk about getting married and having children. He told me he loved me more than he had ever loved anyone, and I believed him because I wanted to belong to this world that I had never known before. We planned our wedding on a beach in Mauritius and I tossed away my diaphragm.

I was delighted when I found out I was pregnant. I felt that normal life was just starting to happen. I wanted us to marry immediately but Nick wanted to wait.

Slowly and painfully he withdrew. Wedding plans weren't made and it took me a long time to see that he didn't love me and probably never had. Finally he told me that he wasn't ready to make such a big commitment.

While I was heartbroken, I had no doubts that I wanted to keep my baby. I had always wanted to have a child and had believed for a long time that it might not be possible. Now I had this chance, no one was going to ruin it for me. Although it wasn't the way I had wanted to bring a child into the world, on my own, I knew I would find a way to make it work.

I had been a fool to think that I could somehow enter a world where I had never been accepted and mix with the normal people in it. Civilians were like aliens to me and I had no idea of how they operated. I wished I had taken up with John White. He might have been a killer but he wouldn't have left me all alone with a child. Civilians were just as dark and nasty as terrorists and killers – they just hid it under a veneer of respectability, and while their victims weren't dead, they were trampled on, disrespected and destroyed. I was reminded of my parents and their fake niceness to the neighbours and wished myself back on the road doing what I did best – war reporting.

After 12 hours of labour and an emergency Caesarean section the doctor put an angel on my chest. Charlie immediately found his way to my left breast then hooked on and sucked away. My heart flipped. I was in love. He was a real-life angel. He was my first taste of a real flesh-and-blood family. Charlie was 'it' for me and remained so. He was my *raison d'être*, my angel darling.

My room was filled with massive bouquets from all the top editors in Fleet Street and there was one from Paul, who'd

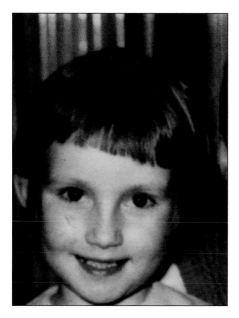

Me aged six.

Making my First Communion.

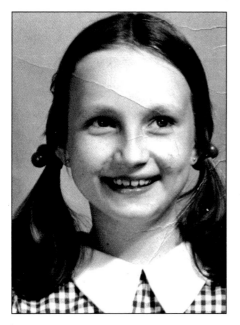

At school, aged ten.

Liam Hart (left), my adoptive father.

Journalist.

Just arrived in Los Angeles and
tired.

Modelling in New York.

At my villa in LA
during Primal Therapy.

My first Lotus.

WE GET INSI

Terror boss boasts · to our girl

1997 Adams (left), with Bertie Ahern and John Hume

1998 Semtex seized in Real IRA bid to bomb Aintree

1998 29 people died after Real IRA blew up shoppers in Omagh

THE chilling truth behind the Real IRA can be revealed today by the Irish News of the World.

Far from being a splinter group manned by a handful of fanatics, it is the new heart of the terror army.

And its members are preparing to shatter Ireland's delicate peace with a sickening campaign of violence starting this week.

In an astonishing move, bosses of the Real IRA invited the Irish News of the World to a secret address to gloat about the mayhem they are set to unleash.

Security forces say the man who spoke to our reporter is second in command of the Real IRA.

And they believe the group is planning to launch an attack in Britain "within the next three days".

The terror leader boasted to our reporter that the Real IRA was armed with advanced bomb-making gear.

Coffin

It is believed the group has a new type of explosive never before used in the Troubles.

And the boss bragged how they are professionally organised and ready for a huge campaign of violence in Ireland and Britain.

The terror leader, who spoke on condition we did not name him, looked our reporter in the eye and said: "The worst is yet to come."

Asked if more civilians would be murdered, he shrugged and said: "War is war."

And he added: "We won't rest until we have sent every English soldier in Ireland back home in a coffin."

He made the sick threats as he revealed the Real IRA sees the Provisional IRA as its biggest enemy.

The group that planted the Omagh bomb – which killed 29 people in 1998 – is so fanatical it con-

NEWS OF THE WORLD **INVESTIGATES**

BY **CHRISTINE HART**

can movement." He bragged that the Real IRA is now **BIGGER** than the Provisional IRA and its ranks have been swelled by veterans of the Troubles.

The Real IRA boss said: "The only IRA that counts is the one that is fighting Britain.

"And the only one the British fear is the one that has active service against them.

"Gerry Adams meeting the Brits halfway was a mistake and now the Provos are split from top to bottom.

"In the peace process Adams allowed the British sovereignty by agreeing to allow the Unionists to have their say.

"The Unionists should only have their say in a Nationalist Ireland."

He added: "RIRA is no longer a splinter group but has sucked in the mainstream of republican activists. We have all the fighting men. The Provos just have the politicians in the smart suits.

"Which is going to be most effective against the British to get them out of our country?"

The Real IRA commander went on: "The British Government has only sampled a tiny amount of what the Real IRA are capable of.

"What has happened so far is merely a training exercise and not genuine terror attacks."

The terror group has already targetted the BBC and MI6. In 1997 it tried to bomb the Grand National at Aintree. But their ultimate aim is to murder one of the British Royal fam-

ily. The Real IRA man said: "The Royal family is our target, the face of the oppression being waged against us.

"It is a symbol of our occupiers. The Royal family is on the walls of our enemy's living rooms.

"A hit against them is deeply prized. Like Mountbatten."

The callous killer added: "We are taking our war to the streets and housing estates of Britain. We have one aim – Brits out."

Speaking at a safe house in Dundalk, South Armagh, the terrorist leader bragged about the taxi bomb which exploded outside BBC TV Centre in London last Saturday night.

He said: "We made it in the

Republic
over the
fore the
regulati
shipped

His h
burned f

He sai
tard race
years of
the Irish
have sub

And h
London
intend te
land as c

"Only
Britain v
know wi
the occu

E REAL IRA

out horrific new bomb campaign

0 Hammersmith Bridge bombing was just "training" for Real IRA	**2000** A mortar bomb was fired by a biker at MI6 HQ in London **2001**	BBC TV Centre is rocked by a bomb planted by Real IRA

nd, smuggled it o the North be-i-mouth disease then had it he mainland." f the English

nglish are a bas-ve inflicted 100 pain not only on very people they occupation."

"One bomb in 80 in Belfast. We he war to Eng-strategy.

ing the war to eople of Britain ave suffered in f our country.

"We are not psychopaths. We are just like all Irish patriots down the ages.

"As long as Britain interferes in Ireland the British establishment plus ordinary people will sow the consequences and reap the Irish great wind."

The Real IRA has laid the foundations for a bomb blitz in Britain by setting up small, highly-organised units called "cells" – just as the Provos did in the 1980s. Security forces con-

firm a cell with five terrorists is working from a house on the border of Buckinghamshire and Berkshire.

It is led by two former senior IRA figures with a savage track record of death and destruction.

Police believe the men – who are known to both fellow terrorists and detectives as Little Dickie and JR – are about to launch a new spate of attacks.

Little Dickie was commander of the Provisional IRA in Ireland throughout the 1980s.

He is the man who directed the 1984 bombing of the Grand Hotel in Brighton during the Conservative Party's conference.

Margaret Thatcher – then Premier – was the target of the attack which killed five people.

He masterminded a string of terrorist outrages, including the killing of SAS Captain Herbert Westmacott in Belfast in 1980.

The ruthless killer also commanded one of the IRA's most successful sniper units, which killed 10 British soldiers in five years.

Little Dickie was also behind the idea of sending IRA terrorists to the Lebanon for training in the 1980s and 1990s.

Hidden

Scotland Yard says his assistant JR travelled to Britain and then disappeared two months before the latest wave of bomb attacks were launched late last year.

Both men were sent to Britain by Real IRA commanders so their experience can be used in a new terror campaign.

Police know they have been visited in London by two IRA killers nicknamed The Engineer and The Surgeon.

There are two more "active service units" known to be operating in London.

They have explosives and guns hidden.

Many of the killers who were released after the Good Friday agree-

tailed knowledge of the old IRA arms-dumps – is being groomed to take over the Real IRA.

And South Armagh Provisional IRA is now said to be completely turned over to the Real IRA.

Police in Britain are planning to launch a media campaign warning of the new terrorist threat.

Security has been tightened in all Government departments and the House of Commons in response to the threat.

It is believed the Real IRA has secret arms dumps all over Britain.

Some of the weapons are thought to have been supplied by the hardline Arab terror group Hamas.

They were smuggled into Britain via a Croatian warlord who is suspected of supplying the detonators used in the Omagh bombing.

Scientists who combed the scene of last week's BBC blast have discovered that the powerful explosive is a new form of bomb never seen in the British Isles.

Despite initial reports that Semtex had been used, the company which makes that explosive has, over the past five years, introduced a chemical fingerprint to Semtex which makes it identifiable.

The new substance is more potent than Semtex – the traditional tool of the IRA – and can be easily stored without regular checks. It can be buried for years.

Police are now liaising with American and European security services to establish the exact identity of the material used in the blast.

But sources say cash is one of the biggest headaches facing members of the Real IRA.

It has managed to raise just £380,000 – mainly from wealthy American donors – to fund its terror campaign, according to police who have examined a string of suspect bank accounts in Ireland.

In the 1980s, the Provos managed to raise £40 million to keep terror cells active in Britain.

But despite the lack of funds, police in Ireland and Britain believe IRA killers are once again at work.

A source told the Irish News of the World: "We fully expect an attack to be launched in Britain within the next three days."

'Every soldier must return to England in a coffin'

With Paul in Cap Ferrat.

Me with Charlie outside Cliveden
House in Taplow.

Hugh aged eight.

My beautiful Hugh 'Dickie' in his glory days.

Hugh with Richard Nixon.

Bianchi in the visitors' room.

Dr Ralph Allison who
discovered Bianchi's 'Imaginary
Companion'.

remained a close friend and had held my hand all the way through the birth, mopping my brow and feeding me ice.

The joy of my baby Charlie was overwhelming. Sometimes, after he went to sleep at night, I couldn't stop wanting Nick and grieving for the family life we could have had. But it wasn't to be and I knew then what I had to do. I vowed to avoid men for the rest of my life. I would be the best mother ever and I would devote my life to making sure my boy grew into a healthy young man. From now on it would be all about Charlie.

Something inside me died after Nick – a tiny sliver of hope that I might be able to trust a man. I didn't want a lover any more. I just didn't. And yet if I thought about it for a minute – the shared rent or mortgage, holidays with another adult instead of being all alone with a child, making love on a summer day, cuddles and laughter – I thought, *Yes, I'd like one*, but then I would get a feeling of deep dread. I couldn't take another knock. Nick had whacked me so hard I didn't have any more stuffing left in me. I feared another man would let me down – go off with another woman, go off me, hurt my son with rejection. I couldn't risk it.

I was happy. Charlie was my reason for living – he was my sun, moon and stars, and my life began and ended with him. Only as my son grew older did I feel the bite of loneliness at times and wonder about finding a good man, but I was sure such a thing did not exist.

Twenty-two
My Soulmate

Sex burns like the sun, imbibing, bright golden,
burning cells afire, breathless, exhausting,
perspiration through tight skin sweating, pores
open, radiant, aroused in cursing splendor, you and
I in momentary forever embrace, becoming one.

Kenneth Bianchi, the Hillside Strangler, prisoner
number 266961, Walla Walla Penitentiary

My beautiful son Charles was a constant joy to me but after he
had gone to sleep I would often sit pondering the breakdown
of my relationship with Nick. Time and time again I had been
drawn to narcissistic men who needed to have power over others.
I had got into a pattern of giving up my own power and sense of
self to make them feel good. It was the dynamic I had grown up
with while living with my adoptive mother – this was how I
thought relationships worked. But now this pattern would have
repercussions for my son.

In order to move on, I sought help from a distinguished man
whom I had both written stories about and been to see once
before. Doctor Mark Collins of The Priory in Roehampton had
apparently treated Princess Margaret for depression and
remained her good friend as well as treating a host of A-list
celebrities, including Ruby Wax and Robbie Williams. Mark could
see I was worried about Charlie and the impact that the absence
of a father might have on him in later life. He told me that all I
could do was to encourage him to grow up confident and strong.
I couldn't prevent the pain that he would undoubtedly feel at

some point but I could help to prepare him for it and attempt to lessen the impact.

He told me that there was nothing wrong with me, so he couldn't help me personally. 'And I can't mend a broken heart,' he added with a kind smile.

But I had heard about a new therapy Mark was practising, called EMDR (eye movement desensitisation and reprogramming), where by a form of hypnotism he took you back to your past. The celebs were nicknaming him Doctor Who! I was a real fan of new therapies and as primal therapy had helped me so much I wanted to see if I could heal further.

'I want the EMDR you're giving to the celebs!'

He chuckled. 'Oh, have you heard about it?'

'I've written about it!'

'Bloody journalists! It's expensive – very!' But he agreed to go ahead with the treatment if that was what I wanted.

I underwent EMDR every Wednesday afternoon as Charlie played with bricks on the thick creamy carpet in Dr Collins' luxurious office. After a few months, I felt as if someone had come in and ripped down all the curtains in every room I had left in my head. It was brilliant – a real trip.

One night I dreamed of Nick. He was on a small wooden raft just slightly out to sea. I stood on the beach holding a rope that kept him tied to me, by the shore. I let go of the rope and as I did the raft started to drift away.

'Goodbye,' I shouted, my voice thick with emotion and loss as he vanished into the mist, and then he was gone.

The next day when I woke up I was free of Nick and all the hurt I had felt over the end of our relationship. Dr Collins had done what he said he could not – he had mended my broken heart. I couldn't remember Nick's smile, the silky dark hair I'd adored, the opulent blue-green of his feline eyes. Sometimes when I looked at my son I saw glimpses of Nick, like a ghost haunting me, and I remembered the man that I had once both loved and lost, but finally I was able to move on.

The cost of my freedom was massive financial debt to The Priory and a fear of relationships. I wasn't about to go through all that pain again, or the expense of EMDR, and so I stayed clear of men.

Work was non-existent now, so I decided to do what I had always wanted to do and write books. I started work on a trilogy based on my work as a private investigator and the criminal investigations I had carried out for the media. One of them was the White House Farm Murders carried out by Jeremy Bamber. Bamber had killed his adoptive mother and father, Nevill and June Bamber, his adoptive sister Sheila Caffell and her young twin sons, and tried to blame the murder on the sister. I had written to Bamber and examined the evidence against him, and on the basis of my findings had written an investigative double-page spread titled 'NEW BIBLE CLUE IN WHITE HOUSE FARM MURDERS' for the *Sunday Express*. Bamber's background as an adopted child was of interest to me, and I had been particularly intrigued to read about his sister Sheila's relationship with her adoptive mother. Apparently June Bamber had found Sheila having sex with a farmhand in a field when she was 17. June had called Sheila the 'Devil's child'. I couldn't help but draw parallels with my own unhappy experience of adoption.

My three unpublished detective novels were called *Phelix Investigates . . .* A literary agent showed them to the heads of the top eight publishing houses in London with high hopes of a securing a lucrative deal. Seven expressed interest but wanted more work to be done on them, while the eighth, the publisher from Macmillan, described my writing as a cross between Martina Cole and Lynda La Plante but said he had just taken on someone like that so I had missed the boat. After these rejections, my agent dropped out as he had wanted to make a killing with the trilogy and it wasn't happening.

I was back at the drawing board and now minus my agent. I felt despondent and put the detective novels away. There was, however, something else I had in a drawer that maybe I could sell. Years ago, at the age of 23, I had written my life story. I had got a good agent for it called Jeffrey Simmons, who I'd heard had discovered Jackie Collins. Simmons believed I had a unique writing talent and he wanted me to publish my life story then get going with other books. Alas, after a year of trying, he had not been able to sell my autobiography. We had a near miss and a meeting with Mark Barty-King, the head of Bantam Press, but publishers just didn't want to touch Brady. Simmons eventually introduced me to a friend of his called Guy Nathan, who wasn't a publisher, he was a businessman. This man published the book, with no advance, and added in lines here and there as well as an afterword in which he expressed a warped opinion of me that I considered to be defamatory. Sickened by the whole thing, I publicly pledged my share of the book to the families of the victims of the Moors Murderers on national television, in an interview with Anne Diamond and Nick Owen.

Brady rang me at my home straight after the programme aired, very angry with me for saying on national TV that he had killed because he was adopted and abused. He told me not to do that ever again and said that if I was angry about adoption I should talk about my own experience and not his, as it would upset the Sloan family who had brought him up. He also was angry that I had publicly pledged my money from the book to the families of his victims, as he wanted it all to go to Mrs Bennett to aid the search for Keith Bennett because he liked and trusted her. He was concerned that if I said 'all the victims' then that would include Mrs West, Lesley Ann Downey's mother, whom he disliked intensely. 'She's made loads of money out of me over the years by talking to the press. I'm no one's cash cow,' he whined.

His request became meaningless, as neither I nor the victims were to see one penny piece from the book after Guy Nathan did a runner with all the proceeds. I considered it a con and reported it to the police but they said it wasn't a crime as he had set up a limited company to publish and then it folded. The debt was owed by the limited company not by Nathan personally, so he didn't have to pay me anything. I had no money to chase him through the civil courts, so he got clean away with it. Jeffrey Simmons later told me to forget about the whole experience, as Nathan had died of stomach cancer.

During the many times the national press had written stories about me and Brady while I was in my 20s, I had never asked for payment. A journalist had once offered me a hundred pounds from his own wallet in a bar but I refused to accept it and he told me that he respected my moral stance. I did, however, want to correct an account that had been printed of a meeting between me and Brady where it had been reported that I said he had sexually abused me. I felt guilty about this, as I felt it wasn't sexual abuse, so I penned a book about it and called it *The Man in the Picture*. I found an agent but once again no publisher was interested in touching a story about Brady.

I sat on it for a while and then, when my son was four, tried to find another agent. This time I found an American who liked it but said it needed editing, as publishers didn't edit any more;

they wanted books ready to go to print. I had to pay for the editing, which took a massive chunk of the payment I received for the book. I was also disappointed with the work that was done, as I had assumed that an editor would make me sound like Ian McEwan but in fact made me sound like Pollyanna on crack. I had to go over it all again, grinding my teeth as I went. The world of publishing wasn't what I'd expected.

After signing a contract for my work, the publishers decided that they didn't want Brady in the book, they just wanted my childhood in the orphanage and felt Brady would overshadow the poignancy of that story. After much arguing, they eventually agreed to include a chapter or two about Brady but I found the whole process very stressful. The Brady chapter was the only one that received a literary review and was described as being reminiscent of *Silence of the Lambs*; the rest was attacked by the same reviewer as being a 'misery memoir by numbers'. I had to laugh.

After the book came out, Ian Brady wrote to my publisher enclosing a newspaper clipping which stated that he had won a High Court battle against the *Sunday Express* when they reported that he had sexually abused me when he was alone with me in his cell.

The publisher's lawyer rang Steven Bacon, the *Sunday Express*'s hotshot lawyer, who told them that in fact the *Sunday Express* had won the case against Brady. The result had been misreported and the paper which had done so corrected their mistake the following day and printed an apology on page two.

After that hideous and unrewarding experience I wished I had never had the urge to write, but I had an inner writer monkey who drove me. I sat chewing my pen. I felt flat and had nothing to write about. My unpublished detective novels sat gathering dust in a drawer and I decided I was better at non-fiction. But what could be my subject?

I still had a massive bee in my bonnet about 'adoption', 'supernatural evil' and 'serial killing', but I had no idea how to combine these three themes into one book.

I knew from my experience of Brady that it was only by getting really intimate with a serial killer that one could get to see their real face; they weren't about to showcase the monster – it had to be excavated.

Could I do that again with another mind society called evil? Strip them bare and continue my hunt? But who would I focus on? I still didn't know what evil was and despite all my searching I was sure I had not found it in its true form. But I was still eager to hunt it down and come face to face with it. It fascinated me, drawing me like a moth to a deadly hot flame. The thought of finding it excited me deep in my gut. In my fantasy of finding evil, I saw it as a supernatural demon that would somehow unlock the mysteries of life for me. It felt like I was searching for a supernatural something. Yet how could I be?

My 'misery memoir' went in at number 17 in the *Sunday Times* bestseller list then came straight out again. Apart from the advance, which went mostly to the taxman and for expenses, it was never to make another penny. I was in the red and I had sold all I had to sell. In the 2008 recession, I listened to an estate agent who told me that houses were going to crash to a hundred grand a pop and I sold him our lovely three-hundred-grand home for two hundred thousand – seventy grand less than I had paid for it in 2003. Charlie and I moved into rented accommodation and the rest of the cash I had went towards repaying the rest of my debts. In a few months it was all gone.

Then I knew what fear really was. Money and I seemed to have an allergy to each other and I had to face the fact that I was financially brain dead and a target for any sweet-talking conman going. I was the typical nerd who only had a mind for academic books and philosophical ideologies. I wasn't streetwise, despite growing up in a children's home. I suspected that I had some kind of inner teenage bimbo who was sabotaging my life.

Being conned out of our home was the final nail in that coffin of naivety. I gave myself a little lecture and planed to evict the bubblegum-chewing, hysterical teenager who was living rent-free inside me. The next time I wrote anything, I would be mature about it and demand fair and full payment. The next time I bought a house, I would pay the fair price for it and when selling it I would make sure it was a fair sale. I would no longer expect others to be honest or fair where money was concerned. I would carefully oversee every step. This, I was told, was the right way to behave in business! My failings in this area were yet another consequence of an abusive childhood. The abused child seeks the 'fair treatment' they never had in childhood. They leave themselves open to betrayals in the naive hope that this time fair treatment will be given and it will salve the past. It was crazy! I had to wise up and grow up. I was both mother and father now to an adorable little boy and this changed me. I became hardened as love for Charlie made me form a protective shield around both of us. I just hoped it wasn't too late and we would get other chances to use whatever talents I had so I could support and house my child.

Despite my financial worries, life was far from bleak. We had each other and masses of love. In 2009, Charlie and I spent the hot summer weekend days in the long back garden of our rented house, Dragonfly Villas, that led to the river. He splashed about in the huge blue paddling pool and made set-ups of countries like Africa with his animals. I sat and made a quilt, knitted or read Graham Greene in a deckchair, both of us chatting happily about everything and nothing. I loved these sticky hot summer days and balmy sun-drenched early evenings when I would sit on the riverside decking or chat to neighbours across the river about child rearing and politics. Charlie, hot and sweaty, would demand a water fight and after getting drenched while running round the garden playing cowboys and Indians we would wrap ourselves in towels and get cosy in the living room in front of a summer fire that I lit to take the edge off the chill. We sat contentedly as logs burned, and played chess; Charlie had already quickly mastered moves to beat me.

'No, Mummy. I've checkmated you. Look!'

'Oh, come on.'

'Ha – you're always so exposed with your Queen!'

'Right, you've won, so now it's your bedtime.'

'You're putting me to bed because I've checkmated you?'

'Yep, I am.' I grabbed him and wrestled him on the settee before we collapsed in a ball of laughter.

I packed him off to bed with a *Diary of a Wimpy Kid* storybook and sat in his attic bedroom with its pirate ships and paper planes, feeling content. Charlie opened his sleepy eyes and looked at me.

'Mummy, how much do you love me?'

'More than the stars, Baby Blue.'

He smiled at my silly name for him.

'I love you more than the moon, Mummy.'

I looked at my six-year-old son. His face and the softness that I saw in it always reached down into the bottom of my heart and claimed all that was there for his own.

I went back down the stairs barefoot, shafts of late sunshine filtering through the tall leaded widows. I threw open the drawing-room windows and breathed in the air that was heavy with the scent of flowers. I was lonely now Charlie was asleep and the large old-fashioned house was silent. I poured myself a glass of gin and tonic and tried to relax despite the deep feeling of dread that seemed to constantly haunt me. I wasn't young any more and I had no income. I worried endlessly about my son having a miserable childhood. I had nightmares about us being cast out in the snow, like characters in a Dickens novel.

With no money to spend, Charlie and I had become experts at taking advantage of everything in life that was free. We both loved long wintry walks in our welly boots in the freezing snow in Richmond Park amongst the hundreds of wild deer. Under mauve clouds and a cheesecake moon, on the slopes of the grey-green hills the cold air rang with our talk of having riches and servants to bring us hot chocolate and how we would each own a Ferrari, his black, mine cream.

In the summer, we visited the tropical jungle of Isabella Plantation with our wide-brimmed straw boaters to protect our skin from a July sun that hung in a parrot-blue sky. We tramped for miles under hanging honeysuckle bushes in pink and cream. We waded barefoot in cool brown lakes covered in green algae, fed the ducks and went on caterpillar hunts. A picnic was laid out under a tree with ginger biscuits, cucumber sandwiches and dandelion and burdock. We sat near the golden hibiscus and admired the green furry bodies in our washed-out marmalade jars. Charlie, with his thin arms, mop of golden blond hair and toothy grin, adored the butterflies our caterpillars would morph into.

I had one female friend, an old neighbour left over from my days of penthouse living and designer clothes. Sienna was a beautiful and talented painter who liked parties and the good time. She had a dark bob cut to her chin and a princess pout under slanting blue eyes. She never bothered to invite me to any of her luxurious Gatsby-style parties at her stunning house in Chelsea, stating, 'Well, darling, you've a child now and of course children aren't welcome at parties, so that's why I can't invite you.'

When she visited us, once seated with drink in hand in our summery back garden she would regale me with descriptions of her lavish parties on St Tropez yachts and decadent dinner parties in the Bahamas. I think Sienna enjoyed it all the more for the way

My Soulmate

I sat there like a desperate little bird gobbling up the crumbs that she scattered for me.

During one visit, Sienna looked at me and frowned. 'You really have got to get a man, Chris, before it's too late.'

'I'm more concerned with providing for my son and finding some way of paying the rent, Sienna. I need money.'

'A man would do that, wouldn't he?'

'Do they? I thought prostitution was illegal,' I grinned at her.

She rattled her diamond bracelet. 'Larry buys me jewellery all the time. I've always had lots of diamonds off my men. My husband takes me on holidays abroad and provides us with our stunning home in Chelsea; I can't complain about men.'

'I don't complain, Sienna.'

'It's because your father sexually abused you when you were a kid. He was a creep, so you went for creepy, bad men. It's not bad luck at all.'

'Thank you, Sigmund.'

'Well, wise up and try to meet a kind one who's interested in you.'

'As Charlie gets older, I am finding myself more and more alone. I'm glad for it, as it means I've done my job, but there will be an almighty crash when he leaves home.'

'Loneliness will hit you even harder.'

It was a summer evening and the sun had not yet slipped down under the rim of the world. I felt tired as I got up to mix vodka and tonics. I carried back a tray rattling with our drinks and sat down with my glass in my hand. I sipped at it, shivered and pulled my cardigan around my shoulders.

'Cold?'

'No, it's just so hot during the day that when the sun fades it gets chilly.' I chewed on a potato crisp and offered her one.

'No thanks, just the booze. Cheers.' Her blue eyes sparkled over the rim of the glass.

'Cheers.'

She nursed her glass on her knee as if it were something very precious.

'So, when are you going to get over your fear of intimacy and get yourself a husband?'

'Where from – the shops?'

The nearby vivid pink rhododendron threw out mottled patterns on the newly mown velvet lawn; I stared at their hot pink petals and thought about my money worries. I turned back to her.

'I'm fine, Sienna. I'm just far too busy writing.' I licked salt off my lips and admired my friend's silky dark hair and her tight body; I had put on weight lately from eating too much Green and Black's and was worried about losing my good figure.

'You're not open to love is the problem, you're too afraid of being hurt. Ever since Nick abandoned you and Charlie, you've never even looked at a man.'

'Golly, you're making me depressed. Got one of your secret cigarettes?'

Her husband hated her smoking, so she came to mine to puff away. She lit us both a Silk Cut and I lay down on the grass and looked up at the hazy blue sky.

I could hear Sienna blowing out smoke and relaxing. Birdsong was raucous in the nearby apple trees, bees buzzed near the flowerbeds and jets thundered overhead.

Sienna was next to speak. 'You know my favourite writer, Ramtha? Well, he says in his book *Soulmates* that each of us is a soul split into two halves. We spend our whole lives trying to reconnect to that other half but don't know it. We unconsciously yearn for them and spend our whole lives searching for them.'

'I don't feel like I'm a half of anything. I'm a whole.'

'No, seriously – come on. Can't you feel a hunger inside of you? That's it – that's your yearning – and if you follow it and be the best person you can be, the universe guides you to him or her – our soulmates – our one true love.'

I sat up on my elbows and frowned at her. 'Rubbish.'

'You are moving towards him each minute of each day.'

'Oh God, such nonsense,' I laughed.

Sienna sipped at her vodka lemon ice and continued. 'He says all soulmates act like mirrors. They are the person who shows you everything that's holding you back. A soulmate will tear down your walls and slap you from your sleep. Chris, it's about time you went and found yours or you'll end up an old bag all alone when Charlie goes off to university. Come on, get yourself slapped awake. You know, you used to be a size ten and now you're at least a twelve. You're even dressing differently, fatso.'

I threw the rest of the potato crisps at her and she laughed cheerfully. Then the French windows banged open and Charlie came running across the lawn to show us both a paper plane he had made before running off into the untidy flowerbeds and the dusty, broken greenhouse that sat neglected at the bottom of the garden.

Sienna went on, 'Ramtha says that sometimes soulmates aren't who we want them to be. They could be a wrinkly old woman or a starving orphan in India – somebody we hate on sight. But the nearer we get to the true us, the more we see our heart's love. Oh, it's all so magical.'

I watched Charlie playing.

'What planet do you live on?' I turned to Sienna and sucked greedily on another of her cigarettes. I closed my eyes as the smoke seeped out from my closed lips and then pulled my knees up to my chin in a gesture of self-nurture. She narrowed her eyes at me, scrutinising. I caught a whiff of her latest perfume; it smelt of oranges, peaches and champagne.

'Wouldn't you like to know what it feels like to love a man? To truly and passionately be in love – to want to merge with them into one as they penetrate you to your depths? Don't you want your soul to be fucked? '

'Oh, my soul fucked! Is that a new G-spot?' I laughed deeply. 'Do you have that with Larry? Good sex, I mean?' I wasn't really interested.

'Larry's a maniac in bed. He brings me to orgasm in seconds.'

Our eyes met and I saw in hers the shiny glint of spite. She wanted me to be jealous; it meant we weren't truly friends. I felt loneliness spike inside me. I sipped my vodka and tonic and focused on Charlie, his golden hair glinting in the evening sun as he ran and jumped with his wooden plane.

'I've forgotten sex and what it's like to have closeness with a man's flesh – complete amnesia. Isn't it strange that that happens when you don't do it any more?'

'It's utterly heartbreaking, my friend.' Sienna pulled out the book from her handbag and flicked to a marked page. 'Listen to this: "When your soulmate bites into a fruit, you will feel the tang on your tongue. When he or she cries, we taste the salt of their tears. What he has been doing in his or her life will have been impacting on yours without you even knowing where that influence came from."'

'Very moving, very D.H. Lawrence.' I drew on my cigarette then stubbed it out on a plate, revolted by it. 'Mind you, years ago, when I was about 20, I saw a psychic who told me that I would meet my soulmate and he would be called J. That was his initial, J, and he worked with his hands, was self-employed and he lived across the sea.' I wrinkled my nose at her.

'Chris, there you go! What have I been telling you all afternoon? It's written in the stars: you're going to meet your soulmate and he's called something beginning with J, and as soon as you find him you will become a god and have this incredibly sensual experience.' She finished off her drink and stretched herself out like a contented cat. 'You must begin looking for this J immediately. You have to search for J high and low, even devote your whole life to it. Do you know that, without you knowing it, your life has been a constant search for your soulmate?'

I looked at the sky as it glowed the bright blue found in Caribbean travel brochures. My whole life, since childhood, had been a search for supernatural evil, so how did that stack up?

'I'll try to keep alert,' I said, grinning at her, 'in between looking for ways to pay the rent.'

'Any plans for the weekend, darling?'

'No, the usual – tea with Charlie, playing games, then early to bed.'

'Is that your life?'

I kept silent. I was OK.

'It's so bloody dull. I couldn't – you're a saint.'

We air kissed.

'A woman wasn't meant to live without a man, and look at you,' she goggled at my breasts. 'Men love big boobies! What a waste!'

We hugged and then she was gone, leaving a scent trail of overripe peaches in her wake.

Later that evening I put down my novel, switched on the television and thought about Sienna's words as I ate a family bar of fruit and nut.

Only a soulmate can help you discover the real you. Your soulmate will find your buried true identity and slap you from your sleep.

I opened the window and let a cool scented breeze caress my face. What an idea – that our soulmates, our true loves, could change our lives and bring ultimate fulfilment. I had worn so many fake faces throughout life and still had no idea who I was. The idea that a soulmate would show me appealed to me. I had once dreamed of true love and passion but I had long since given up on them. The idea seemed like bullshit.

I went out to the garden to fold up the deckchairs and put

them away in the shed, then arranged mineral water and biscuits on my desk and set to work, hoping that the children's book that I was now writing would turn out something like my own favourite, *A Wrinkle in Time*.

The house was quiet and loneliness sat on my shoulder like cold ice. I felt depressed. I had no real belief that I could make it as a writer. I focused on my son and making his life as pleasant as I could. I braved the dull ache of loneliness and pushed myself on into the early hours until tiredness took me and I slept on the settee. The alarm went off at seven and it was time to get ready for the pain-in-the-arse monotony of the dreaded school run.

Twenty-three

Enter the Hillside Strangler

Even when our eyes never meet they pass each
other in spiritual glances, and I miss them ever so
much. My guilt overflows, over having eight hours
of sleep, and yearning for a two-hour stir and your
contented bliss on my shoulder on your journey
back to dreams.
Can you feel my love?

Kenneth Bianchi

I turned on the television and channel-surfed, remote in one
hand, drink in the other. I stopped at one programme. It was an
American crime show featuring a picture of a good-looking man,
dark-haired and in his 20s. The room was airless and I fanned my
face with a copy of *The Independent*. As I listened, I realised that
the man who had caught my attention was a notorious serial
killer. He was called Kenneth Bianchi and he had been convicted
in 1979, along with his cousin Angelo Buono Jr, of the Hillside
Stranglings. Together they had raped and killed ten young
women, one of whom they had tortured with electric wires.

I felt compelled to keep watching. The two rapists had terrorised
Los Angeles by strewing the bodies of tortured, naked girls over
the hillsides and for a long time had fooled the police. Eventually
the man I was looking at had gone to Washington State and was
caught after he raped and strangled two more women. I was so
fascinated by his cool, boastful confession that I turned up the
volume and pulled up my chair. He was the personification of
evil. I felt like a scientist who had suddenly had a breakthrough.

In for the Kill

On the screen, Bianchi was in a police station being interviewed by a cop. He stood smoking the butt of a cigarette like a gangster and boasted about murder. He wore a blue overall and his back looked strong. I felt an immediate hunger to sexually violate him as he had done to his victims.

The cops had laid out photographs of the dead girls in a row. Bianchi was standing pointing at them and he said, 'I killed that one. Angelo did that one. I did that one. That broad, I don't know. That one he killed . . .' And so it went on.

He sounded like an angry young child I had once known on distant childhood streets, long forgotten.

I studied his face: he had a perfectly straight nose, chiselled cheekbones and a sensitive mouth. How could he be guilty of such evil acts when he looked like a choirboy and had been, according to the narrator, a trainee Catholic priest? This was fascinating: the Devil and yet with the face of an angel. It was Wilde's Dorian Gray in real life.

It was ten o'clock and I needed to go to bed to get ready for the school run in the morning. I got up and closed the window to shut out what had now become a chilly draft. I poured a glass of vodka and wondered about what this image on the screen was doing to me. Then I went over and turned off the television. I went to bed feeling sick. I fell asleep thinking of how it must have felt to be in a house with two men playing with you sadistically until they exorcised their demons by torturing and then finally putting you to death.

After the school run the next day I opened my laptop on the round kitchen table and searched the Internet for information about Kenneth Bianchi. Was he really as bad as this programme had made out?

I discovered, as I researched, that he was adopted and had not been treated well by his adoptive parents. There seemed to be a number of serial killers who had experienced early separation from their birth parents. Ted Bundy, for example, serial killer, rapist and necrophile, was originally raised by his grandparents, and his grandfather was described as being violent and abusive. Jeremy Bamber had been adopted and Ian Brady had been fostered. Louis Schlesinger, who wrote *The Sadist*, believed that adoption could leave men prone to cataclysmic homicide, that is, in the right circumstances they would be likely to kill. Adoption results from rejection, so it causes anger that can be easily triggered.

Enter the Hillside Strangler

As I read Bianchi's story, I saw interesting parallels with my own life. A teenage mother had abandoned him as a child. A childhood of beatings and terrorising by his highly religious Catholic adoptive mother was recorded in Bianchi's medical records, as was the theory that he may have raped as a form of revenge for the intrusive medical examinations she made him undergo. My own Catholic adoptive mother had beaten me mercilessly and my father had sexually abused me. Reading Bianchi's notes, I felt intrigued by the similarities with my own life. It was creepy.

Amazingly, Bianchi had turned up in Los Angeles in his mid-20s with only a battered suitcase and hope in his heart, just as I had turned up in LA at a similar age looking for something, all alone with just one battered suitcase.

His trip to LA had led him into the underground world of the sleazy sex trade and from there into rape, sadism and serial killing. I had drifted off into a zany, hippy world of primal therapy, trying to find a cure for the overwhelming numbness I felt as a result of my childhood torment.

I poured a cup of coffee from a freshly made pot and returned to my laptop. The information I found on the net suggested that some doctors believed Bianchi suffered from multiple personality disorder. While Bianchi was under hypnosis another personality had emerged – an evil 'twin' of the normally 'nice' Bianchi, a loving partner and father – and it was this personality, who claimed to be called 'Steve', that had committed the murders.

The demonic personality on the clip I had seen was Steve. I was fascinated. Where was Steve now, if he wasn't still in Bianchi? Floating around in the ether looking for someone else's body to use?

I found a YouTube clip of Bianchi in the police station. He was politely answering questions in a mild-mannered way. I stared at the screen. I had no chemical reaction to him like I had when he was being Steve, and then all of a sudden he changed, standing up and turning on the cameraman aggressively.

'YOU . . . you're the one who's trying to get me to leave him.'

That was Steve revealing himself. I was mesmerised. Saliva came up in my throat and I felt like I couldn't breathe. This was fascinating. Steve was pure evil and I was engrossed. *Oh my God – look at you.*

That night I sat in the kitchen thinking about all I had read and seen. I was intrigued at the mass of contradiction that I was finding in this fascinating case. Was this man acting up, was he mad or was he really possessed as he claimed? I knew one thing – Ken and Steve were completely different. I could feel it.

I told myself that I had my work head on and that this story was of professional interest to me. I told myself that maybe I could further my career by writing an investigative book about one of America's most infamous serial killers.

Twenty-four
Pure Demonic Evil

When I am asked how many demons there are, I answer with the words that the demon himself spoke through a demonic. 'We are so many that if we were visible we would darken the sun.'

Father Gabriele Amorth,
chief exorcist of the Vatican, Rome

I sat sunbathing in the back garden. It was a hot early August afternoon and I sank my feet into an ice-cold bucket of water, enjoying the fantasy that I was at the seaside.

I began to think about Bianchi's crimes, especially the torture. It was disgusting. Why had he done it? I had no inside information about him; he was a mystery. But I felt that he was evil in as concentrated a form as I had ever come across it. I was like an archaeologist who had found an ancient bone I had been searching for my whole life.

My son was at the nearby village school and I had the whole day to myself, so I decided to get to work. I flicked through my Filofax, looking over all my journalistic contacts and wondering who could help me start to pick away at the dirt that surrounded Bianchi to reveal the truth about this man.

I rang an ex-colleague who was a well-known crime journalist in Fleet Street. He listened to me for a moment and then said, 'I can help you out, Chris. There's another writer called Chris Berry-Dee who's been over to America to see Bianchi. He told me all about how he had been threatened through the bars and spat at. Hang on, here's his home phone number.'

In for the Kill

I rang Dee to introduce myself.

'Hello, Mr Dee, I'm Chris Hart, a journalist. I've found an interesting character in America called Ken Bianchi and a colleague told me that you've been over to meet him.'

'Oh, I've met him all right,' started the friendly Dee. 'He's a human monster! When I went to see him in jail in Walla Walla, he was brought into the visiting room in manacles. I hated the look of him; he had piercing black eyes like a great white shark.'

'Why were you so scared of him when you're a crimey like me?' I asked.

'There's something weird about someone who injects bleach and gasses his victims. That murdering sado-psychopath is even more evil than other serial killers! You know one of his victims – he tied electric wires to her hands and tried to fry her before he murdered her. He only got caught by accident because he left his cousin Buono, who had got fed up with him. He got caught as he tried to hang another two girls in Washington State.'

'I know some of this. I've read about it on the Web.'

'Thank God there was a guard there when I visited him. Bianchi leaned forward, grabbed my lapels and hissed, "If I have the chance, I'm going to smash your skull to bits." The guard had to restrain him. Then as he left, he said, "Never, ever, come near me again."'

'That's pretty scary,' I replied as I lifted my bare foot up to paint my toenails in Red Queen. I painted two straight vertical lines in red along my big toe and sniffed. Dee was enjoying trying to scare me, I could tell. His regional twang rose in pitch as he described his adventures in America's toughest prison.

Creamy-coloured butterflies flitted above my flowerbeds and alighted on the pink and yellow rose bushes. There was no sound apart from the occasional jet screaming overhead.

I got up with my mobile in my hand and took a reporter's notebook out of the drawer in the kitchen, came back out into the garden and started to scrawl down what Dee was saying. He stopped talking; I held my breath, my pen suspended in mid air.

'Are you doing a book? I can hear you scribbling notes.' He sounded tense. 'I'll be glad to send you my files on him if you want. Some writers say that Bianchi was the subservient partner to Angelo Buono but that's not true. Bianchi is as highly dominant as they come. He killed before his cousin and he killed after he left him. Chris, I'll tell you something odd. I had this really strange experience when I was with him. As I sat opposite him I felt something almost alien search around inside my mind. He can project the killing side out of him. I felt him inside my head, but not him. It was the Steve part, the killer.'

The sun was making my head pound.

'How did you know it was the Steve part? Are you joking with me?'

'I'm deadly serious. He's got the ability to project the killing part of himself into the minds of other people. It's the killing part that comes in and out of his body. I tell you I felt him trying to get into my mind. It felt like a reptile was looking out of my eyes.'

'So he can project himself out of his body?' A profusion of pink roses alongside the garden wall were being tossed around in a warm breeze and sent their pollen flying at my nostrils, making me sneeze violently.

'Bless you.'

'Thanks.' I wrinkled my nose to stop it itching.

'Yes, he can, so be warned and, hey, what are you up to with this man anyway?'

'Dunno – I'm out fishing.' I jutted out my bottom lip thoughtfully. Now I was scared but even more curious. I pointed my face at the hot afternoon sun. I had to say I didn't like the idea of someone who might be able to project himself into my mind.

He went on, 'We don't know much about serial killers, so if you rattle their cage all sorts of unknown stuff can happen. I'm not trying to scare you; I'm only giving you a warning.'

'I know, I have experience with serial killers and close-quarter assassins.'

'Kenneth Bianchi is different, Chris. He is the real demonic deal. As I approached his cell, I felt the evil choke at my throat. The prison governor of Walla Walla once told me a young woman called Cathy had started writing to Bianchi out of pity for him. She ended up having a nervous breakdown. Her father wrote to the prison and complained. He asked them to prevent Bianchi from having contact with a woman ever again. He said Bianchi is a very dangerous man.'

'How could he have made her go crazy?'

'Easy. He got inside my head. If he can do that to me, he can do it to her. I tell you, he's got evil powers. I could feel it oozing out of his cell as I walked down towards it.'

I was having trouble believing that this was true but I said nothing. I felt excited. I remembered how, as a kid, I had longed to find something demonic to fly down and kill my mother for me. Here was what I'd been so interested in and it was being shoved in my face. Bianchi sounded like a real-life vampire locked in his coffin.

'Bianchi claimed he wasn't guilty, didn't he? He said he was possessed by the demonic Steve?'

'Yeah. But that may have been because he was faced with the electric chair, like the girl he wired up. By the by, he injected bleach into one of his victims, for God's sake. He bit them, beat them and sodomised each of them before strangling them with rope. I suppose you know that he's in the sex-criminal part of the prison, which is a separate block? If they didn't put him there, the other prisoners would try to murder him for his bloodletting.'

As Christopher went on, telling me more about Bianchi, my stomach started churning. This was getting really nasty.

Charlie had just come out into the garden after walking home with the school-walking bus that went past the front door. I called him over and hugged him. His angelic qualities were much needed due to the conversation I was having about Bianchi.

I pulled Charlie back and searched his face to see if he had enjoyed school. His soft eyes were all summer: sky blue and flecked with pale gold.

'How was it at school today, buddy? Playground OK?'

'Yes, Mum, fine.'

'Who'd you play with?' I kissed his warm cheek and pulled him close, feeling protective.

'Mm, no one. I sat on the friendship bench.'

My stomach sank. 'Oh God, darling. You'll make friends soon, I know it.' I felt nausea rise into my throat. Bugger this bloody village, it was so close-knit and the rich boys were in a clique, as their parents dined together every Saturday night. I wasn't in with the in-crowd; in fact, I wasn't in with any crowd. I blamed myself for being socially inadequate and not being a married to a wealthy man with a million-pound house like the other mothers.

'Go and play while I finish up and I'll be in in five minutes to join you, OK?'

'OK, Mummy.'

A stabbing migraine started to gather in my head; it was worry and fear about Charlie. Rubbing my forehead, I turned back to work to escape my son's pain and my own guilt.

Pure Demonic Evil

I made sure Charlie had disappeared back inside and then said to Chris Berry-Dee in a quiet voice, 'Chris, was Bianchi ever physically violent to you?'

'Later on, after I interviewed the governor, she showed me around the prison. As I passed his cell I saw Bianchi lying on his bunk listening to music through headphones. The cell was so tiny that the bunk of the prisoner next door cut through into his. He's stuck in there 22 hours a day. He told me he had a bigger cell than anyone else but it was the smallest.'

I started to feel breathless.

Dee was still recounting his story. 'Bianchi looked up and saw me, and he flew at the cell bars, screaming obscenities and spitting at me. I ran off down the corridor. I was terrified and so was the governor. He was like something inhuman.'

'God, spooky.'

'I've also interviewed Ronnie DeFeo, Chris. You know, the Amityville Horror case? Demonic possession. I'm psychic and I'm into all that. I believe in it and I can suss it.'

'I was interested in that case. I found it fascinating. It's the idea of something evil possessing someone. Does evil mean demons and devils, or is that bullshit? It's like I need to know!'

He laughed. 'You and I are so fucking alike. You know, Chris, we both have to excavate evil. We want to know it, explore it, find out its capabilities, pull it out and feel it.'

'I know – yeah, me too! Others think we're attracted to it.'

'Maybe wanting to know it is an attraction to it?'

'An attraction to knowing its mysteries.'

'I tried for Brady, you know – Daddy of the Devils, or so he's called. I couldn't get near him, so well done, you. I investigated Bianchi but I never got through a thick layer of plastic coating. Bianchi tries to be very private. He never lets anyone into his inner sanctum. I got an introduction to him through the prison and I was making a film, but he refused to be in it. You won't get anywhere near him. When he wouldn't reply to my letters I sent two ex-models to write to him with their photos and he blanked them both. They were stunningly beautiful and yet they failed to get near to him. I know about 20 American journalists who are gagging to talk to him but he won't answer any of their letters. A lot of writers are interested in Bianchi but you won't ever reach him – no way.'

I knew that I would – somehow it felt as if Bianchi was just sitting there waiting for me.

'I still have to investigate all of this myself, Chris,' I said, 'so I'd be grateful if you'd send me all your files, letters from him and anything else you have.'

'I like the sound of you, so you can have what I've got.'

'Thanks a lot, Chris, and any time I can help you, please let me know.'

'Yeah, you can. I used to give tips to a girl on the *Mail* who'd write up the stories. She's left now, so you could have them if you like and we could split payment.'

'Cool – send 'em through.'

'I've got a photo from the Amityville case. It's a photograph that was taken by the crime-scene officer at the time. It has a hazy outline of a little girl on the bed but it's not the present-day victim. She's wearing an old-fashioned nightdress and if you look closer there's an oil lamp in the photo. You know they thought it was the same crime being committed in that house over and over at 3.06 a.m.'

'Email it over and I'll place it and write the words.'

I pointed my face at the afternoon sun and felt good; the conversation had been fruitful. My book on the case would be intriguing.

Just before I hung up he spoke again. 'Chris, one thing! Years ago Bianchi made me a tape from his prison cell. His mother's interview with the cops is on the other side of it along with a tape Veronica Compton made me from prison, the woman who attempted murder to try to free Bianchi. I'll post it. Some of my letters I sent to David Cantor, the celebrity shrink. Ring him if you like and say I authorised you to have all Bianchi's letters. The rest I sent to the FBI in Quantico. They need letters from serial killers. They go through them line by line. We know nothing about them, so that's the only resource they have – us.'

'Send me the tape.'

'I worked hard for it. I'll sell it to you for forty quid?'

'OK.'

I was short of money but I wanted the tape of Bianchi, to feel who he was by hearing him.

When Dee rang off, I felt numb. What was this monster in Walla Walla?

Inside, Charlie was playing soldiers. 'Mummy, want to play?' he shouted.

'One game and then we'll have our tea outside, near the river. I'm going to make your favourite: milk rice for pudding, and sausages, onion gravy, cabbage and mash for dinner.' I grinned at him.

'Hurrah, hurrah. I'll start setting up the battle now. You can be the good guys. No, on second thoughts,' he said earnestly, 'I will be the good guys; you, Mummy, can be the bad guys.'

I went over to my desk and switched on the computer. I pulled up a photograph of Bianchi on the Internet. He had clear blue eyes, a straight nose, Byronic dark hair and a face like an angel; it was hard to think he had done any of the things that Chris had told me. I went onto YouTube again and viewed the clips of him. The one of him in court didn't interest me; it was only the one of him in the cell confessing that drew my fascination. They seemed to me to be clips of two different people.

I printed out two photos of him and stuck them onto the large corkboard I used while investigating cases. It seemed to me that one of them was Steve. He had a dark, brooding, very male look in his eyes. 'Hello, demon.' I took my marker pen and wrote 'Steve' above it.

The second photo was a still of Bianchi sitting in court. He looked composed and gentle, almost feminine. 'This is just some really wimpy guy.' In one of the videos I had watched he had appeared remorseful, saying, 'If I did do this, I'm so very sorry, but I cannot remember doing any of it.' Over this one I wrote 'Kenneth'.

I could smell both of them using my sixth sense. One was not worth my time, while the other had something other-worldly about him, even his voice was different; in it I could hear something and I couldn't put my finger on what it was. It was like he was unsocialised somehow. He was incredibly dominant, even in his body language, but was somehow detached from humanity – not by coldness like a psycho but by entering into another world and he seemed to echo from that world. I saw him as a kind of a gateway to the world I wanted to explore. I wondered if he had spent a long time alone as a child. Had he been psychic? What had he tapped into? Was there any scent of the occult or Satanism around him?

I searched the Internet for any links from the Hillside Stranglings to the occult and learned that Bianchi had a tattoo saying 'Satan's Own' on his left upper arm. Joining the seminary was also a clue – he had been looking for something. Michael the Archangel was, after all, one of God's most beloved and beautiful angels, but he never would have felt at home in a church.

In for the Kill

I switched off the computer. I would have to get really close to him to see anything at all, as he hid. Angelo Buono would have seen it all clearly but maybe not all at once. He got scared of Bianchi and started to tell his girlfriends to avoid him as he was 'nutty'. Had he been let into the furnace and found Bianchi's world all too much for his common-or-garden rapist mind to cope with?

Charlie and I ate a late dinner while we talked about his day. After I cleared away the plates, washing them in hot water by hand at the sink, I made our dessert, stirring the rice pudding in the pan and adding in cold home-made raspberry jam from the fridge. As I stirred, I wondered if a book on Bianchi might bring in some much-needed money. Financially, we were at rock bottom – we had no house, no money in the bank and no relatives to help out. Despair throbbed through me and I felt like crying.

I poured the steaming hot rice pudding into two crystal glass bowls and sat in the warmth with Charlie on the doorstep. We watched the evening sun slip behind the clouds as we ate and I began to relax. Charlie was watching ladybirds as they flew around our doorstep.

'Do they believe it, Mummy, that when we tell them to fly away home, they believe us, you know, that their houses are on fire?'

'Maybe . . . don't know.' I thought of Bianchi as I let the scarlet spotted insects crawl all over my bare feet.

'What's the matter, Mummy?'

'Nothing, I'm fine.' I was lying. I felt as if I was walking down a dark corridor that would lead to an escalator that would take me down into something horrible, yet hunger for something unseen wouldn't allow me to cease my descent.

I bathed my son, read to him and then put him to bed, and soon after showered and went to bed myself. Later on, in the middle of the night, the curtains were drawn and I had been brooding for hours. It almost felt like Bianchi was food and I was salivating. I told myself that it was work, but was it? I sat up in bed and pulled out my cream embossed writing paper from my bedside desk.

> Dear Mr Bianchi,
> I am a British journalist who has seen a programme
> about you. Like you, I was adopted, and, like you, I was
> abused by my adoptive parents. I would like to write a

Pure Demonic Evil

book about your childhood abuse. Maybe we can then both help children who have been abused. Please let me know if you can help me make something good out of something very bad.
    Sincerely,
    Christine J. Hart

I looked at the full moon that hung just outside the bedroom window. I was tired but pleased that I had got it out of my system. But I suddenly realised that I wouldn't get a response from this devil unless I put in some candy. What was it that made most men putty in the hands of a woman? I reached into a nearby drawer and pulled out a photo of myself. I had slightly mussed blonde hair, looked sexy, and my top was low cut and falling off my shoulders, revealing my full, knockout figure. It was a treasured snapshot. I looked like a beauty, but in an unthreatening way, like I was also the girl next door.

I put the photo in with the letter. I wanted him to want me to set up a link. I knew what I was doing. In a book by Shelia Isenberg, she quoted a cop called Frank Salerno, who had arrested Bianchi, as saying: 'Bianchi's ex-wife Shirlee was thin and had no teeth, and his long-term girlfriend Kelli Boyd was overweight, short and plain.'

I thought that the Hillside victims had been attractive girls and women, especially Karen Mandic, who also had brains. Did Ken fear female power?

Dee had used models to try to get close to Bianchi. It was a mistake. A model would have the effect on him like Karen Mandic and he might have felt threatened by them.

I licked a stamp and addressed the envelope to the Walla Walla Penitentiary in Washington State. Then I propped the letter up by the clock ready to post on the school run in the morning. I turned the lamp off and settled down under the duvet. It was hot. I tried to get to sleep but still couldn't. The curtains billowed open with the cool breeze. I got up and went to the bathroom. I blinked at my reflection in the mirror.

What are you doing? I asked myself. *Why? Why really? Forget evil – you'll never find out what it is – never!*

I sat on the edge of the bath that was still full of cooling water and stared at Charlie's boats and yellow ducks, then I looked back at my reflection in the mirror. I arranged Charlie's toys along the edge of the bath and on my way back to bed I knocked them over one by one until they floated in a line in the water.

My old need to hunt down and investigate evil was surfacing. I wanted to make an important discovery and write some kind of worthy book about the subject. I was going to put major effort into getting as close as I possibly could to Bianchi – I needed it to raise my self-esteem. I hoped it wasn't my old need for revenge on rapists like my adoptive father working in me and hidden from even myself. There was a victim in Bianchi and I could feel something dark and vengeful inside myself baying for rapist blood.

Twenty-five

The Man in Cell 3

This is the myth, as raindrops fall in muted rhythm
like sweat dancing, while we grope and embrace the
day away.

Kenneth Bianchi

It was a cold late September day by the time I received a reply
from the Hillside Strangler. It landed on the mat in a long
white envelope with an American stamp on it and some type
saying: 'This is a letter from an inmate incarcerated in a
Washington State Penitentiary.' On the left-hand corner it had:
'Ken Bianchi, prisoner number 266961, cell number 3, tier 5,
Rainier Wing, Washington State Penitentiary, Walla Walla, USA.'

The letter inside was on white paper and it was typed. Even the
signature was typed. *This man is hiding*, I thought before I read it.
Murderers in jail get lots of mail – serial killers had sackfuls of
mail. When they respond, they hide themselves, not even giving
their signatures away.

In the letter he suggested I contact a former LAPD cop called
Ted Ponticelli. He had apparently written an as yet unpublished
book called *Without Evidence* and had investigated Bianchi's case
for the book. He suggested that Ponticelli might be able to help
me and enclosed his email address.

Hmm, that's interesting, I thought. *He seems to be saying that he's
innocent.*

I dressed quickly, putting on my panama, a red silk dress and
black pumps. I left the house and walked to the village green,
where Richard Hugh Burnett lived in a Grade Two listed house

next to the old castle ruins. His large yellow-brick house reminded me of the one in Dickens' *Great Expectations*. The high walls of the front of the house hung with green ivy, it had leaded windows and a long walled front garden with a heavy wrought-iron gate.

Hugh came from a bygone age where all was Trevor Howard, cocktails on the camomile lawn and clipped vowels. Dickie, as he had once been known, had been in MI6 and based out in what used to be Ceylon. After MI6, he entered the Foreign Office but eventually ended up working for the BBC and produced a programme called *Face to Face*. This had been his own series, featuring interviews with Carl Jung, Martin Luther King, Cecil Beaton, Evelyn Waugh and Richard Nixon. He loved to talk about the people he had met and used to reminisce about the evenings he had spent in a cafe on Sunset Boulevard chatting with Marlon Brando.

He was a widower and had been my friend for the past 20 years. I liked to go round to his ivy-covered mansion on the green to talk about my work, as we were both writers. When I met him, he was sleepwalking through life and trapped in grief over the loss of his wife and also two of their three sons. I woke him up through our discussions of the projects we were working on, and Hugh loved it that my mind longed for adventure as much as his. When his third son, Max, passed away suddenly at only 40 years old, we grew even closer.

Hugh now answered his heavy white door in a royal-blue dressing gown and slippers and grinned at me. 'So!'

'Hi,' I grinned back and followed him into his shady drawing room and sat down on his chesterfield. He was a rabid intellectual and had a set of even white teeth he often bared at some terribly wicked joke or other and penetrating grey eyes that hypnotised me. Hugh was wolfish – he even had the head of a Canadian gray lupus hanging on his wall.

'I've got some interesting news,' I told him as he lounged behind his drawn curtains. 'I've got a letter from a murderer in America.'

'What?'

'I told you about the guy who had murdered 12 women. I got interested and talked to a friend who said he was a case of demonic possession.'

Hugh sat down, stared at me and smiled. I smiled back at him. He was older than me but there was a strong chemistry between us as we were both high dominance and saw the world as a mystery that we had to delve into. The theory of high dominance was one I'd read about in my many delvings into psychology. An American psychologist called Abraham Maslow believed that human beings could be divided into three categories – low dominance, medium dominance and high dominance – and they all mate within their groups. High-dominance humans need to self-actualise and are often leaders. I was high dominance and so was Hugh, so we got on.

'What made you do that, for God's sake?'

'He says he's not guilty. He says he was possessed by another spirit called Steve. It's interesting.'

'You mean because you're a bloody Catholic that you believe in possession by some kind of demonic power? Are you nuts?'

'All Catholics believe in demons, didn't you know that, Hugh? You've covered stories on Catholicism.'

He went to make us tea and came back with a tray laden with blue, gold-rimmed china from Mauritius and a plate of his favourite ginger biscuits. I poured the tea and watched him as he went back to his leather armchair. He was good looking in a refined, James Bond-style, British way; his hair was neatly cut and swept back off his face, his aquiline nose was strong and sat over his gentle mouth, his eyes were heavy and his sharp intellect beamed out of them, so that his age became unimportant. I found his voracious mind seductive and I knew he also enjoyed me. We played with our sexual chemistry like a ball of fire that we threw to each other but never held still.

'Exorcism is the biggest rubbish they've ever invented. They even believe that children are born evil with original sin. It's nonsense, Chris, you dizzy blonde.'

'Bugger off. I'm not going to sit here and bicker. I've just come to see if you think I'd get anywhere with him. I've my eye on doing a book.'

'All Catholics are crazy to believe that crap. Mind you, they are entitled to believe anything they like. Where do these demons live? Have you read the Bible?

'Not much.'

I nibbled on a ginger biscuit and watched him as he openly admired my black-stockinged legs.

'Try the story of Legion. Jesus goes to see a man nicknamed Legion and casts demons out of him. It actually says that Jesus talked to them and he asked them if they could go into a herd of pigs. Guess what happened next, Chris?' He got up to pour us both another cup of tea and then went back to his armchair.

'I don't know.' I sipped my tea, looked around his drawing room and felt bored.

'All the pigs jumped over the cliff and drowned. Now what happened to the demons? Did the demons drown? Have you ever heard of such a load of nonsense?'

'I do believe in possession. There have been so many stories – there's the Amityville story and many others. Bianchi might have been possessed; his story ticks all the boxes.'

Hugh wasn't listening. He read the letter, ignoring me. His long, green velvet curtains were drawn against the mid-afternoon sun and they billowed slightly. His shady drawing room was full of old books and artefacts from his TV programmes about South Africa and Jerusalem. He had DVDs of his interviews with Marlon Brando, Henry Kissinger and Carl Jung. I enjoyed the musty smell of books and his glass cases full of large butterflies and moths. I noticed that when he'd gone off to make tea, Hugh had also changed into a beige pair of summer slacks, a white cotton shirt, open at the neck, and worn brown felt slippers, one of which hung off his foot as he crossed his legs in his wingback armchair. I imagined us kissing, with me undoing his shirt and touching his chest.

He looked up at me with his sexy wolfish grin that showed his neat row of white teeth and my fantasy faded. I was a coward who couldn't take human intimacy, I knew that much. What a shame I couldn't be a woman, marry Hugh and come here to live. Charlie would call him 'Father' instead of 'Uncle Hugh'. Hugh was a very loving uncle to my son, ever enjoying Charlie's boundless energy, telling him stories about his time spying in MI6 or teaching him to draw cartoons, of which he had published eight books. We would often come over for Sunday dinner. I would make roast chicken and imagine that we were a family. I loved his fine house, particularly the small kitchen with the black china cock watching out of the window and the blue jugs in a row along the leaded windowpane. In the summer he and I sat in the front garden and had tea with strawberries and Rose's lime juice as we sunbathed and discussed Evelyn Waugh and their friendship after Waugh had appeared on *Face to Face*.

Hugh looked across the room at me and woke me from my thoughts. 'When you rang me last month to say you'd seen a

programme about the Hillside Strangler, Chris, I researched him
on the Internet. Bianchi never replies to letters, so you've done
well to get a response. What are you going to do? Reply?'

'No, I'm going to ignore him,' I said sarcastically.

Hugh pulled a wry face. 'What is it you want from him?'

I scratched my chin and looked at Hugh's wispy hair; it was so
clean. I felt a surge of affection for him that made me feel
uncomfortable.

'Dunno. It's this nagging voice in the back of my mind that
tells me I have to get to know him. I have no idea what it means
but I'm a writer, so my hunches and feelings are my only compass
and they tend to lead me to worthwhile writing projects.'

'Serial killer number two for Clarice.'

'I am hunting down supernatural evil.'

'No such thing, I've already checked it out before you. It made
me curious too, Chris. I did a good few programmes investigating
the supernatural. I find this thing about Bianchi interesting too
– keep me in on it, won't you?'

'OK, and, Hugh, if you don't mind I'll do my own research!'

He stood up, saying, 'Broads!' He went to the toilet, which was
out near the door, and started singing loudly in a mock American
twang: 'Cigarettes and whiskey and wild, wild women – they'll
drive you crazy – they'll drive you insane.'

I smiled as I heard him. He came back, pinching a ginger
biscuit off the tray on the table as he passed, and winked at me.

'Chris, come on, cheer up. I've got something for you. You
know I've been all over Rome, looking up the dirt about the
Roman Catholic Church. I went all around the Vatican. I went
to a house where the beams were out of shape and they believed
that the Devil had done it. I found some nuns living under a
huge mural of the Devil. And I found a photograph from
Palermo of nuns holding the Devil's signature – this shows you
how mad they all were. And that's just the beginning of the
rubbish that's hanging around Rome. There's even a bit of the
true Cross, not to mention a footprint of Christ that I filmed in
Jerusalem.' He left the room and then returned dragging a
battered green antique trunk.

'In Italy, St Catherine of Sienna's head is on an altar and she
believed her wedding ring was the foreskin of Jesus.'

'God, how gross.'

I eyed his trunk with trepidation. What was he going to pull out, a load of dried foreskins? I felt sick.

Hugh clicked it open. 'Do you want some of these photographs that I have collected for the programme I was making for the BBC on heaven and hell? Take your pick. I found them last night and thought, *Hmm, these will interest that blonde of mine.*'

I looked through the green trunk; it was full of beautiful photographs of paintings of angels and some of demons.

'May I send this angel painting to Bianchi?'

'Yes, send him an angel; he's probably a bit short on the heavenly hosts.'

I picked out some stunning photographs of the work of Michelangelo, Caravaggio and Rembrandt. I picked one of the Martyrs in the Coliseum lying on the floor in terror, surrounded by lions with blood around their mouths. Death for no reason except pleasure.

I put them all into a brown envelope I managed to find in Hugh's sideboard and addressed it to the Walla Walla Penitentiary with a note saying:

> *Dear Kenny,*
> *Thanks for the email for Ted but I talk to you or I talk to*
> *no one. I haven't got time to waste playing games. By the*
> *by, why not get your side of the story out with a memoir?*
> *I've just published mine and I could help you write yours.*
> *I'm sure my publisher would be interested. I'm enclosing*
> *some photos of paintings, you can have them if you like.*
> *You probably need some angels.*
>   *Best,*
>   *CJ*

Hugh was watching me thoughtfully. 'Do you talk to Jesus when you go to church, Chris?'

'Yes, of course I do. I love talking to Jesus.'

'Do you know he's not actually called Jesus?'

'No.' I felt exasperated with him and wanted to get away.

'And how do you envisage Jesus?'

'I see him as suffering on the Cross.'

'And you relate yourself to his suffering on the Cross?'

'Yes, I compare my own hard-done-by life and I look at him and I say, *You had it bad too, didn't you, pal?* and then I feel not so alone.'

'And you call that praying?'

'Yes.'

'Poor you, looking at the tortured figure on the Cross and feeling that you and he are alike. But you've got a right, Chris, to your dreams of a saviour who cares.'

'Everyone needs to know that somebody out there cares. I know Jesus loves me and Charlie. Nice things happen to us and that's when I know.'

'What about when bad things happen – is that him, too?'

After I had listened to Hugh, his friend Rick arrived with some groceries. I smiled at Rick and left to cross the green to go to the post office. I knew that I wanted to do something worthwhile with my life. I was starting to feel my inner self and know that it had good in it, not just bad as my mother had taught me. I wished others well and I hated hearing of anyone being hurt.

I posted the letter to Kenneth Bianchi and went to pick my son up from the school gate, dreading having to face the school-gate mothers. I had found it hard to mix with them from day one. It was all small talk at the gate and I had always found it hard to do small talk; it was a skill I just didn't have. But I said hello and tried to get in and out as quickly as possible.

The year before, Charlie had been bullied at school. It had been a little fight that had started between a close-knit group of boys and my son and his little friend. The situation had escalated and turned into a living nightmare for both Charlie and me, leading to him being ostracised at school and me being treated as an outcast by the mothers. On reflection, my loneliness during this time perhaps spurred me on to seek solace in my work, pushing me further down the road to Bianchi.

In an attempt to help Charlie deal with the situation, I had bought a water-filled blue plastic punch bag. I went crazy punching it, then turned and said, 'See, that's how you make sure no one bullies you. And that, sweetheart, is what I'd like to do to the mothers who deny their sons hit you and then leave you out of their parties.'

He sat and cried as he watched me. 'Mummy, I don't want to learn to punch and be mean. I don't want to be a spy like you were. You were mean; I'm not like that.'

I stood watching him with my boxing gloves on and out of breath. Charlie was everything I wasn't – gentle and free of resentment. But now I was teaching him all about my world – a hateful place where you had to learn to attack. I left the punch bag and instead we jogged around the park together, lifted weights and I told him about the vulnerable points of a face and body, teaching him the skills of defence I had learned in karate. I wanted him to be able to defend himself.

On days when Charlie was left out of their sons' parties, I used to cheer him up by having our own parties at home, with baked cakes and balloons, just the two of us. As I watched him laughing and fooling around, I knew that somehow they didn't quite reach him. My love for him was like a solid rock and he knew it, and I could see it had built in him such amazing strength. It would be hard to ever knock down this boy who would one day become a loving and compassionate man.

It was around this time that Nick Davies came into my life. Davies was a very good-looking, well-respected reporter who had written a brilliant book exposing dirt in the media called *Flat Earth*. He wrote for *The Guardian*, who were focusing on the story of phone hacking at the *News of the World*. In 2007, Glenn Mulcaire and Clive Goodman had been jailed after being convicted of intercepting phone messages. *The Guardian* had smelled blood and continued to investigate the issue. Nick was one of the journalists most actively pursuing the story and he had been given my name as someone who had worked for the investigations unit of the paper.

When he contacted me, he aroused my curiosity. It seemed as if the hacking scandal was about to blow up into a much bigger story and so I agreed to meet him at my old tennis club, for which my membership had lapsed but I could still get into for lunch. I had snuck into their pool for a swim and he was already sitting having coffee when I breezed up late with soaking wet hair.

He smiled at me in his charismatic way. Davies oozed a profound goodness from every pore. I wondered what type of woman would interest him sexually. He was a man who flew above evil, reporting on it. I got my wellies on and waded knee-deep in it.

'What exactly was it like to work in the newsroom for a man like Greg Miskiw back around that time?' he asked me. 'And how did all the hacking start? Where did it come from?'

It was early days and no one knew at that point that the hacking scandal would spread much further than the intrusion into the royal household. I didn't really feel I had any information that would help him, as I had left just as Mulcaire joined the paper. Nick wondered if I could use my contacts to get any more information for him and I told him that I would consider maybe helping him and let him know.

That night I went home and went to bed and I dreamed.

I was walking along a country lane and it began to get smaller and smaller. As I walked, I saw little tiny rabbits lying in the streets. At first I thought that they were cute. But then, as I moved on, they got under my feet and I started to walk on them. I looked round and others were stroking them or feeding them. I began to feel sick at the sight of them – there were so many. I could smell bunny fur. It seemed like rabbit country. As I walked on, the rabbits got bigger and bigger. I began to feel real paranoia. I knew that if one feels fear in dreams it's best to turn and ask whatever is scaring you what it wants. I turned and spoke to the giant army of rabbits.

'Who are you?'

All the rabbits turned in unison – millions upon millions of rabbit faces all turned to face me at once and answered with a roar 'MURDOCH'S EMPIRE'.

Then they all attacked me, jumping on me – millions of them until I was buried alive beneath their rabbit fur. I woke up terrified, with my heart bashing against my chest. I went to splash my face with cold water and could practically taste their fur and feel them as if they were squashing me. What a terrifying bunny nightmare.

I rang Davies the next morning and told him that I was really sorry but I couldn't help him at all.

In July 2011, a reporter called Sean Hoare, a young guy who was a good laugh and with whom I had worked on many stories, was found dead in his apartment. Sean had spoken to the *New York Times* about phone hacking at the *News of the World* and at the time of his death had also been talking to Nick Davies and exposing a few things that I felt it was nuts to be talking about. Sean had well-reported problems with drink and drugs, and his health had suffered badly as a result. His death wasn't treated as suspicious and I couldn't help but wonder about the stress he must have been under. After reading *The Independent*'s headline – HACKING ENQUIRY TAKES A SINISTER TURN WITH THE DEATH OF WHISTLEBLOWER SEAN HOARE – I was glad that I had decided to stay out of the whole affair.

Twenty-six
The Goddess of Truth

Since I gave birth to this part of you, I'm going to name her. Let her be named Minerva, Goddess of Truth.

Kenneth Bianchi

The American prisoner's long, handwritten letters came weekly throughout the icy winter of 2009.

I sent Bianchi my memoir that had been published a year earlier. I knew my experiences were very similar to his own but he didn't comment on this, merely remarking that he admired my bravery in both telling my story and in helping others by writing it. He said it would have been worthwhile if it stopped just one parent from hurting a child.

'Yes,' I replied. 'Most of the bravery is in facing your childhood abuse and not acting it out on innocent victims.'

He ignored my hint and wrote back with more details of prison life. He was apparently kept in his cell for the majority of the time and the conditions were so bad that the water in his toilet bowl had frozen during the winter. He told me that he had studied law and joined the American Bar in 1989. He now worked in the law library and gave free legal advice to the other inmates and prison guards. He also mentioned his son Ryan, whom he hadn't seen since his conviction in 1979. Ryan had been two years old when his father was convicted but was now a grown man. Bianchi seemed sad that his son was a stranger to him, saying that not a day passed during which he didn't think of him.

In November, when snow lay thick on the ground both in my

quaint English village and in the north-west American prison, Bianchi sent me a copy of a yellowing photo of the mother of his child with his son. The plump blonde called Kelli in the old photo resembled me in her colouring, and oddly his son looked like my Charlie. I wondered whether Ryan had been taught to hate his father.

In my letters, I told Bianchi about my financial worries and about the anxiety I felt about being a single mother. I told him that I felt ashamed about some of the journalism I had been involved in and he wrote back saying that I should try to work for the better newspapers in order to make a difference to the lives of others.

He's a right creep, I thought. *What an awesome difference he made to the lives of others when he was free.*

I told him, 'With respect, yes, the tabloids can look crummy, but they pay the rent. I haven't time to pick and choose.'

I was trying to get close to him to find out about Steve but his letters were full of hypocrisy and self-pity. They were, however, making me have dreams and I wrote to Bianchi, describing them. He wasn't impressed at first and told me to stop, but when I continued he told me that he felt 'honored' that I would share such intimate information with him.

I was enjoying myself, playing mind games with Bianchi. I was no longer a writer, grovelling around news editors; I was an intrepid reporter digging into the mind of a serial killer and checking out what real evil actually was. Bianchi was the real deal. At last I could make a study of supernatural evil and find out what it actually was.

A few weeks later he wrote again in another white airmail letter with the prison crest in the corner that I would feel better if I knew that I was bringing my son up with a worthy set of morals.

Morals! I thought. *Coming from a murderer, this is incredible.*

Were these letters coming from Steve, I wondered (the Steve part of him). Or were they from the innocent-looking family man that I had seen on the TV? Either way, what right did he have to lecture me on my life?

I was halfway through a book about him and the details that I had discovered in it were nauseating. But I was fascinated by Steve and I asked Bianchi to tell me more about him.

Bianchi now started to write about the crimes and about the confession he had made in which he explained that he was taken over by 'Steve'. Only now he told a different tale. He wrote that

The Goddess of Truth

Steve was the demonic imaginary friend who had consoled him in his childhood, a figment of his imagination that had grown more and more full of evil as he grew older. Now he said he had not killed at all; Steve was the reason he had falsely confessed. He had confessed after reading the police files that had been given to him to study. He now claimed that in the television interview I had seen he had been under hypnosis and was merely playing a role, acting out the part of a psychopath who had committed murder. Bianchi now asked me to believe that he thought the real killer was still out there and even said that the thought of this scared him.

Was there a serial killer still on the loose, lying dormant as Bianchi was claiming? This correspondence was becoming intriguing.

His next letter was a twenty-page diatribe in which he accused me of not listening to anything that he was telling me and also picked apart all the personal information I had revealed to him in my letters.

I rang Sienna in tears. 'That bastard Bianchi has picked me apart so badly that I hardly know who I am. Clearly he's been listening to my every word and now he's catalogued it and flung it all back at me in one go. I feel as if my head's spinning. What the hell has he done to me?' I started to cry.

'He's an armchair shrink is all. Come on, calm down. Which way do you feel spun?'

'Er – anticlockwise. What use is that?'

'Imagine yourself spinning back the other way. It's a trick for the mind I read about somewhere.'

I did as she recommended and amazingly I felt better.

That night as I slept I saw Bianchi in his cell. I felt fear as he approached me. I was terrified. He said, 'What are you afraid of?'

He came towards me and I said, 'Keep back – don't touch. I don't let humans near me. They're dangerous.'

He seemed upset to see me so scared. I explained. 'I'm not just afraid of you, I'm afraid of everything human. I don't normally come out.'

'You mean you're like a ghost?'

'Yes, I guess. I don't actually live. I never come out. I just stay back, watching. My child side is all that lives.'

I looked down again and saw myself in a body. 'Oh, you've brought me back to life,' I said. 'How did you do that?'

In for the Kill

I woke up and made notes about this new me who had awakened in the dream. As I believed she had emerged as a result of the shock I'd received from Bianchi's last letter, I wrote to tell him about it.

He seemed pleased by this development and suggested that I think of the new persona as 'Minerva, the Goddess of Truth'.

I made a note: 'He thinks he's Carl Jung.'

But that night I dreamed of Minerva again. She was wise, clever and caring but had been repressed. I felt that she held the key to my heart, my feelings and my sexuality. She was my femininity.

I woke up in a cold sweat. Bianchi had birthed Minerva somehow by ripping me apart with words. I began to develop a need for his insights. He was playing the role of psychiatrist to me, when I had intended to do this for him.

Bianchi also had needs of his own he wanted me to fulfil. He had apparently been working on an autobiography. He said he had written the real truth about his life but needed a writer to work on it and asked if I would act as his ghost. He suggested that in this way I would get to know the real man behind all the headlines.

That was an easy request to answer. Bianchi was so notorious it sounded like a licence to print money, and I had to think about supporting Charlie. I would be the Hillside Strangler's ghost. I felt excited by the prospect. As I fanned my face with his letter, I could detect not only the odour of the American Penitentiary but also the hands of the lonely man who had written the letter.

Twenty-seven
Ghostwriter

He who doesn't believe in the devil does not believe
in the Gospels.

Vatican Archives, Address of the Holy Father

I contacted my therapist Glyn Powell to tell him what I was
doing. I'd been in touch with Glyn since living in Los Angeles.
He was a 50-year-old musician who worked as an analyst. I loved
to be in analysis and believed everyone could benefit from it.

'This is amazing, isn't it, Glyn, me working as a ghost for Bianchi?'

'It's not that amazing. You were a renowned crime reporter and
you're already a published writer. You've been busy being a good
mother, now it's time to get back in the driving seat. He's onto a
good thing and he knows it.'

'I'm a little out of my league with him. If I say anything out of
place he tells me all my shortcomings and he doesn't hold back.
Last time he did that I didn't know who I was for a week.'

'Yes, you did.'

'He was brutal. I felt kind of weird and out of sorts.'

'I think our Ken isn't all roses around the door.'

'I know that, Glyn. He's not got that hate thing going on,
though, that other serial killers have.'

'Come on, what do you expect? He's America's worst serial
killer, so he'll be the best at pretending that he's a decent chap. I
couldn't think of a better person to ghost him, Chris. You've
worked your way up to this. Being the ghostwriter of an infamous
American serial killer is a wonderful chance.'

'I'm going to be the new Truman Capote.'

In for the Kill

I waited for him to contradict me but he didn't. So I went on in a boastful way. 'Only thing is, he says he didn't kill anyone, so the autobiography he writes will be delusional.'

'Don't get caught up in his web of lies.'

'He hasn't got a web of lies, he's got his own world and it's impossible to get into it. But it will just give me more time to examine his psychosis and really find out what makes him tick.'

'Use your charm.'

I chewed on my fingernail. 'Oh Glyn, I feel to know him I will have to let myself fall down the rabbit hole, sip from the bottle labelled "Drink Me", get smaller and smaller and then enter into his world. You need special glasses to see it and make sense of it but he won't let me in.'

'Yes, you'd need to be a psychiatrist. Careful, Chris. Evil is an area of the mind we know little about.'

'Glyn, I'm glad I'm going to be his ghost.' I squinted in the evening sun and reached for my panama and Ray-Bans.

'I'm so pleased for you.'

'I'm worried that I'll screw it up.'

'You'll write a bestseller and then you can buy a solid family home for you and Charlie.'

'That's what I want.' I felt pleased; success was in the air. I took off my Ray-Bans and frowned. 'Why hasn't he asked a Yank, though, to ghostwrite for him? Why me? Why an English writer?'

'Yes, that is odd. Be careful of him, Chris. Remember he's said to be a real ladies' man with charisma and also to still have his spellbinding good looks.'

But I wasn't listening to Glyn's warnings. The American book-buying market was so much bigger than ours and I was consumed with thoughts that I might be able to earn enough for a down payment on a house of our own. I wasn't heeding the warnings that I should be wary of Bianchi.

'He's just sent me a yellowing old manuscript that he kept in his cell. Here, listen to this. Judy Miller, one of his first victims. He's written about her murder as if she was killed by another man. He's even described the man and how he must have done it – walking up behind her and tapping her on the shoulder, describing her turning. Is he secretly gloating over Miller turning to see her killer's face and it was his face, do you think?'

'Don't know!'

I read out sections of the manuscript to Glyn but then had to go as I realised Charlie would be home at any moment. As I hung up, as if on cue, the doorbell rang and I ran to greet Charlie. How lucky was I – a healthy, handsome, clever son I adored and a fascinating career. No man, though, or a house or money in the bank. *Oh well*, I thought to myself, *I can't have everything. Who does?*

Just before midnight I emailed the celebrated American forensic psychologist J. Reid Meloy to ask his advice for dealing with Kenneth Bianchi. Meloy was a consultant on *CSI* and he had been described as a 'rock star' in his field. I had befriended him when I came across one of his books and we had emailed back and forth. Meloy had written about the infamous Bianchi in his respected work *The Psychopathic Mind*. He was generous with his knowledge and I had learned a hell of a lot from him. I now told him that I felt he was incorrect in his diagnosis of Bianchi as a psychopath, as it seemed more likely to me that he was a multiple.

Meloy wasn't convinced and told me that he wasn't impressed by journalists acting as armchair psychiatrists. He added, as an attachment, a paper he had written about psychiatrists who had worked with serial killers and fallen under their spell. Apparently it was something to do with the serial killers' omnipotence. Meloy said that nothing is as seductive as life and death.

'Read that,' he said, adding that he felt I might have a 'transference' with Bianchi. Apparently I was showing in the way that I talked about Bianchi that I cared about him. How had this happened? He warned me to be careful, saying that although I might find it amusing to try to get close to Bianchi to extract all his secrets, there was a chance that he would draw me in by simulating a bond between us, then he would start devaluing me and I would end up being emotionally battered by him. He ended by saying: 'That's why work like you're attempting is best left to doctors.'

Meloy was quoted extensively in textbooks on psychopaths and homicide. He was an internationally renowned expert, so I couldn't ignore his opinion. But there was no way I was going to stop my process of opening up to Bianchi so that he would open up to me in return.

I looked through the crime-scene photos again. Two dead teenage girls had been thrown in the back of a small car. Other girls had been laid out on grassland, naked, one face down, another lying naked on her back with her legs spreadeagled.

Another picture was a close-up of the neck of one of the victims, showing a dark red mark where she'd been strangled. There was a bite mark on her body. Another girl's palm had been seared by electric wires that had been taped on them in the position of stigmata. It was really sick stuff.

I had tracked down an American cop called Frank Salerno who had arrested and interrogated Bianchi. He was now working as a private eye in LA. Salerno had replied to one of my emails and I'd also spoken to him on the phone. He had told me that Bianchi had been planning to change his modus operandi. Whereas up to the point of his arrest he had strangled all the victims, he had decided that he would take any further victims up into the Santa Monica mountains and shoot them in the head, then leave them there for the public to find the bones. This had never come out about Hillside before.

'Execution?' I chewed my lip. 'What was he like when he said that – facial expression and tone of voice?'

'Matter-of-fact – glib.'

I thought about Bianchi's mother, Frances, and how when interviewed by the police she told them that Bianchi had four distinct personalities. She said she knew three of them well but the fourth had always been a mystery to her. Frances felt that the fourth was the killer. I asked Salerno whether he had seen any evidence of Bianchi's other personalities.

Salerno was clear that he didn't buy into the multiple personality disorder (MPD) theory. As far as he was concerned, Bianchi was a psychopath who had feigned MPD in order to plead insanity. He believed that Bianchi was as clever as they come. Serial killers were chameleons who only showed what they wanted you to see – nothing else.

I sat by the fire and read some of the notes from the trial by lamplight. At 3 a.m., an email came in and the beep of its arrival made me jump. At this hour, it had to be from America. I opened it. It was from Frank Salerno – one line, written in red capitals, saying: 'KEN BIANCHI IS A COLD-BLOODED KILLER.' I went to bed and as I lay in the dark I felt afraid – as if I had bitten off more than I could chew.

I woke with a start the next morning and found a letter from America on the doormat with Kenneth Bianchi's name and prisoner number across the top of it. He'd apparently had a change of heart about the idea of me being his ghostwriter, saying he wasn't sure whether or not he trusted me. He'd worked with other writers before who hadn't gone along with his claims of innocence; he needed to be convinced that I believed him.

I put down the letter and decided that he was trying to manipulate me. A cool draught blew into the drawing room and I went into the kitchen to make scrambled eggs for breakfast. Charlie was playing soldiers on the floor and the television was on. I sat eating my breakfast and enjoying the wintry sunshine that was streaming in the French windows as I thought about what I was trying to achieve with Bianchi.

Lately, in an attempt to get him to open up, I had been confiding to Bianchi what I did each day, down to my cupcake making, what I ate and how I cooked. I sat at my computer, night after night after Charlie went to bed, and opened myself up. It was incredibly enjoyable. I had been alone for seven years and had gotten so used to it that I wasn't aware how isolated I was as a single parent. I had forgotten the sheer joy of showing oneself to someone who didn't reject you.

In his letters Bianchi came across and being kind and charming. He sounded so normal – there was no hate, no dark messages. He seemed like Mr Nice Guy! But in reality he was one of the most brutal serial killers in American history and I was being naive in letting my guard down.

Charlie had pulled out paints and paper and was busy painting a house with a sun over the top of it on the table. He was covered in paint like a Native American and he was having fun. I brought through the CD player and, inspired by the music, I began to use Charlie's paints to sketch what my mind was telling me about Bianchi.

I dipped into cerulean blue with a thick-tip brush and began to wash it over the top of the page to represent the sky.

Then I stopped. *No, that's not right*, I thought to myself. *If I'm painting Bianchi's childhood days, then it had to have been a grey sky. Yes, it was grey and terrifying, wasn't it?* I dipped my brush into pewter grey and mixed it with titian red.

And it was raining, wasn't it? Yes, it was raining all over your sky. I splurged dark wet splodges all over the page. In the corner, I painted large dogs, vicious ones, barking at the budding young serial killer in a school playground, growling and snarling.

I closed my eyes.

Who were your dogs?

I could see them in my mind's eye. Bullies. School bullies. Bigger boys jeering at him. I felt for a moment as if I were a small boy filled with utter dread of bullying.

The Pink Floyd song 'Pigs' was blaring out from the CD player. I drew a large pig's face. Two pigs: one who gave him up; one who abused him. *Like me.*

No one bothered to look and see who you really were, did they? Like me.

I covered the whole painting in black pencil.

He had no idea who he was. It was too dark to see, too much black rain. Like me.

I found myself painting another boy at the edge of the playground, watching. Then I put down the paints and stared at what I'd done.

Charlie came round the table. 'Mine's much better than yours, Mummy. Mine's happy; yours is ugly. And that boy in the corner looks mean.'

'Why?'

'Dunno. He just looks like he means the other one harm.'

Later that night, after I had put Charlie to bed, I poured myself a vodka and orange. My painting stared up at me from the kitchen table. I homed in on the boy at the edge of the picture as I slowly sipped my drink. I got up, opened the back door and walked out into the back garden to breathe the fresh air. As I stood in the pitch-black silence, I suddenly knew that Steve was real. I also knew that Steve wasn't human. And if he wasn't human, then what was he? I felt as if I was getting closer and closer to something I had wanted to meet all of my life – 100 per cent undiluted *evil.*

Twenty-eight
Mr Good Guy

A murderer from the beginning . . . a liar and the
father of lies. Satan is the deceiver of the whole
world. We know that we are of God and the whole
world is in the power of the evil one.

John 8:44

Bianchi's attention was a magic potion that had no label on it.
I began to take larger and larger swigs; there seemed no harm
in it. Good-looking Ken was clever. Ken was kind and concerned,
and Ken the good guy was innocent. I began to realise that I was
growing dependent on this unknown man who shivered under
his blanket. *Am I going mad?* I asked myself. Most of my feelings
of need for Bianchi's attention were because I was lonely. I was in
complete isolation in the village after the bullying fiasco.

Charlie came home saying that the boys had had yet another
party and he was left out of it. The hurt on his face made me want
to kill the other mothers. Instead, I ground my teeth. To me the
village was a mix between *The Village of the Damned* and *The
Stepford Wives*. I felt like Stephen King's Carrie in my longing for
revenge on them. I wish I had never heard of the place. Being a
single parent was the hardest thing, as all the problems were
there for you alone; there was no one to lean on. Bianchi was
offering me himself to lean on and doing it in such a way I was
forgetting who he was and accepting his version of himself as the
innocent victim.

I wanted to ring someone and ask them what to do, but there
was no one. I felt at that moment that life was becoming a real

struggle. My close friends were few. I began to feel very bad about it. Yet I hadn't even been aware of it until Bianchi. I had begun to confide things in letters to him that I would under normal circumstances have shared with a friend, such as my car getting impounded by the police for being a day late for paying my insurance and Charlie and me having to walk back from London in the cold night's rain.

Something about him felt genuine. Was I being taken in by his sweet talk? He told me that he was lonely and asked if I felt the same way. Something about my letters was making him feel alive. He drip-fed little details about his life – about the tiny cell with a concrete shelf on which he slept on a thin blue plastic mattress with just a single grey blanket under which he tried to keep warm. I knew that he had a radio that he played for company and that he was listening to a play with Jenny Agutter the last time he wrote.

After reading his latest letter again I picked up my mobile phone. I knew Sienna didn't welcome a call from me unless she rang me first but I felt utterly alone. I rang her number, hoping that she would chat.

'Larry's here,' she said in a voice that told me my call wasn't welcome.

'I'm sorry. I just feel so alone.'

'Can't. My husband's here.'

'Oh, I'm so sorry.' I hung up and felt consumed by pain. I poured myself another glass of vodka and poured in some lemon concentrate. There was nowhere to go with my hurt and my loneliness, and it was overwhelming me. I needed love and kindness, and it was like a giant pregnant ball of need that I had been carrying around for so many years while bringing up Charlie all alone. I felt like I had ruined things for my son and that I was a useless mother.

From day to day I soldiered on without the comfort and joy of love and sexuality in my life. I was in a posh little village where there were no single parents; it was all well-to-do, happily married couples with huge Edwardian villas, four-by-fours and tweeds by Boden. My single status was rubbed in daily when I did the school run and witnessed most being accompanied by their husbands, holding hands, before the booted-and-suited hubby went off to London. I didn't find the men in the village or London men very appealing – they were too refined. But I was getting older and not having sex made me feel I was missing out; it was like being pressed up against the cake shop window imagining how it would feel to sink my teeth into the large slice of sweet white cake, the warm red jam at the centre and the sharp tang of the fruit, the ice-cold sugary fresh cream, curling around my tongue, then the lick of my greedy lips and the taste of icing sugar, soft and talcum-powdery, providing that sweet swirling bliss. The idea of a very male man entranced me but it was like looking for an extinct life form. I knew that I would feel differently if I had some sexual contact. It would take away some of the boredom about the humdrum nature of my existence and make me feel like a woman again.

I went over to the computer. It felt nuts to pour it all out to a caged American that I was supposedly investigating. But as I typed another letter I knew that he would listen carefully, even though he was 6,000 miles away from my lonely, cold English village.

By the time I had finished offloading this pain to Ken Bianchi in his isolated cell, I had stopped feeling down. I somehow felt better after offloading all my shit, and his response, when it came, brought the comfort I had been so desperately seeking. He had stopped attacking and criticising me, and it was like he had become a magic mirror that reflected back only good things and ignored all my faults. After the low feelings brought on by his attack on my character I now suddenly felt a high from the unconditional positive regard.

According to the eloquent Bianchi, I was the world's most unique and beautiful woman, and my superior brains would get me out of this hole I was in. He told me to stop beating myself up. He thought I seemed very soft and very funny. I should believe in myself and believe that my luck was about to change. He reminded me that I was a stunning blonde who had already been very successful in my career as an investigative journalist and a published author, so there was no reason to believe this wouldn't happen again. My financial worries were just a blip and in no way my fault. I should focus on all the good things in my life – I had a roof over my head and I sounded like I was an amazing mother. He reminded me again to count all my blessings and think about God. He even included some poetry he'd written that he said he hoped I would enjoy. I folded the letter and felt an immediate lift.

An idea came to me. I would play a role to Bianchi of a woman who needed him and was lonely and desperate for attention, and then I would get inside his head and find out all his secrets. I read his letter over again and sat and answered it. I wrote about how I was grateful for his words and how in my lonely life he was an oasis, the only thing I had to look forward to. As I wrote, flooded with journalistic ambition, I leaned, stumbled and then I fell down the rabbit hole into a land warmer than any other I had ever found. It was like nothing I had ever known before. I looked around me and everything was warm and pink – it was nice. A large metal gate suddenly clanged shut and as I heard it lock behind me I found myself emotionally dependent on the mysterious American prisoner who had wound his way inside my mind.

Twenty-nine

Exorcism

Love is that thing, smiling, with claws and feathers. My eyes opened to the chill of longing, my empty palms feel wet, my veins surge for that first rush of desire.

Kenneth Bianchi

Bees hummed over the lake and a gaggle of ducklings swam up to us looking for bread. I relaxed and enjoyed our picnic in the park after school. The air was full of deer musk and wood chippings.

'Don't wipe the jam on your school shirt, sweetheart. I was going to make it last another day.'

'Sorry, Mummy.'

We stayed until the breeze grew fiercer, like wind off a cold sea, and the sun began to go down. Some nearby deer began to look as if they were going to charge at us. My hair blew into the butter and stuck in the apricot jam plastered onto sourdough bread. Charlie ran around feeding our madeleines to the black crows as our hair tangled in the wind. I watched my son, entranced by his youth and beauty. One day he would be gone and I would be sitting here alone but today I could feel the warmth of life in the presence of Charlie and for the very first time I knew that the beauty of life was in relationships.

We drove back to Dragonfly Villas in the twilight and I went into the sunroom to get some milk for a cup of tea. There were flying ants all long the top of the plastic roof. I got out an aerosol and sprayed them, feeling dirty that they had invaded our home. They fell off the roof onto the floor one by one.

In for the Kill

I went upstairs to have bath to feel cleaner but when I went into the bedroom I saw that there were little brown creatures moving around on my best rug that lay beside my bed. I quickly rolled it up and heaved it out of the window. It lay in the back garden and I enlisted Charlie's help to roll it up and put it out for the bin men. Back in my bedroom I realised that there were more dark speckles and tiny moths where my Persian rug had lain. The carpet was covered with hundreds of tiny moths crawling on top of each other. I shrank back in horror and ran to get the vacuum cleaner. I cried as I cleaned off the horrible creatures, cursing this house that seemed to be teeming with insects.

I came down from my bath. Charlie was doing his homework at the dining-room table. I pulled up my email and found I had a message from an American psychiatrist I had tracked down called Dr Ralph Allison. Allison had interviewed Bianchi at the time of his sentencing and given him the CPI, which is the California Personality Inventory. I was intrigued and wanted to talk to the US doctor in person. We talked over email and I asked him some questions.

'Is it the same invisible friend haunting him now as was there in his childhood?'

He replied: 'I haven't seen him since his conviction for murder in Bellingham, but I doubt if he has had any treatment which might help him get rid of Steve or Billy. They can stay around for a long time, until he wants to get rid of them.'

I asked Dr Allison: 'Was Steve his protector?'

He replied: 'No, Steve was not a protector. He was something Ken created from emotional imagination to defile and kill females.'

I asked him: 'So, is Steve is a totally separate person from Ken? What is he? A person?'

He replied: 'Steve is what I eventually came to call an Internalized Imaginary Companion, or IIC. He was made by Ken's personality as a way to get back at his mother when she was yelling at him at home, during his youth. The story he gave me was that, at age nine, he was hiding under his bed while his mother was screaming her insults because his father kept losing his pay at the local racetrack. It was then he first imagined "Steve" into being, and he became Ken's hitman in expressing his hatred of women who were like his mother.'

'Was Steve a real creature?'

Exorcism

He replied: 'Steve was as real as is any imaginary companion. But he was fashioned to meet Ken's juvenile need, in this case to be able to survive living with his very difficult mother.'

'What exactly is an IIC and is this your own theory? Why did you first believe that Ken B. was a multiple? When did you change your mind? What is the difference between an IIC and a multiple?'

He replied: 'An IIC is what has been called a "Thoughtform" in parapsychological literature, or an imaginary playmate or companion in pediatric psychology. However, the pediatric doctors assumed that all imaginary companions exist outside the bodies of the children who created them. That is false, as the child can place it anywhere he wants it to be, outside sitting in a chair, inside a doll, or inside his body taking over his body to do its deeds. It is designed by the child to take care of the child's emotional needs, whether that be to combat loneliness or to avenge some insult to the child by a hostile adult. It is made voluntarily by the child with a vivid imagination and can therefore be destroyed by that same child as an adult.

'Yes, IIC is a term I invented to describe these "other selves" which were not alter-personalities. Initially I called them IMPs, for Internal Malignant Personalities, which seemed to be a good acronym, as an IMP is a playful spirit. But I realized that only some were malignant, and others were benign, so I changed the label to something that was morally neutral, Internalized Imaginary Companion or IIC.

'I thought Ken was a multiple when I first saw him, since he clearly showed at least Steve as an "other self." At that time, I did not have enough experience with "other selves who kill" to know the differences they had from my male MPD patients, who were not killers. No one did at the time, not even the top experts in the field.

'Several years later when I testified in the preliminary hearing in Los Angeles for Angelo Buono, Ken's partner in crime, I realized that Ken did not meet my latest criteria for MPD. In my testimony, I listed over 20 items which disqualified Ken from being a "multiple", but I still didn't have a label for Steve and Billy, whom I had met when they took over Ken's body. But alter-personalities, which exist in patients with Multiple Personality Disorder or Dissociative Identity Disorder, are created by the essence of the patient, not by the personality. Alter-personalities are created by the essence to save the life of the patient, when he

217

or she is threatened with death, usually by a parent. Ken was never in danger of losing his life from his mother, but he got mighty angry at her because of her need to control his every action. Alter-personalities are not likely to kill anyone, as that is not a life-saving method of behavior. But IIC can be created, by the personality, with only murderous hatred-energy and no means of control. They have no conscience or sense of social appropriateness.

'To clarify, when I write "essence", I mean the spirit or soul of the human. In dealing with multiples in my office, I learned that the essence and personality are bonded together from birth on. They can be separated in hypnosis and by life-threatening trauma before the age of six. The personality is the only part endowed with human emotions, while the essence is intellectual and nonemotional. The essence is the wise "still small voice within" which we should listen to. The personality is driven by emotions and various neurochemicals and can be very foolish. Under hypnosis, I believe that I met Ken's essence, which called itself "Ken's Friend." Unfortunately it did not have much influence over Ken's social behavior.'

I next asked him: 'Can you explain who Martin Orne was and why he was against you and Doctor Watkins and your opinion of him and why he said what he did? Were you and Doctor Watkins in agreement?'

He replied: 'Dr Martin Orne was a professor of psychiatry and psychology at the University of Pennsylvania, one so high up in the field that he testified before the Supreme Court regarding use of hypnosis in criminal cases. He was well known to the prosecutor to be a skeptic of MPD, so he was hired to disprove the diagnosis of MPD initially offered by Dr Watkins, from the University of Montana. We were aware that Dr Orne was not likely to diagnose anyone with MPD, so we were not surprised when he maintained that Ken was just a liar. In Buono's preliminary hearing, he also stated that Ken had never been hypnotized by any of us, something I greatly dispute.

'Dr Watkins was convinced Ken was a multiple and apparently never changed his mind, in spite of new facts. I had given police lots of leads during my interviews with Ken, which they followed up on between Ken's trial and Buono's trial. They never found any boyhood friends who had ever witnessed evidence of personality changes, for example. I was caught in the middle of a "battle of the experts", with Dr Orne on one side saying Ken was only a liar, and Dr Watkins saying Ken was a bona fide multiple. I knew he wasn't a multiple, but I didn't then know just what he was.'

'Why did Ken pick the name Steve Walker, and didn't this prove that the IIC was a fraud? Why does Ken now say that Steve was an aberration brought on by the hypnosis and he is an innocent man? What can be done to cure Bianchi?'

He replied: 'I don't know why the name Steve Walker was picked. Often the name is chosen because someone nearby had the name, or the name represents something to the patient. What name he picked doesn't prove anything. In my patients, alter-personalities sometimes came with a personal name, sometimes not. If not, I might ask them to pick a name so I had something to call them.

'Ken is not an innocent man, but his personality could well seriously object to believing he is responsible for killing those women, and in the way he did it. His shame could make him suppress or repress the memories, as happened to many of the wife-killers I met working in a state prison. In the best of therapy situations, it would take them several decades to accept the fact that they killed their wives, and they should stop blaming the unknown burglar they had always blamed for her death. It is possible that the terrible traits of Steve Walker were in Ken since boyhood, but not crystalized into something so specific it appeared as another self, until we examiners got to him. Then our curiosity and use of hypnosis forced him to bring all the evil elements inside him together so he could "explain" to us who killed these girls and why. I didn't think of this option at the time of my examinations, but it is possible our forcing him to look into himself so much did bring about the final result we called Steve. But his behavior showed that the elements of Steve were there well before we met him.

'If by "cure Bianchi" we mean "get rid of Steve Walker", there is nothing we outsiders can do. But I have seen enough such patients who have had vigorous IICs who got them into such trouble that they were eventually more trouble than they were worth. At that point, the patient wanted to get rid of them, and could do so, by an act of will. Sometimes, it was done in their own minds by themselves. Sometimes it took a special ritual, which meant expulsion of evil to them. But they had to get rid of the hatred in themselves first, and that can be hard to do. It might mean forgiving those you hate so much you want to destroy them, and that can be hard to do.

'However, he is in prison. In one other similar case of a killer I evaluated, he was sent to Death Row, where I interviewed him two years later. At that time, his killer IIC was still intact, dealing drugs to his Death Row comrades. He got along well with the other inmates that way. At the same time, his ordinary personality was on excellent terms with the guards. He had another IIC who was conferring with his attorney on his appeal. So all three were needed to take care of his various needs in prison. Fortunately, his appeal was successful, and he eventually was removed from Death Row when he got a life sentence instead. So I have to wonder if Steve isn't providing some benefit for Ken while "they" are still in prison. After all, someone has to live by the "inmate code of conduct" to survive there.'

'Why did Bianchi plead guilty and then change his plea to insanity?'

He replied: 'That isn't the way I remember it. Nobody initially pleads guilty to multiple counts of first-degree murder. When Dr Watkins found Steve and told his attorney Ken had MPD, this laid the grounds for an insanity defense. That is why I and the other psychiatrists were hired. But when Dr Orne's report came in, the defense attorney realized that he could not persuade a jury that way if even one psychiatrist said he did not have MPD. So then they started plea bargaining to avoid a death sentence. That brought him to L.A. to testify against Buono, but his testimony was so erratic it didn't earn him prison time in California as he had hoped for. He was then sent back to Walla Walla, Washington, to serve his two life sentences there.'

'Can you explain why Bonnie Waldrop, a friend of his girlfriend, reported that she knew he wasn't Ken? In an interview she said that one night before the last of the murders she had seen Ken but had been left feeling very confused by the encounter: "When Ken got here . . . and, you know, when I talked to him before – it was just really weird. Um, I was frightened when he came through and I didn't want him around me – I always liked him and he and I, well, we've talked, we have always had a good relationship – to me that wasn't Ken, I didn't understand it."'

He replied: 'I know nothing about Bonnie Waldrop and she played no part in my report, as best as I can recall.'

Exorcism

I told him I found it interesting that Rorschach tests were carried out on Bianchi which confirmed he was different people. He also underwent handwriting tests. On each he was asked to sign and put the name of his parents underneath. Ken wrote his parents in by name. Steve wrote underneath his name 'I HAVE NO PARENTS'. 'If he had no parents then what was he? Where had he come from and why attack the world he had emerged into with savage murders?'

He replied: 'Steve was created in the emotional imagination of Ken Bianchi. He was designed to deny Ken's parenthood, since mother was seen as evil and father as distant and unprotective. We have people all over the world destroying each other, so what is the surprise of one man doing this to women he sees as worthy of nothing but raping and killing? The human imagination is the most powerful force our minds have, and it can create great damage if it wants to. It can also create great benefits if we use the "inspirational imagination" of our essences instead.'

I ended the email conversation with Allison and after putting Charlie to bed I began to write my book on Bianchi from my notes. The house was deathly quiet. I started to write about Steve and, as I typed, I started to feel as if I was being watched. I glanced around the room nervously and realised that I was getting scared by this strange idea of an invisible murderer.

I passed it off as imagination and carried on writing. After ten minutes, I felt heavy breathing on my neck. I got up in fright with my hand over my neck and looked out of the French doors. Was the window open? Had an intruder come across the moonlit garden? I checked that the window was closed and locked it tight. As I stared at the black glass, I thought of Bianchi's victims and felt as if I could see the shape of one spreadeagled on the grass. I knew then that I was going crazy. The case had got to me. I went back to the computer and switched it off; this whole business was scaring me.

It was midnight. I picked up the new contract that Bianchi had sent me, requesting my signature as an assurance that I would go ahead with his book. Although he'd written to me earlier, voicing his doubts about using me as his ghostwriter, he'd gone on to do another U-turn and convinced me to go ahead with the autobiography. I'd decided to agree so that I could continue to gather information for my own book at the same time. I signed my name in black ink next to Bianchi's curled signature and

In for the Kill

folded the contract I had made with the Hillside Strangler. I tucked it into an envelope, licked it closed and addressed it to the American penitentiary.

I went to get a bottle of red wine from the basement and took a torch as the light down there was broken. On the way down the rickety wooden steps I thought about how Bianchi had strangled two college girls on the stairs down to a basement. *Why do it there?* I thought as I stopped on my own basement stairs and banged my head on the single light bulb that had blown, making it useless to illuminate the dark. I switched on the torch and saw scratch marks over the banister. I knelt down and saw the words 'Help me'. I thought that this must have been written by the previous occupants. The door swung shut behind me and I panicked and sprang back up the stairs. I decided to forget the wine.

In an attempt to relax, I poured myself some vodka instead and switched on the television; it was a programme about someone who had found the skull of a young girl buried in their back garden. I quickly switched over.

My eyes were wandering around the walls of the drawing room as I sipped the vodka, admiring my paintings, when suddenly it was almost as if there was someone in the room with me again. I felt icy cold. I felt a presence come nearer and nearer and then I saw it was a cloud of tiny moths in the air. I screamed.

The phone rang and I scrambled to pick it up in case it woke Charlie. I got to it after the third ring. As I picked it up, an American male voice spoke to me.

'This is the operator from the United States, ma'am. Will you accept a collect call from Washington State?'

There was a pause. Bianchi had mentioned in one of his letters that he wanted to talk to me and I had been waiting for him to call. Alternatively, I had also rung one of the staff at the prison who worked with Bianchi and left a message for him to call me back.

'Who's calling?'

'Washington State Penitentiary.'

I felt afraid. Was it him or the worker there ringing me back?

'No, sorry, I can't afford it at this time. Sorry.' My hand was sweating while holding the receiver.

'That's OK, ma'am, thank you.'

I opened my mouth to speak and before I did the phone line went dead.

I could feel him. All of a sudden I could hear in thought form the words 'BITCH, CUNT, WHORE'. Then the ugliest images came into my mind – gay male pornography of the very worst kind. It was a fraction of a second but it felt alien and I most certainly didn't like it – here was what Dee said he had experienced whilst dealing with Bianchi.

I ran upstairs, lay on the bed shaking and said the 'Our Father'. I was OK – it was gone. But I was concerned that what Dee had warned me was true. I rang him immediately, lying on my bed trembling. It was one o'clock in the morning.

He started to laugh. 'Don't make me say I told you so.'

'As if anyone could believe what you said – it's spooky. I'm terrified, Chris. What was it – evil? '

'It's Bianchi, of course, and it's commonly known as astral projection. The prison walls can't hold him.'

'It's not true – it's our imaginations.'

'What, both of us?'

Dee seemed to find it all amusing. It was odd. I didn't. I was terrified. He took it in his stride.

'No one tells us that serial killers are poltergeists,' I said.

He laughed. 'They aren't. But Bianchi is the real deal. There's something odd about him. It's the killing part of him – Steve, or whatever he chooses to call it. It's not in a body, so it can float around and get into other people's heads. This is the real deal – evil ground zero. I told you he got inside my head. I felt him inside, looking around my mind. I warned you about Bianchi, Chris, and you went ahead. Whatever you do, love, be a smart girl and don't let him get inside your head. Don't tell him things about you or your life and you'll be fine.'

'I don't know if I believe I wasn't just imagining it, Chris. I've been reading a lot about the case and I'm sensitive.'

'Just be careful. If he gets into you, he may not want to get out again. We're out there, Chris. This is tough stuff, what we do. You're on the edge of the abyss, Chris, and I tell you this, the abyss does look back at you and try to check you out. They should call us something, you know.'

I began to laugh. 'Absolute fucking morons?'

'Nah – ghostbusters.'

'Mulder and Scully? Oh, I love them! I like aliens – the reptiles and the greys.'

'You're so like me, so do I. Hey, let's call ourselves Murder Incorporated.'

I laughed. I was cheering up and after chatting for an hour with him I hung up and felt better. Chris was good medicine. But as soon as he'd gone off the phone the fear returned with a crash. I was beginning to sense that there was something supernatural and fundamentally evil about the whole case but no one had wanted to look into it as they had been under pressure to convict his cousin. And Bianchi himself had wanted to hide it. There was something about Bianchi that wasn't like other men – he had a shaky hold on his body and clearly something had come into it.

The next day was Sunday and Charlie and I drove to Mass. After the service I went to talk to the priest in his private rooms to ask for his help. I told him about what had happened, while my son waited in the priest's comfortable drawing room for me with some children's books on Jesus, so I could talk in private.

Father Blanchard was tall, lean and well into middle age. I remembered him from when I was a five-year-old child in the school nearby. He had a chiselled face and clear grey eyes that looked kind and a mouth that looked like it only uttered good things. He leaned back comfortably in his black leather armchair and put his fingers to his lips as he listened to my story about Bianchi and the work I did.

'It was only for a fraction of a second that I saw the images but it was connected to the man in Cell 3, I know it.' I realised just how crazy I sounded only after I had said it out loud.

Father Blanchard looked at me carefully and then said, 'I'm not an exorcist but I can refer you to some Scriptures from John. John explains what evil is. You could also try contacting one of the Catholic Church's top exorcists, if you wish, but I also have a friend who is very good at blessing houses. He's a Jesuit called Father Borgia and he's down in London next week. He may help you if you ring him. I have his contact details here.' He reached for a red book in his desk drawer.

'Do I need to ring him?' I asked, hoping for some reassurance.

He smiled at me kindly. 'Give me your email address so that I can send you the Scriptures that you need to read. I'll add his number and you can call him at your leisure. I think you should, given this man's devotion to evil. Most people would avoid a man like that. The Catholic Church has specialists who deal with evil.'

We went back out into the priest's drawing room, where Charlie was sitting playing with a five-inch plaster Virgin Mary.

Father Blanchard took the Virgin Mary-shaped bottle from

Exorcism

Charlie and poured some holy water from a large font near the door into it before handing it to me.

'For you.' He frowned at me. 'Of course, the only real protection against evil is a mind that won't let it in. Pray daily and attend weekly Mass. I have heard priests say they have experienced something similar to what you have described while carrying out exorcisms. Be careful. He is evil, this man is dangerous, be warned about him. It's not a trivial force – even God himself cannot fight it.'

I thought about how I had searched for true evil all of my life. It was a force even God was near beaten by, yet I had sought it. How arrogant was I to feel that I would unlock all of its mysteries? Even though I was afraid, I still had a burning curiosity. I was inches away from something I had always wondered about. How pathetic it would be to lose my nerve now.

The thought of Dee gave me strength. He had experienced the same phenomenon yet found it par for his course. If he could cope with it then so could I. He even seemed to find it amusing. I found it about as amusing as being knocked down by a car. What if Bianchi or whatever it was attached to him came inside my head and decided he liked it and never left? What if he drove me bonkers, so I couldn't look after my little boy. What if – what if?

I thanked Father Blanchard, hugged Charlie to me and left. My real protection was my determination not to let anything stand in the way of being a good mother to my son. I drove off with the holy water in my handbag, while Charlie laughed in the backseat and spread his bubblegum over the side of the car.

When I got home, I checked my email and found that Father Blanchard had already written to me, including a verse from John that discussed evil:

> You are of your father, the devil, and the desires of your father you want to do. He was a murderer from the beginning, and does not stand in the truth because there is no truth in him. When he speaks a lie, he speaks from his own resources, for he is a liar and the father of it.
>
> John 8:44

In for the Kill

I had attended theology lectures for over a year at a seminary in Osterley and I was familiar with the Bible but I didn't ransack it for spooky lines. It felt unpleasant to sit and read the verses after I felt as if I had experienced something supernatural.

Later on that night, after my son had gone to bed, I rang Father Borgia from my mobile. When he answered, he sounded kindly and had an Italian accent. I told him that my parish priest had given me his number and then told him my story.

'Do you want me to bless your house for you?'

I was shocked that he came out with it so quickly.

'Do I need you to?'

'I feel the problem is that you've been telling this mass murderer all about yourself – he has your scent, so to speak. Now you've attracted his demons.'

'I didn't know evil was like catching nits?'

I heard a sigh down the phone.

'If two men are possessing one body in a multiple personality, then one of them may be possessed. There is of course the possibility that one of them may be a demonic entity in itself.'

'Demons and possessions aren't talked about at Mass on Sunday.'

He seemed to smile down the phone. 'We don't advertise for the other side.'

I felt sick and thought of the vile images that had come into my mind. 'Why am I having these visions?'

'The evil is based in the serial killer, that's its earthly dwelling place. You are dealing with the house of the devil. You have entered the house and are trying to explore it, are you not?'

'Yes, I suppose so.'

'You only wanted to dip your toe in?'

'No, I wanted to see everything. I wanted to see the evil. I knew it was there. But now I'm afraid. I didn't expect it to come to me. I wanted to peer at it from a distance.'

'You to it are the most trivial of things.'

'Is it possible for it to be transferred from him to me?'

'I would say this man has been its host for decades and will stay its home. You have an interest in studying evil. It is very ambitious. It has killed men who have joined the Church – eaten away at our exorcists, and they are armed with the Bible. You are armed with only your curiosity.'

'Is the evil in him a lost soul?'

'Yes, a lost soul, but it has found something. Clearly it has made evil its god.'

'It's possessed.'

'It has bathed itself in evil and become one with it perhaps.'

'God.'

Chris had told me it was Steve who had projected himself into his mind and Steve who had driven the female penpal of Bianchi's mad. Steve who I felt powerfully drawn to.

Father Borgia made an appointment to visit the following Thursday, when my son would be at school.

Thursday afternoon came and there was a knock at the door. I was upstairs in bed having a nap after working all night on the book. I hurriedly put on my clothes and went to the door. There in the rain stood the priest in his black garments. He was in his 60s, had cropped grey hair and was short with a slightly wrinkled and pleasant face. He brushed the rainwater off his face and said, 'Hello, are you Chris Hart? We spoke on the phone. I'm Father Borgia.'

'Come in,' I said.

He dripped his way into my hallway then put down his black bag and took off his beige overcoat and handed it to me. It was soaked. I ushered him inside to the fire.

'Would you like some tea or coffee?' I said as I offered him a towel.

'Not right away. After I bless the house it would be nice.'

He opened the gold clasps of his bag and brought out a leather Bible with heavy metal binding. On the dining-room table he then spread out a purple silk cloth with golden tassels on the edges. He had something that looked like chrism oil in a clear glass bottle.

'Now,' he said, and looked at me with his pale blue eyes, 'where have you had these experiences?'

'Mainly in my study, which is over there.' I took him through and pointed over to my computer.

'Well, we'd better start there.'

He sprinkled water over the floor, blessed it and then started to read from the Bible. He then went up to my bedroom and made a sign of the cross and prayed. He repeated the ceremony in the hallway.

After he had finished he went downstairs and put his stuff away in the black bag. I heated him a vegetable samosa and we

227

both stood in the kitchen as he ate and I drank hot tea and ate a chocolate croissant.

He looked over at the kitchen window.

'Have you seen faces there?'

I stared at him and my chewing stopped.

'Of the victims?' His eyes were wide and intelligent.

'No, I haven't.'

'I can feel them here.'

'Who?'

'The women. Were they beautiful?'

I felt like I couldn't breathe.

'Some of them had had hard lives but, yes, they were all knockouts.'

'You've a strong sixth sense. It's a curse. Satan likes nothing better than to demolish God's most pleasing handiwork.'

'Why would they be here?'

'I don't know, it's for you to find out.'

I rang for a taxi to take Father Borgia to the station. After he left I draped rosary beads over the handles of most of the doorways and put up some pictures of the Sacred Heart I had bought. I vowed to pray nightly and make sure I went to confession and Mass weekly.

That night I was afraid to shut my eyes in case I saw vile images again. Eventually I fell asleep with the light on and the same thing happened again in my dream. I saw again images of horror and people dismembered. Then I saw a man who had been buried in sand in the desert up to his neck. He had a red face and he was dying slowly. I half woke from the dream but it was so real I had to go back to it and I was too tired to shake myself awake. I clasped my rosary beads and prayed as hard as I could. I went into the body of the dying man and he became me. As I prayed, I felt taken over by Jesus and dying was somehow not a scary thing any more. It took him a long time to die and I have never prayed so hard in my life. When I finally woke up I was still afraid – was this going to go on every night? I would end up exhausted. I was afraid something had got me and would chip away until I gave up praying for protection – and then what would happen?

I went to Mass again on Monday but Father Blanchard didn't mention the situation, so afterwards I drove over to Hugh's for advice. I stood at his door and admired the roses that clambered up his garden wall. They were a much deeper pink than mine but looked unkempt and I made a mental note to tidy them up for him.

Hugh opened the door in his warm beige cotton shirt and favourite brown cords. I sat in his dark front room on his low black leather settee and watched him as he ate sour cream and chive flavour Pringles and gazed at me in the languid way that I found beguiling.

Hugh had his heating on far too high and I moaned at him as I took off my cardigan.

'It's dry in here and it dries out my skin.'

'Put up with it, Chris. I'm cold and I like it hot. Now what have you really been up to with this American?'

'My priest told me I needed my house blessed, so he sent over a friend of his.'

'That's crazy. What did he say to you?'

'He said I had a demon.'

Hugh grinned mischievously. 'Do you really believe in demons and blood-sucking vampires? Surely you don't believe in such rot?'

'I don't know.' I smiled at him and cheered up a bit.

'Look, Chris, Catholic priests are all exorcists and they are all mad. Did he really believe you had been in the presence of Bianchi's evil spirit? A serial killer thousands of miles away?'

'I don't think that distance means the same thing to the undead as it does to us – they don't need to take the bus!'

Through his floor-length leaded windows I could hear the thwack of a ball on a cricket bat and the cheer from the watching crowd.

'He said Bianchi may have another spirit in his body that is unborn – not in a body permanently – with nowhere to go.'

'What did he give you to get rid of it?'

'Prayer and some holy water.'

He guffawed. 'Holy water! What a load of superstitious tomfoolery. Your priests are involving themselves in the madness of all of it. Leave Bianchi alone. He is the one disturbing you, Chris. I had bad dreams after you lent me that book on him. His crimes were terrible and it can make you have bad dreams. I couldn't sleep for a few nights after reading it but I never told you.'

'Christopher Berry-Dee was right, Bianchi has got special powers.'

'There truly are no such things as supernatural powers to mind read or time travel.'

'Of course there are such things as psychic powers. I can't help but feel that Steve has always been there, waiting for me to find him.'

We talked for hours over some smoked salmon sandwiches and a fresh pot of Earl Grey with honey that I stirred in, and eventually, as he always did, he cheered me up and made me laugh with his wolfish grin and his wicked mind.

'At least I've managed to make you laugh!'

Hugh always made me laugh and I loved him for it, but I kept my feelings well hidden from him in case this put me in the vulnerable position of needing somebody.

I put my blue leather gloves on as I prepared to leave.

'How are the school-gate mothers?'

'Terrible. They ignore me. One of them said to Charlie recently, "Your mummy's a scumbag because she's not married."'

'One of the mothers said that?'

'Don't be daft. They keep it oh so polite. It was one of their sons that had bullied Charlie. These women make Victoria Beckham look fat and ungroomed. I'd admire them if it weren't for them leaving Charlie out of their posh parties. Charlie was ever so upset. Why do they find it scummy that I'm a single mother? Is it the fact I was dumped by a man or the fact I couldn't find a loving one? Or is it because I shagged before I was married or am I a "scumbag" because I'm broke?' I mused thoughtfully.

'You should have got respectably married before you had Charlie,' Hugh told me in a haughty voice. 'He's beautiful but he'll suffer because he was born out of wedlock. He'll be judged for it by polite middle-class society. It's all about land and ownership of land. They will leave him out because of that round there. I know that lot at that little stuck-up school, Chris. English suburbia is a hive of snobbery. Blame your God for not doing anything about it.'

I slammed the door as I left.

Thirty

The Reincarnation of Jack

Someday I'll walk amongst the unstable footpath
and crush all that turns me around.

Kenneth Bianchi

It was early January 2010 and the air had an icy bite. Charlie was in the back garden, running around in the white mist by the river. I watched him as if he were a dream – a child of sunlight and shadows, the child that I never thought I would have.

It was a Saturday morning. I had written to Ken Bianchi a fortnight ago, telling him again about the upset I had suffered over losing our family home when I had panicked and sold it for a loss at the start of the recession. I told him how I often thought of the apple trees in the garden, our bird tables where we would leave out nuts and seeds, and the dew-covered cobwebs in the morning sun in the bushes in the front garden. I told him how I used to stand in our wooden front porch and watch the summer rainstorms lash against the black tarmac of the road outside. I thought of my bedroom, where I would wake and feel happy because we had our own home. I reminisced about the small front garden that I used to enjoy mowing and the friendly neighbourhood.

The postman noisily stuffed a bundle of mail through the letterbox and in it was a reply from Bianchi. I made myself a cup of coffee and sat down at the kitchen table with the letter. Hoots of laughter echoed in from the open French windows as Charlie played in the garden. As I read Bianchi's latest offering I wondered if I was risking my sanity by confiding in a man I didn't know and had never met, but ambition to write a good study on him pushed me forward.

In the afternoon I took my son up to Richmond Hill, and as I drove past the huge houses I looked at the For Sale signs. I always felt sick with bitterness when I looked at those houses. I was angry with myself for not buying years ago. Other people had bought property instead of living for years in rented homes. Therapy to get over my childhood abuse had taken up all of my resources, money and time. In between, I also had to build a career as a writer. When I was building my career as a top investigative journalist in Fleet Street, I didn't have time to worry about investing money in pensions or property. Because of my difficult start in life, the damage that had been done to me and the struggle I had gone through to get over it, I was late in starting my career and had my foot firmly on the accelerator. I had worked very hard for years and yet had nothing to show for it. When I finally did manage to buy my own home, I lost it as a result of bad advice and poor judgement on my own part. Whereas before that I had had no idea what I was missing out on, now I was feeling the reality of it. I had few close friends, I didn't own my home and had no money in the bank to go on holiday. Charlie would need all of those things but I didn't know how to give them to him. I began to feel panic as I looked at the houses we were passing. I didn't have a home and I was getting older and had no energy left in me to get one, nor did I know how. I had a hundred pounds in my bank account and no work.

I thought of Bianchi's new letter. He had listened to what I told him about my yearning to have a home of my own but questioned whether the people with big houses and cars were really happy. Was that where happiness really lay? He believed that happiness lies in the moment – in really feeling the present. That was where he believed God came in – just at that moment. When God flew in, he said, he couldn't breathe; it was such a spiritual experience. He advised me to find that in my own life by making the small things bigger.

What a load of shit, I thought as we parked by the riverside.

We wandered around the woods, chatting and looking for deer. On the way back to the car I watched my son running along the side of the stream. He looked stunningly beautiful and so healthy, his golden hair flopping as he ran. Horses were galloping behind him in the backdrop. The whole scene was elegantly lit by a sunset so pink and spectacular it was lilac and gold.

Charlie turned and called to me. 'Mummy! Look how fast I can run.'

All of a sudden I couldn't breathe. I had a son – a son – and he was *so beautiful*. Tears swam in my eyes and I whispered up to God, 'You've not forgotten me.' Fear of having no money had blinded me to all of my blessings.

Later on, back home at Dragonfly Villas, I opened the French windows and stood in the garden sipping an aperitif of gin and tonic and thinking about Bianchi. How could such an evil man make me aware of God? Since the odd mind thing I had experienced nothing, so it was easy to tell myself it was all just imagination.

I picked up his fifteen-page letter and re-read the last few pages where he talked again about the murders and the false confession that he claimed he'd made. He said that he'd been hypnotised and this had led him to make the confession about raping, torturing and murdering the girls. After that, he said, everything was like a blur and he barely knew whether it was night or day. Whenever he fell asleep the cell door would swing open and someone would clang their baton along the side of his bed. He would be hauled out of his bed on what felt like an hourly basis, pushed up against a wall and the interrogating officers would yell at him, telling him he was the Hillside Strangler. He would be stripped to his underpants and have cold water thrown on him. He said he could taste urine and faeces in his food and most of the time he refused to eat it. After a few weeks of this kind of treatment he said he was ready to confess to anything. He said he told them what he had confessed to under hypnosis was true, as he just wanted to put a stop to the questioning. He had been sure that someone would contradict him because he knew all the details he had come out with were incorrect. He wanted them to realise that he had confessed due to the way he had been treated. He was convinced that someone would stand up for him but this never happened. He had been a stupid kid, he said, and now here he was, 30 years later, lying in a cell, forgotten about by the world.

Could this be an innocent man locked up? I thought to myself. Then Charlie came running in, breathless from his exertions in the back garden, and woke me from my thoughts. I poured him some orange juice and got on with cooking us supper. I pulled sausages out of a packet and began to peel potatoes. I felt lucky to be able to make my son happy with something as simple as a cooked meal with gravy. I smiled at the thought of how pleased he would be that it was sausages.

'Mum, are you OK?'

'Yes, honey, I'm fine,' I replied as I rinsed the potatoes. But I wasn't fine. I was confused about the innocence or guilt of that man in Walla Walla.

Later on in bed, wrapped up with extra blankets as it was icy cold, I wondered if my loneliness was making me throw myself into the Bianchi book too much and I was going to end up stressed by it. I had nothing else to lean on in my life and my need for a strong man was overwhelming – he must have picked up on it.

I fell asleep whilst studying Bianchi's letter again. As soon as my eyes shut, I immediately saw an old-fashioned black-iron lantern. I was a little girl of ten and I was walking behind a lantern that was on the back of some kind of horse's carriage. I felt very desolate, afraid and unhappy. I was in the company of two rough-looking older men who I didn't like.

It was a very dark, snowy and terribly cold night. I could hear the horses pulling the carriage, their chains and their hooves clopping. It was hard to walk along in the deep snow and I was very tired and felt very heavy and dispirited. Suddenly the old-fashioned Christmas-card carriage stopped moving. I stood there behind the lantern and stared at the half burnt-down candle inside it, feeling terribly depressed. I knew that I didn't want to live any longer. There was someone in my heart whom I needed to be with very badly. It was like a yearning so strong I thought I was going to be sick with love and need for him.

I knew that if I ran off into the darkness, into the endless slopes of snow, then they would swallow me up and I would surely die, so in my dream I broke free and ran.

The two men called out after me. 'Hey, come back here, you.'

I ran on and on into the thick snow. They didn't chase me. I heard them say in a contemptuous way that I would die anyway. I ran on and on in the dark and the snow and eventually I found him. He was my 12-year-old brother Jack. He was walking on his own out in the dark and the snow.

He called me Rachel and we hugged. We were tired and hungry

but with no hope of any food we sat down together in an icy ditch. I was so happy to be with Jack that I didn't care that the terrible cold was painfully cutting through to my bones. I knew that I could face even the most terrible of experiences with Jack beside me. I felt safe with him and we huddled together to try to keep warm. Jack said, 'Rachel, please don't fall asleep. It's dangerous. We'll die, it's too cold.'

'No, Jack, I won't, don't worry. I just want to be with you.'

Eventually, sick and weak with the cold, I let sleep take me. I woke in my dream and to my surprise it was warm and there was a tunnel of bright light. I stood up and looked around me. Jack was standing up and looking around dazed and afraid. I looked down to the vision beneath us. It was the two of us frozen together into one solid lump of ice. I said, 'We're dead. Look, they were our bodies.'

We watched in horror as the two men came upon us and sneered at our dead bodies. 'Look at those two dead idiots – frozen solid.'

My brother was upset but I said, 'It doesn't matter. We're OK, look at us.'

He said, 'But, Rachel, we're dead.'

I said, 'Jack, so what? At least it's an end to that terrible, terrible cold. Look at us. We're OK, aren't we? And we're together.'

We walked up the tunnel towards the light. As we walked towards it, my brother's hand slipped away from mine. I screamed out after him as I was pulled towards the light and he was sucked another way. 'I'll look for you, Jack. I'll find you again. I'll search for you and search for you and I'll never give up. Never.'

I woke up in a cold sweat, my eyes wet with tears. It was still dark outside the window. I looked at the clock – it was 4 a.m. My dream came back to me. I noticed that I was still holding Bianchi's letter. Was it a dream about his life? I let his letter fall from my fist.

I thought about the 12-year-old boy, Jack, from my dream. I remembered, as I lay in bed, that ten years ago I had visited a psychic for a lark with a friend. This was the incident I had recounted to Sienna. Amongst other things he had told me that my soulmate had the initial J. He had said, 'This J is the one for you. You and J are two sides of the same coin. J is not only a match, he is THE match.' I knew somehow that J was for Jack. But where was Jack now?

In for the Kill

I pulled the curtains to block out the sun coming up and went back to sleep again. I thought of Bianchi as a child as I tried to sleep. When his adoptive family moved to a new house, he told me that he had sensed great evil behind a locked door in his attic bedroom. It was there every night. He said he would dream that it overwhelmed him and he would wake up screaming. I wondered whether his family had found a house with a demon in the attic like in the Amityville Horror and that was what had possessed him. Or maybe the 'great evil' was the childhood abuse he had suffered that he couldn't integrate into him.

Perhaps it was earth that was the hate factory of the universe, a bad-apple planet polluting the galaxy with its toxic waste, I thought to myself as I fell asleep.

Thirty-one
Invitation to America

A simple nest, love does make, brittle straw,
marigolds lace upon a cliff, overlooking many hills
and valleys sunlit, as chants of courtship await.

Kenneth Bianchi

It was still January and it was freezing. Intermittent fog was making driving difficult and the roads had constant black ice. We stayed in a lot and I cooked us thick stews and soups to keep us warm and healthy against the threat of swine flu and winter infections.

This particular night was icy cold and Charlie and I sat at home and did colouring in and played marbles. That morning a parcel had arrived from the States. It was Bianchi's yellowing police files that to my surprise he had sent me. I now cut open the cellophane packet and read the letter that fell out. Bianchi wrote that a prisoner had stabbed another man in his part of the prison and they had been locked in their cells for over a fortnight. The prison was snowed in and there had been a blizzard. His cell was unheated and the air conditioning used during the summer months was still running. He said that the prison authorities always forgot to turn it off, as the staff didn't like the smell of sweat from the prisoners' sleeping bodies.

I had to use a magnifying glass to read some of the fine print on the police files. The crime-scene photos were revealing about the special signature of the Hillside Strangler and the variance in his modus operandi. One very unusual factor was that the all the murders had been carried out within a month and sometimes there were two victims. In Robert Keppel's book *The Riverman*, he quotes

In for the Kill

Ted Bundy as saying that this indicated that the mind of the Hillside perpetrator was unusually extreme. Bundy said that it meant that the serial killer was intense. Rape and torture were supposed to satiate hunger for the three Ds of sadism. The three Ds were to make the victim experience dependency, degradation and dread. The fact that the Hillside Stranglings were carried out mostly over the space of one month made the case unusual – like a rampage.

When I had first read the facts of the killings it had taken me two days to get it out of my system each time. In all my years of journalism, I had never come across anything like it. Was the man I was writing to really connected with all this?

It was the eye of the storm. Pure evil was present in all of these crimes and it had seemed to me from the outset that it was some kind of Satanism. I had asked Bianchi if he was interested in Satanism or the occult and he told me that he had tried Tarot cards, but just for fun, and also messed around with a ouija board. He'd watched *The Exorcist* a few times and enjoyed it – why was I asking, he wanted to know.

Jeffrey Dahmer had played *The Exorcist III* to his victims, I told him.

He got cross and asked me why I was trying to make a connection between him and Dahmer. He said: 'I hate these killers. I think they should be given the death penalty.'

The garden was white with frost. Foxes' footprints ran across the grass. I shivered and pulled my cardigan around my shoulders as I looked at the ice-covered river that ran past the end of the garden.

To my amazement, another letter arrived the next day. Out of the blue, Bianchi had sent me an application form for a prison visit. He wanted me to visit him! On a calendar he had blocked out the date of 14 February with a green biro. He wanted me to visit him on Valentine's Day! He said it would be hard for us if I went to visit him but all he asked was that I be myself. I couldn't believe this was happening.

Along with the printed forms was a list of rules for visits. I noticed that it said visitors were allowed a four-minute hug with the prisoner, which was clearly intended for married couples or those in a relationship. He had also enclosed a photo of himself with his adoptive parents. He looked handsome in it, with dark hair and a moustache. He was dressed in casual clothes. I didn't take it as a hint that he liked me. Maybe I should have. I felt that all of a sudden I had broken into a vault. I felt overwhelmed by him, as he was very intense. I wondered what he wanted from me, as he clearly wanted something.

I rang Chris Berry-Dee and told him.

'He likes your tits, I tell you that now.'

'Chris, that's a bit rude!'

'So's he, dirty ol' bastard, I've seen the photo you sent him. He's after wife number four.'

'Rubbish – he's knows I'm a writer.'

'Oh, that won't stop him. He's arrogant as they come. He'll see you as a challenge.'

I wondered if he was jealous. Often writers who know serial killers can feel as if they own them.

'You jealous?'

'You can let him roger you away behind the Coke machines, Chris, and I won't get jealous.'

I blushed; he was flirting with me.

'You're not going to actually go, are you?'

'Of course I'm going! I'm gong to ring the airline now. No, on second thoughts I'll try to write a piece and file a story first so that I can get a newspaper or a magazine to pay for me to go and interview him.'

'Chris, have you any idea of the journey to get to Bianchi? He's on the other side of the world. It's the farthest side of America! It's over a day's solid travel to get there – about thirteen hours on a plane and that's only one of the planes. Not to mention Walla Walla prison is in the middle of a set of mountains and the only way of getting to the actual prison is on a really tiny plane that flies over the jagged mountains, and if that won't get you puking up, the turbulence or the neon-green carpet in the tiny shack of an airport will. And that's before you've even sat down with the scary bastard and got to know him, God forbid.'

'I will go.'

'Why? Why go? Looking for his alter? I told you already that Steve isn't real.'

'It's on Valentine's Day.'

'Sorry?'

'I'm going on Valentine's Day.'

'You have to go on the day he gives you.'

'He's given me Valentine's Day.'

'You're going to go under the circumstances that that bastard dictates. You're treading on very dangerous ground. I kept my distance from Mr Bianchi. And you think it'll be fun and games to fool around with him and have a Valentine's date. Mad! Even by accepting, he'll see it as a green light.'

We hung up on each other and I felt confused.

I rushed round to see Hugh as soon Charlie was off to school on Monday.

'God, it's so bloody hot in here!'

'Put the kettle on, sit down calmly and tell me all about it.'

Hugh had just finished eating porridge and was still licking the spoon greedily. I felt a surge of affection and attraction for him.

'Bianchi has invited me to go to America and visit him on Valentine's Day.'

'That's incredible.'

'Why is it incredible?'

'Going to see a mass murderer on Valentine's Day, are you crazy?'

'Why is everyone making such a big deal about it being Valentine's Day?'

'I thought this guy upset you and scared you? Why get all lovey-dovey with him?'

'I think it's a coincidence, Hugh, that he's picked this day to meet me.'

'How innocent can you get?'

'What do you mean?'

'You've just been taken in by this man.'

'In what way?'

'He's deceiving you with his Valentine's Day invite.'

'How do you mean? Deceiving me how?'

'He's leading you up the garden path, for Christ's sake, even sending you his love poetry – wafting away like Byron. Who does he think he is?'

'I don't know.'

'God knows there's something sick about all this.'

'How do you mean? Do you mean you think *I'm* sick?'

'No, Chris, you're not sick; I mean the situation. You're a very attractive single woman and he's an imprisoned man. You're getting far too close to this chap. You're no longer being a professional journalist, so how can you see him clearly?'

'I am being professional. I've rung around editors I know and one of them has agreed to commission me to fly to America and interview him.'

'Which newspaper?'

Invitation to America

'*The Guardian.*'

'Well, that's a bloody good newspaper.'

'I know it. I'm a damn good investigative writer.' I frowned at him; he wasn't truly on my side. 'They want me to write up an investigative piece on him and his assertions of innocence. Bianchi told me to apply for a visit as a friend, as that way we get eight hours together and full contact. He said if I apply as a journalist I would only get an hour and we wouldn't be allowed bodily contact.'

'Well, there you are then. He's cosying up to you so you'll write nice things about him. He sees you're lonely and stupid. He's a murdering shit and you're completely under his dishonourable spell. Now he wants to have full contact with you. How is that anything to do with *The Guardian*? I can't believe you've conned them into paying for you to go and have your despicable "full contact" with a mass murderer on Valentine's Day.'

'I wish I hadn't told you, Hugh,' I said as I stood up.

'Don't go. Hear this. You've been searching for pure evil most of your life. I cannot understand anyone who would seek out evil to try to come to grips with it – no one can. It's one of life's great mysteries. Who do you think you are, a theologian?'

'Yes! Yes, I've done a course in theology!'

'A tin-pot course for lonely people on weekday evenings is what you did, Chris. You're not a bloody theologian. You're misguidedly going to seek out the Steve character, I know that. Who the hell do you think you're going to see? There is no Steve, it's all Ken.'

'I don't believe that to be true.'

'So you are flying thousands of miles to see Steve?'

'Yes.'

'I think you're nuts. And you've conned *The Guardian* by making out that you're investigating Bianchi when really you're chasing a demon. They'd never commission you for that, would they?'

'Who cares?'

'Demon chasing! I implore you to not go. Don't carry on conning *The Guardian* and don't visit a mass murderer.'

Hugh was being insulting and a little too precious about *The Guardian* for an avid reader of *The Times*. I got up and went out, slamming the door behind me, feeling tired of our love–hate relationship. He was jealous but I couldn't work out why. He had made a television programme about demons and haunted houses, so why was he angry at me for getting on a plane to interview a subject from the same area of interest? I saw him glance at me through his window. If we had been the same age, we would have been a power couple, but we were from different times.

Feeling as though I needed someone's support, I went round to visit Sienna in her Chelsea home to ask her opinion. When I got there and rang the doorbell, there was no answer, so I knocked on the neighbour's door to ask if she knew where Sienna was.

'She's gone into The Priory.'

'What happened?'

'She and Larry have been having problems. She's had a nervous breakdown over it.'

I rang The Priory from my mobile as I sat in the car.

'You can come and visit her at three o'clock on Wednesday,' said the matron on the phone. 'She'll be a bit calmer by then.'

On Wednesday afternoon I drove up the long private drive to The Priory, parked outside the massive white castle and looked around, admiring the place.

I found Sienna slumped on a wooden bench in the spectacular grounds. She had her head down and was reading a battered copy of *Atonement*.

I sat down and put my arm around her shoulders. 'How are you, darling?' I asked.

'I can't stand the bastard,' she said through a flood of tears.

'What do you mean?'

'Larry's always up in the city making money. He never takes any notice of me. I'm lonely in that boring old house of ours.'

'What about all the glittering friends you have and the all the champagne parties?'

'I have to put a stop to all that. My psychiatrist told me that I was an alcoholic.'

'Oh, Sienna, you're not.'

'I know I'm not. One titchy bottle of Pol Roger a night doesn't an alcoholic make. He's far too strict.'

She had on a long purple silk hippy dress and a golden headband. I wondered if she was trying to pretend she was one of the pop stars that roamed the corridors of The Priory. She stood up and did a mock dance of the seven veils, her four fingers pointed into V shapes and twirled around her face. I noticed she had far too much sparkly green kohl around her eyes.

'I love it here – I'm like a celebrity. It makes me feel important. You'll never guess who I've just seen in the canteen.'

Invitation to America

I smiled at her benevolently and looked around the grounds. There was an air of peace and tranquillity. A young man in a white coat came walking over. He handed her a plastic cup of three tablets.

'Sienna, you need your tablets.' She swallowed three bright pink pills obediently.

'You've got to go, Chris. I need to rest.'

I had to tell her about Bianchi's invitation as I was in two minds about whether to go to America or not.

'You remember the American mass murderer that I'm writing to? He's invited me over for Valentine's Day.'

Sienna pulled a face. 'Really, Chris, you're taking your despair for a man to a whole new level by having a Valentine's Day date with the Hillside Strangler.'

'It's not a date; it's an interview. I'm a journalist, that's what they do.'

'No, they don't. Journalists write mind-numbing stories for tedious newspapers. They don't go off and have dates with serial killers.'

'Whatever, it's not a date.' I stared at her. She looked less luminous than her usual self; life had somehow crushed her, yet I still felt judged by her vacant blue eyes.

'What about the personal feelings that you've developed for Bianchi?'

'I haven't.'

'Why, then, would you go and see him on Valentine's Day?'

'He asked me to. I'm hardly going to bring him a big chocolate heart.'

'He's got that hot photograph of you, don't forget that. Your boobs were hanging out – so unethical for a journalist. '

I stared at her for a full minute, not speaking. Her tablets were taking effect and she seemed to melt in front of me like the wicked witch of the west. Amazingly, it seemed to make her nicer.

'Yes, yes, yes. OK, you're a professional,' she slurred. 'Go along and find out whether he is telling the truth about his innocence for your newspaper. But keep in mind why you wrote to him in the first place.'

'Hearing the voice of Steve is what drew me.'

'And?'

I killed that one – he killed that one, that one I did, that one I don't know. Could that one have done her hair differently or something?

'When I heard the voice of Steve confessing I sensed something not human there – something otherworldly.'

'It's the cry of the vampire. It's what you heard that drew you – you knew he wasn't human. You've hunted evil since you were 13. You're a real-life Bella.'

'Give over with that *Twilight* shit, you're too old for it.'

She stared up at the sun and her golden headband slipped down over her eyes.

'Vampires exist!' she exclaimed to the asylum walls.

'Maybe Steve isn't the killer; maybe he was just protecting Ken. Maybe Ken is the killer. No, he can't be, he's too medium dominance.'

'God, you're so like Miss Marple.' She opened her blue eyes, lazy after the pills, making her look like a lovely cat. 'Meeting him will tell you your answers.'

I cuddled up to her, pleased that she was listening. 'I do feel like Miss Marple, Sienna.'

'Lovers meeting all over the world,' she said, but then turned to me seriously. 'He's after you, he must be! It's like a date he's fixing up on Valentine's Day. Be careful. Bianchi's playing you, I can tell, and you're falling for his bullshit.' She scrutinised me. 'You're so lonely for a man it makes you vulnerable to him and he's dangerous.'

'Piss off, am I lonely for a man. I'm getting close to get all his secrets out of him.'

'Sorry, Chris, you're a pro, but don't you think you're going to forget who you are and really fall for him? Wasn't he the serial killer who got a woman to kill for him from behind cell walls and isn't he supposed to be a big Svengali?'

'I'm fine. I know what I'm doing.'

Sienna and I hugged tightly and she started to weep.

'I'm sorry. I'm a bitch of a friend.'

'You're not.'

'Yes, I am, I'm a cunt.'

I helped her into the reception and left her slumped in the arms of a nurse.

I didn't really know where to go. I felt lost, so I ended up driving round to the green and calling back at Hugh's. Whenever we argued, I was like a homing pigeon. I wanted to be close to him again, as without him who would I have to turn to? He was my first port of call and my safe harbour.

Hugh was in the mood for brain stimulation, so he got stuck in straight away, leaning forward in his armchair so that I could smell lavender soap and newly ironed cotton. He had his warm beige shirt on undone at the neck and his hair looked freshly brushed and neat.

'The Catholic Church drinks the blood of Jesus, or thinks they drink the blood of Jesus because they're all out of their minds.'

'I do it. I believe in it.'

'What do you think drinking blood does for you?'

'It's supposedly Jesus Christ's blood and it gives one eternal life.'

'Load of bloody vampires! Do you know there's about 12 vampire series on Sky at the moment?'

'I know. Why do the kids like it? It's weird.'

'They hunger for spirituality. We have made religion weak, pappy and dull, so they turn to the dark to find an escape.'

'I was like that as a 13 year old. Hey, I was ahead of the times.'

'Young girls that seek evil – it's common, I think, but God knows why.'

'I'm angry at the book that first influenced me – Brady was no demon!'

'How's Charlie?' Hugh asked, changing the subject. 'Bring him round today after school. I've some cartoons ready for him to finish off. He's learning from me. He'll be a great artist one day, Chris.'

I smiled at him and felt love curdle in my stomach as I ached with need that I wasn't about to reveal to him. It was great, though, to have emotional support while bringing up Charlie.

Charlie and I still went to Mass and that Sunday we sat up at the front. I paid special attention when the priest performed the transformation. I bowed my head as the bell rang, then I drank the blood of Christ.

Did I believe in it and did I feel closer to God because of it?

I was going to fly many thousands of miles to America to visit the Hillside Strangler on Valentine's Day to seek out the Devil. I wanted to find Steve and examine him. I felt it would be easy. I would get Bianchi to relax and hopefully out he would come. I felt angry at the idea of having to put up with Bianchi for all that time but I felt sure I would be able to say things to trigger Steve.

Bianchi learned that I'd been commissioned by *The Guardian* to write about my trip and we bickered over what would make the visit a success. He wrote and said that it meant I would learn all about his case. I was angry about that, as I wasn't going there to do a PR job for him. I said, no, a successful visit was one where he didn't wheel out the nice-guy act and I saw it all. He said that he didn't know what I meant but suggested that if I was going to have an attitude like that I should stay in England. I apologised and told him I was stressed out.

I knew that Walla Walla was the hardest prison in America. I had to fly from London's Heathrow to Seattle and then transfer to a tiny plane to land near to the penitentiary in a small village. I booked tickets for me and Charlie and arranged a hotel. The Hampton Inn was the only one that would give me free room and board when I told them *The Guardian* had commissioned me to do a piece. They wanted to be plugged in the article. I planned to get a babysitting agency to look after Charlie while I was at the prison.

I had sent off my application forms to the prison and now I phoned them to ask about visiting regulations. I didn't want to depend on the copy I'd been sent, as I knew that the rules often changed. The prison sergeant told me what to wear: 'No low-cut dresses or tops. Skirts must be three inches below the knee. Do not let your bra strap show, or your panty hose, or we will not let you in. Dress like you would if you were going to church. Nothing sexually stimulating, Rainier is a sex-offenders' wing.'

I then asked her if I might have a third day's visit.

Bianchi had written just after I'd accepted his invitation suggesting that, as I was coming all that way, 'Why not come in on 13th too, then we can have two whole days together?' And if I could arrange that, 'Why not get the 15th too – that way we could even have three days.'

But the officer said, 'You can have two days with Bianchi, that's it. Not a third day when he's in Rainier. They can't have a third day in the visiting room as they'd get murdered if the general prison population saw them.' The visiting area was used by the whole prison.

I remembered Bianchi had told me in a letter that he'd been put in Rainier because he'd been accused of a sex crime. He said that this humiliation was just one of the many indignities that he had to live with.

I sat in my kitchen and made myself a cup of tea with honey. Then I packed a large suitcase for myself before pulling out a smaller yellow one for Charlie and filling it with clothes and toys. I took some fresh notebooks and my Olympus digital voice recorder. My laptop would have to stay at home, as it would be too much hassle to lug it on the plane and the hotel had an Internet room.

That night I slept for an hour and when I got up I checked my email. Ted Ponticelli, Bianchi's biographer, had emailed me an urgent message, saying: 'Bianchi says not to come. He says to stay in England.'

My heart began to beat rapidly and my throat went dry. It was my fault for being stroppy in my recent letters. I had screwed it up royally. Shit! It was a catastrophe. I hated myself. *The Guardian* was expecting a 6,000-word story to follow up the 3,000 words I had already written for them. They had paid the airfare for both of us. There was a taxi booked for 5 a.m. to drive us to Heathrow Airport, the plane tickets were paid for and the hotel was expecting us. I felt sick with anxiety. I had no idea what to do, so I drank a large glass of vodka.

I went into the kitchen and took the cover off the painting I had done of Bianchi's childhood. The strange boy in the picture looked back at me. I leaned forward and blew dust off the paintwork. I got a duvet I had brought down earlier and cuddled on the settee in the dark. Before I knew it, I had fallen asleep again. In my dream, I was sitting in front of two houses. They were black and white and somehow looked like Dorothy's house in the *Wizard of Oz*. Bianchi appeared and he was so young that I looked down at myself. I was young too. We were about ten or eleven. In front of us was a picnic. I spoke to Bianchi.

'Want to join me?'

'Yes, please.'

Bianchi sat down. All of a sudden another boy appeared who was dressed in rags and looked as if he had been beaten. He looked sullen.

I stared in silence then asked, 'Who's he?'

'Oh, just ignore him. Steve comes with me everywhere. He's my best friend.'

I stared at the boy, who didn't seem able to speak. What an odd boy, so scruffy and uncared for. Like an orphan that nobody loves, with no home. I felt a fascination for him. He looked as if he had a spiritual hunger gnawing at him.

I turned back to Bianchi. 'Where do you live?'

'Over in that house with my mother.' He pointed at a white clapboard house on a hill in the distance. I looked at the black and white house and then back at him. We picnicked for a while and I gave a sandwich to Bianchi's silent friend.

He didn't eat it. When I looked at him again, I realised that he looked pale as death.

I looked at him curiously. 'Why is he see through?'

Bianchi looked at him and then back at the house. There was terror in his eyes.

'He thinks Mother is bad but she's not. He protects me. Look, we have to go.'

'Will you come back and play tomorrow?'

'Course.'

'Oh, and bring him.' I smiled at Steve, whose skin was as white as marble.

"Don't worry, he'll come. Steve comes with me everywhere, he's my invisible friend. No one else can see him. I'm glad you can see him too.'

It started to rain before he reached the house. Heavier and heavier the rain fell until it became blood dripping down. There was blood dripping from the trees and from the sky – blood everywhere. It covered me and I looked down at my arms that had blood running down them. The blood drips sounded heavier and heavier – like knocking. There was a constant knocking sound in my dream. I tossed and turned until I woke and sat bolt upright in the dark with my heart beating fast.

There was someone at my door in the middle of the night knocking hard. Fear shot through me. I jumped up and went to the door, saying through gritted teeth, 'I'M CALLING THE COPS, ARSEHOLE.'

'Miss, I'm sorry. I'm your taxi to go to Heathrow Airport.'

I turned to look at the grandfather clock in the hallway, my heart still pumping. It was 5 a.m. and time for us to get to Heathrow to fly to America.

'Oh, I'm so sorry. Hang on a minute.' I wasn't even dressed.

Kenneth Bianchi was refusing to see me and had sent me a message telling me not to come. Surely I couldn't fly all that way for nothing? But it was too late for me to stop fate. *The Guardian* was waiting for my article to be emailed over as soon as I had met him. I wondered if I should just go and then possibly tell the paper that the prison was on lockdown. My tenacity as an investigative reporter made me decide that I wouldn't let Bianchi screw me around. If he knew I was out there he would have to see me or it would be a sign of disrespect, and he needed me to ghost his memoir. I was coming. I had the power. I was the writer.

I got dressed and then dressed Charlie in the half-light before we headed out into the ice-cold, foggy village street.

Thirty-two

The American Prisoner

As long as life is the rain, as long as it had a voice, I
will listen and I will try to be real.

Kenneth Bianchi

What was I doing in a plane full of business people that were
flying long haul to America? I hated flying. I felt panic rise
as the plane shook and dipped in the sky. My ears popped as we
rose higher and higher at cloud level and anxiety surged. Here I
was, trapped for the next eight hours on this flying elevator.

After three hours, Charlie woke and grinned at me. It was his
first long plane ride. As we watched TV, laughed and both grew
excited at the adventure of travel, my fear of flying miraculously
lessened. The cabin buzzed and the plane tilted as a shaft of
bright hot sunlight suddenly shone in the window. I pondered
Ken Bianchi in Walla Walla. What did he mean by full contact
and why did he want it? Loneliness I supposed.

The prison authorities had made me sign a form to say if I
was attacked or hurt in any way it was my own responsibility. I
knew he was segregated in the sex offenders' unit but the visit
would take place in the main visiting hall. The air hostess came
round with breakfast and as I ate my bacon and eggs I wondered
what sort of food you get in an American jail. In my letters I had
often asked him what they fed him but he wouldn't answer.

The voice over the tannoy said, 'Cabin crew, prepare for
landing,' and the hostess went round to make sure that everyone's
safety belts were fastened. The plane touched down at JFK airport
and my stomach lurched with anxiety. We had to queue up for

immigration and reclaim our baggage before our next flight to Seattle. We had a four-hour wait, so I introduced Charlie to what an American hamburger tasted like.

We boarded the next flight and Charlie slept. I sat and read *In Cold Blood*. Nearly five hours later, I looked out of the dark window at the lights over Seattle; the city looked golden and opulent from the sky. *What am I doing?* I thought to myself. *You're on a commission from* The Guardian – *you're a top-notch investigative journalist,* a part of me replied, but I didn't believe her.

After landing in Seattle, we made our way to the departure gate for our Alaska Airlines flight to Walla Walla, our final destination. The tiny ten-seater plane was to take us over the rugged mountain range to the small village nestled inside Walla Walla where Bianchi had been locked up for thirty years.

The village was an old Native American stronghold whose name meant 'place of many waters'. It now housed the toughest jail in the whole of America. Walla Walla, I knew, had a segregation unit for America's most violent criminals. I remembered that Bianchi had taken immense trouble to avoid being sent there by the Los Angeles court when he was tried for murdering and torturing those 12 girls.

I was feeling sick with anxiety at the idea of travelling on this tiny plane. I was also apprehensive about meeting this man who in his letters had painted a picture of himself as being kind and considerate. I was meeting him because I wanted to study the nature of evil. I wasn't sure what to believe about him – did he have multiple personality disorder or not? Was he a cold-blooded killer or had he been wrongly imprisoned? Would this visit bring answers to any of my many questions?

I noticed that a man slouched opposite us in the departure area for the shuttle was trying to talk to me. He had a big paunch and his blue shirt hung over his trousers as he gave me the eye.

'Hey, girl, long day travelling?'

'London.'

'Wow, England, that's pretty far. What brings you to Walla Walla?'

'Work, I'm a journalist.' He was irritating me as I was so tired.

'We all know each other in Walla Walla. May I know the name of your interviewee? He must be famous, you coming all that way from England?'

'I can't really say.' *I'm being picked up*, I thought with dismay. I was far too tired to make small talk.

'Here's me!'

He brought out an identity pass.

'Here. This here is me, Lou.' He waved it under my nose. 'See – Lou.'

I glanced at his card and saw that he was a member of the fringe religious group the Seventh Day Adventists.

Lou moved in and helped me with my bags as we boarded the plane. The plane felt as if it was made of cardboard and the inside was tiny. I felt terrified. I strapped myself and Charlie into our small seats and took a deep breath. We veered down the runway and took off, fear shooting through me as my stomach churned and my ears popped. After we were airborne, the two hostesses started to pull out a large crate of bottles.

'Red wine?' said the rough-looking young girl holding a large bottle of newly uncorked red wine. I got the feeling that the cheap wine was being thrown at us to lessen the impact of the turbulence.

'Tea, please?'

'We only have red wine,' she said stonily and slopped some red wine into a plastic beaker. I drank it quickly as I looked around at the other passengers; they were a strange lot – slugging cheap red wine on a plane that was juddering so much it was like a fairground ride. It felt as if I was in a plane with a bunch of yokels who were all staring at me. I lowered my eyes and pretended I was back in London where nobody takes any notice of you.

I sipped at the beaker of vinegary red wine to calm myself. The plane was bucking and dipping badly. It then seemed to drop about 500 feet and I screamed. I put the cup of foul wine to my lips and gulped back as much of it as I could stand to take away my fear. The hostess came round again and offered me a refill, and I held out my cup with a trembling hand.

We landed after about an hour and soon we were in the shack that passed for the Walla Walla entry point. It was now ten o'clock at night in Washington State and I adjusted my watch. We picked up our luggage and a well-dressed old lady milling around nearby asked us where we were going.

'The Hampton Inn.' I was exhausted and held Charlie's hand protectively.

'Listen, I'll give you a lift,' she offered brightly.

In for the Kill

'OK, yes – that would be lovely,' I lied. Unused to such friendliness, I became worried about our safety and didn't want to go off with her in her car down a dark country lane. I was, after all, in a strange American town with some weird old lady who might have been the head of some kind of coven. The locals were all watching this well-spoken, well-dressed blonde English woman with piercing eyes.

She heaved our suitcase into her boot and the three of us drove off in her large white Cadillac with us in the back.

My anxiety levels were sky high.

'This is our hotel over here,' I said, pointing to the first inn that we passed.

'I thought you said the Hampton Inn, dear,' she called from the front seat as she drove at ten miles an hour.

'No, no – it's definitely this one. You can drop us right here,' I said calmly.

I got my suitcase out of her boot and Charlie and I sat in the hotel reception and asked the friendly young receptionist to call us a cab to our real hotel. A yellow minibus drove us through the deserted town; it was as silent as the grave.

'Where is everybody?' I asked the driver.

'Oh, most folks round here go to bed about nine.'

'That's odd, isn't it?'

'Oh, this town's full of nutcases,' said the driver. 'It's run by a bunch of Seventh Day Adventists.'

'That's interesting. How do they affect the community?' I was mentally writing up my piece.

'They don't allow drinking or sex before marriage, they like us all in bed early. In fact, they don't allow anything that is any fun.'

Bianchi had told me in a letter that it had been alleged that he was a member of the Seventh Day Adventists and they had made him a reverend. He said that the story was untrue, but I had my doubts. It seemed to me that 'Reverend' Bianchi would do anything to show what a nice guy he was. Nice was so very important to him, yet the world itself was far from nice.

As we drove along, I looked around at the mountains surrounding us and thought to myself that I was now a prisoner in a small village from which there was no escape for us except by a tiny plane. What if they found out I was visiting a murderer? What had I got myself into?

I was exhausted and anxious by the time we got to the Hampton

The American Prisoner

Inn; Charlie was in good spirits. The night manager showed us to our suite; it was warm and comfortable. As I was settling in, the manager walked in with a bottle of red wine. I put it on the table and went to undress for a shower.

'Aren't they kind, Mum? They've left us fruit and this room is super.'

'Yes, darling, they are kind.'

Charlie ran around the suite, exclaiming in joy about the large double beds and the even larger TV set. He flopped onto his bed and turned on the TV with the remote.

'America is so cool, Mum.'

'Yes, it's cool all right.' I smiled at him. He was happy and life was an adventure for him. I was glad of that.

I closed the bathroom door and stood naked in front of the bathroom mirror. My blonde hair was in a bun and I unpinned it and let it cascade around my bare shoulders. I laid out my bra and knickers in the top drawer, hung up my Chanel suit and laid out my glossy black stilettos and black tights. He hadn't known any classy women in his life, so it would be my first weapon – my classy British reserve. Bianchi had been kind in his correspondence but I would see through any masks on my visit. I wasn't the blonde bimbo he thought I was. I would strip him down and see the monster that lurked within. I showered and slipped into my pyjamas. Then Charlie had a bath.

Charlie and I both watched TV in our pyjamas and ate chocolate biscuits and drank cocoa to chill out and adjust to our new surroundings. At twelve o clock, with aching bones desperate to sleep, I unpacked his Enid Blyton *Five Go to the Lighthouse* and his yellow bucket, red spade and binoculars.

'They may come in handy,' I said as I looked through the binoculars.

'Are you being a detective, Mummy? I thought you'd given that up for journalism?'

I raised my eyebrows and smiled at him. 'Spies never give up, Charlie!'

'Are we on an investigation?'

I tucked him into the bed opposite mine.

'Maybe.'

He snuggled down. 'Great!'

'Come on, close your eyes and off to sleep! There's an exciting day of solving mysteries ahead of us,' I joked.

In for the Kill

I went to my bed tired from the long day. I screwed up my face as I thought of Bianchi in that dark cell and its haunting loneliness. I sat up anxiously. Charlie was sleeping soundly. I lay down again. Outside, the American village was silent and still. I hated the atmosphere of Walla Walla with its secrets; I felt watched.

At three o clock in the morning, I woke in a cold sweat. I wondered where the hell I was. I lay awake in the strange warm bed in the inky blackness and thought of the man in a cell a few miles away that I had travelled thousands of miles to see. I could smell the mountain air and hear the hawks swooping outside. I was going to meet a man I had confided in. Yet I was also carrying out an investigation for an internationally respected broadsheet newspaper. *Who am I?* I thought to myself yet again.

I turned over in bed and watched the branches of a tree make patterns in the silver moonlight on the ceiling. It was no good. I knew I wasn't going to get to sleep. My mind was in turmoil and I wondered about the blood-sucking demon that he told the cops about called Steve, who he had said committed the murders.

I was not only moving closer to Kenneth Bianchi, I was moving closer to what Father Borgia had called *pure evil.*

Thirty-three

The Visiting Room

Babbling Babes, Bandy boisterously bellowing, beautiful but bad. Ballads, Bestowing believable ballyhoo before brunch.

Kenneth Bianchi

It was morning. I must have fallen asleep again, as I woke up with a start as hot American sunshine streamed through the hotel's ground-floor windows. I looked at my watch; it showed it was 7 a.m. I lay on my side and gazed out the window. I had expected to feel excited when I woke but instead I just felt sick with nerves. Was I going to be afraid of meeting Bianchi? Was I going to be repelled by him? I thought of Karen Mandic and the way he had strangled her with so much fury it had cut into her flesh. I saw his victims swim across my vision one after another, most of them bitten and beaten until their bodies were lifeless and bloodless. Outside the window, the water in a turquoise swimming pool was splashing against the sides.

Charlie woke up and rubbed his eyes. 'Wow, Mum, we're in America.'

I grinned at him. Charlie was always able to lift my spirits just by his voice and the sight of his face. 'I know, sweetheart, it's exciting, huh?'

'Mummy, can we go for a swim after breakfast?'

'OK, darling! But let's get half dressed and get some eggs first.' I squinted my eyes at the sun as it streamed into our suite and bounced off the gilt mirrors. My head was pounding unbearably from the glasses of red wine I'd consumed the day before.

255

In for the Kill

We walked down the corridor to the dining room and saw a buffet of hash browns, gravy, freshly made waffles with syrup, hot scrambled egg and crispy bacon alongside an urn full of hot coffee with various tiny creams with hazelnut and French vanilla; it was a good spread of American fare.

We piled our plates high and went back to our suite in a jovial mood. I laid out our food on my bed and was just wondering what to eat first when the phone rang.

'Hello?'

'How are you? How was the flight?' It was Ted Ponticelli, Bianchi's biographer. I had left him a message late last night on his mobile to tell him I was in town and had given him the number of the hotel and my room.

'I'm good, we just woke.'

'All set to meet Bianchi today?'

'Yes, I guess I am.' I felt slightly irritated. What was this, junior journalist week? What did he want?

'Why did you send me an email to say Bianchi didn't want to see me?'

'Aw, never mind that, you're here now. Bianchi gets moody is all. He's not seen anybody bar me in 20 years. He gets suspicious and he's not big on trust. By the by, you know you're not meeting an infamous serial killer today?' he drawled in his East-Coast accent.

I sighed. Not only was he annoying, he was patronising.

'Look, I've met IRA men. I've met gangland assassins. I'm very experienced in crime writing, Mr Petrocelli.' I got his name wrong deliberately.

He ignored the hint. 'Bianchi rang me this morning. He thinks that he will be pleased to see you.'

'Great. I won't get turned away at the gate then.' I sounded cold and sarcastic but I was still nervous that it was on the cards.

'Nah, he'll be OK!'

I put on my white Chanel suit and felt anxious. I slicked on some pale pink lipstick in Baby Doll and sprayed on Chanel No. 5. I decided to arrange the babysitter service even though it was only 8 a.m. and the visit was set from 2 p.m. to 8 p.m., but the manager of the hotel gave me a shock.

'There are no babysitter services in Walla Walla.'

I let my mouth hang slack.

'What do you mean, no babysitters? Are there no teenagers? I need a nanny agency then, please.'

The Visiting Room

'No such thing. People mostly use relatives or don't bother going out. Sorry, I can't help you at all.' He pulled a sympathetic face.

I was going to criticise and then remembered I had never had a babysitter for Charlie as I felt it wasn't fair to leave him with a stranger. But this was America, I was working and I needed and expected childcare. I went back to our room and rang the prison for advice. I spoke to a senior member of security, explained I was a journalist from England and the problem with Charlie. He told me, 'You just come on and bring him along. Everyone brings in their kids – don't you go leaving him with a stranger! There's a wonderful crèche area overseen by all the guards and it's a great place.'

I felt relieved. So, there was a crèche. I looked over at Charlie. This was a better idea. I had always felt bad about planning to leave him in a US hotel room with a stranger. The prison with its vetted security couldn't be safer. I made a decision to take Charlie with me but if the prison was grim I would cancel the interview.

At half past one, I was so nervous I was pacing the floor. I felt like a drink but thought it would be risky. Then I thought again and uncorked the bottle of red wine the hotel had comped me. It was gorgeous but I wasn't used to drinking in the afternoon. I took two mouthfuls then, paranoid it would cloud my judgement, I poured away the rest and brushed my teeth again.

I stared at my face. The room's dehumidifier had been on all night in the bathroom and I looked about ten years older than I usually did. I felt disappointed and questioned myself, *Why are you here? Why really? You like him. No, no, I don't. Yes, you do, go on, admit it, he fascinates you.*

The room telephone rang. It was my taxi and it was Rick, the same good-looking young driver who had brought us to the hotel last night. I felt glad to see a familiar face.

'Sleep OK?'

'No, awful, I think it was the jet lag.'

It was only a mile to the prison, which stood in the middle of the countryside. I noted the address 13th Avenue on a road sign. This was the address I had put on all my letters and now I was looking at a road sign saying it. The grey buildings were surrounded by high barbed wire.

Rick was talkative.

'Lucky man that you're going to see. You look – wow – you look great. Can I say you look hot – can I?'

'It's Chanel,' I replied as I eyed him from the side.

'It's beautiful. Who's the lucky guy you're going to see?'

I smiled at him. 'I'm a writer working on an investigation for a British newspaper,' I said as I fiddled with my bracelet.

'Oh, wow, that's really cool.'

I bit my lower lip, praying he wouldn't ask me again who I was going to visit.

We jumped out and Rick drove off after handing me his card so that I could ring him as soon as we came out and he could take us to a swanky restaurant in town.

I went through sliding glass doors into a sunny large reception area and up to a wide desk; the decor was all monochrome and leather. I felt safe here; it was elegant, clean and professional, like the entrance to a smart American law firm. A young guard behind the desk asked me for my name and typed it into the computer. He had on a black cop-style uniform with a peaked cap and asked me who I was visiting. I gave him the name Bianchi. Without looking up, he said, 'I can't look up by names, Miss, number of the prisoner, please.'

I said, '266961.' I knew it off by heart as I had put it on top of every letter.

He called over a female guard standing nearby and said, 'Her skirt's too short.'

The attractive female guard in a similar uniform told me to come over to one side. As I moved behind the desk, I tugged at my Chanel skirt until it lay on my knee. She looked at the hem and said to the man. 'It's OK – it's long enough.'

I smiled over at him.

The guard instructed me to go and buy a white card from the machine that would allow me to buy goods for that amount to give to the prisoner. I put in ten dollars. She patted me down and ushered us both through a metal detector, where I had to take off my solid gold bracelet and put it in a little white dish with my purse that then sat waiting for us at the end of a conveyor belt after it had been X-rayed.

There was a row of lockers and I was given a small key so that I could put my purse and anything else I was carrying into one of them. The only thing allowed in the room with us was the tiny plastic white card.

Charlie got talking to another boy his age who was sitting waiting and they started running around the room playing make-believe planes.

The Visiting Room

Eventually all the visitors were ushered down a short corridor to the inner waiting room, and we found several other women waiting there, some with more children.

I stared at the smartly dressed kids and the attractive mothers. It was sticky and hot in the room. An older woman with short grey hair and a delicate face, well dressed in a pink dress that looked like she was set for church, spoke to me.

'I noticed that they let you off with having that miniskirt on, dear,' she said with a smile.

I smiled back at her. 'Oh, did they? I had to tug it down.'

'They will make all the exceptions for you, dear, because of who you are.'

'Who I am?' I felt my anxiety levels shoot up.

'Everyone knows who you are and why you're here. You're interviewing Ken for the English newspapers.'

The place began to fill up with more mothers and children until there were about 30 of us. Charlie and the boy who was the same age sat talking. I wondered what Bianchi would be like – unpleasant – obnoxious – would I like him – get on with him – all those hours stretched ahead of me like an appointment for major surgery.

I stared at the woman. Talking to her might ease my anxiety.

'I'm Chris!'

'Phyllis!'

'How do you know who I am?'

'Everybody knows who you are, honey – get real!'

'Really?'

'They've got the red carpet rolled out for you. You can get away with anything.'

I eyed the silver cross that hung around her neck and wondered who she was visiting. I wanted to ask Phyllis a whole host of questions but I felt increasingly claustrophobic and wondered how many doors we would have to pass through to get to the visiting area.

She carried on talking to me. 'When I visit my husband Bob, I tell Ken, "Boy, you get better looking every time I see you." Ken is the dreamiest-looking man that you're ever likely to meet. You're in for a real treat, and he's a real ladies' man.'

I thought to myself, *Well, not quite the ladies' man, lady killer maybe*, but I bit my tongue and glanced at Phyllis's friendly lined face and her flowery summer dress and pink cardigan. She was a really good and kind woman – I could feel it oozing off her. What was her husband Bob in here for? How long had she been coming here and known Ken? I wanted to ask her but felt afraid of her answer. She thought Ken was dreamy. Did she have any idea of what he had done or didn't she mind?

I ran out of time to ask her any questions, as the guards came in and we were all told to line up to get ready to go in. We were all led across a muddy yard and followed a uniformed guard with peak cap, handcuffs, chains and a wooden stick that he ran along the bars to make a noise. We went down long, wide white corridors that resembled those in a hospital. We all followed the guard into a massive hall that seemed like a picnic area in a holiday camp done out in dark wood and light brown walls. It was packed with about 20 armed guards milling around the 20 or so tables.

Charlie tugged at my sleeve. 'Wow, look at them.'

I leaned down to him. 'Yeah, wow.'

I could see a bright, well-displayed *Jungle Book* collage in the large cordoned-off play area/crèche for children on the far side. The guards strolled around and everybody was mucking in to look after the kids, who were running around nosily and watching the large TV set playing the Disney Channel non-stop. It was nothing like the grim poverty of English prisons; it was pleasant. I left Charlie with the boy he had made friends with, and the computer games, and told him if he needed me to tell one of the guards to come and fetch me. He was knee-deep in play on the Wii with the other boy, so I left him and walked over to the senior guard.

'You know who I'm seeing today?'

'Yes, I sure do. We have an extra five guards on, just for you and him.' He grinned at me.

I stared at him, unable to think of a reply, then managed to get out, 'Is that needed?'

'No way. Kenneth Bianchi is pretty well respected here. He's not going to do anything. He's our resident legal eagle. You're a million times safer here than you are walking down the street, lady.'

I smiled at him. I was being treated well. They knew *The Guardian* was a well-respected broadsheet and he assured me he would keep a close eye on my son for me.

I saw two uniformed guards sitting at a desk in the front of the hall. A man with a huge ledger asked me to sign in and I wrote in

The Visiting Room

Bianchi's name as the prisoner I had come to visit. He looked back at me sternly and I knew he knew who Bianchi was.

'Table 12 – the prisoner sits facing us. You can sit anywhere,' he said gruffly.

I searched for table 12; it was one back from the guards' table. I assumed they had picked this one as he was their most notorious prisoner and they wanted to watch his every move. I sat down in the chair right next to his rather than opposite, I felt that there was no point coming all this way without finding out who he really was – if that was at all possible. I was so curious to find out how many fragments of ego or personalities there would be on display here today. I didn't know what to expect. No situation in life had prepared me for this moment apart from meeting the Monster of the Moors all alone in his cell for so many hours. The two infamous serial killers were not alike. Kenneth Bianchi was a puzzle wrapped in a quandary. Was there a monster concealed within him or was it something pure evil that had used his body?

We were surrounded by other tables, like diners in a busy restaurant. The tables were wooden topped. The term Hillside Strangler went around my head. I wished the voice would turn off or shut up but it would not. My palms were sweaty. I started to feel spaced out, surreal and very, very anxious.

Suddenly the varnished wooden door in the corner opened. I held my breath. Was Kenneth Bianchi going to enter the room? Things I had said in my letters went round and round my head. My demands to see the invisible Steve seemed ridiculous now. About five prisoners along with another ten guards filed into the room, the men were wearing matching beige suits. I breathed out.

A good-looking prisoner with grey hair walked up in front of me like a film star strutting onto a yacht in sparkling white gym shoes. He stood in front of me, nodding his head and smiling, and I remember thinking that he looked like Robert De Niro. I stared back at him and recognised him from the black-and-white court videos I had watched on YouTube. Apart from his hair colour, his appearance hadn't changed one bit. It was uncanny. I also felt very uncomfortable. He looked too much like he did when he was younger and an active serial killer. It brought all his crimes to the centre of my mind along with the question *What are you doing here with the Hillside Strangler?* I answered myself in my head, *You're a journalist.*

As I stared at the tall, looming figure that was Kenneth Bianchi, he continued to stand in front of me as if waiting for me to get over the shock of seeing him in the flesh for the first time. He was handsome and had a chiselled face, dark eyes over a mouth hidden by a thick moustache. I noted that he was going to be the confident one. He was tall and looked as if he had been working out; his chest was strong looking and his arms looked hefty. His hands protruded out of the prison garb – a beige shirt and pants that made him look like he was on safari.

I stood up. I had no idea what to do, so I let him lead. He reached for me with his hands and pulled me close to him in a hug. It was a strong hug and I felt his chest press up against me tightly. He smelt of pine and wood chippings and a deeper sniff brought the scent of olive oil soap from his neck that was beside my nose. He spoke into my ear quietly.

'Hey, how are you? Was your flight OK, Chris?'

'Yes, thanks!'

I felt very embarrassed by his closeness and the feel of his hot breath in my ear. He was incredibly male and it oozed out of him.

'I'm really glad you're finally here!'

'Great, thank you.' I pulled away and we sat down. I still felt embarrassed.

He had pulled me so tightly to his chest I could still feel the massive heat of his body clinging onto mine. But I was glad he was going to be informal with me.

He started in a lazy New York drawl. 'Did you recognise me at all, Chris?'

I was going to ask, *What from, the courtroom dramas I'd been watching on YouTube?* He seemed to have forgotten what he was doing in prison or that he was in prison at all, and instead he seemed to be assuming the role of a film star I was interviewing in a top Los Angeles nightspot.

'You haven't changed since your arrest.'

He spoke softly and leaned forward. 'Don't you ever be embarrassed by anything you've ever written to me in your letters. Don't you go feeling you've made an idiot of yourself.' He smiled coolly.

It was too much. He was really trying to make me squirm. I wanted to say, *Oh, my flirting you mean? Don't worry, it wasn't real.*

'Oh, I'm not one bit embarrassed by my words!' I said.

'Great.'

I noticed that his smile looked a little frozen.

The Visiting Room

'Did you recognise me from the photograph I sent you last year?' I asked.

'Yeah, of course I did. But you had long blonde hair in that picture, now it's shorter.' I was again reminded of De Niro with his softly spoken American accent. I had expected him to be shy but he smiled at me disarmingly and seemed over-confident, like a talk-show host. His short hair was grey, his skin olive-toned and smooth. His shirt had his number on the back of it: 266961 sewed onto a white patch.

'I'm sorry, I should have said I'd cut my hair.'

'No, no, that's OK. It looks great.'

'Thanks.'

'Look at you sitting so close to me, Chris.'

'Pardon?'

He indicated that we were inches apart with our knees knocking under the table.

'Oh! Yes!' I felt tired. What did he mean?

'All this shit that I hate women, Chris, when I love women. You're so close to me and am I a monster?'

It was odd. Why did he kill 12 of them so cruelly if he loved them so much? Loved killing them more like. I opened my mouth to say something then realised if I challenged him so early on he would close up.

I tried to keep my composure but now he had mentioned his feelings about women, I was all of a sudden thinking about the Nazis. I started to think about the heinous physical experiments the Nazis had done on the Jews and how Bianchi, who had carried out similar forms of torture on women, looked like one of the actors in the film *The Boys from Brazil*, Gregory Peck even.

'No, you're not a monster,' I heard myself say, but it felt like my lips had gone numb, I was so anxious.

'Do you feel uncomfortable at all sitting so close to me, Chris?'

I hadn't but now he had said it I was starting to feel extremely weird. I could sense something but I didn't know what it was and it made me feel afraid.

'People call you a monster, though, evil, inhuman.'

'All lies, Chris. You don't believe the lies now, do you? I invited you here because you believed me.'

'I know.'

I met his eyes; they looked clear and impassive. Yet almost as if I was above a clear, calm sea I could also sense the large, sharp blade of a shark looming underneath the surface.

'Would you like to get yourself a drink? Over there we have the machines.'

Something told me that he had decided that I was an idiot. He gestured to a long row of huge vending machines along the far side of the room with his powerful arms. I noticed that his pale hands were incredibly well shaped, like a priest in an oil painting. They didn't seem like hands that had been used to torture and kill; they oozed spirituality, as if he had been praying non-stop in his cell.

'No thanks, but would you like a drink?' I asked, picking up the white card in my hot fingers.

'No, I'm fine, thanks.' He smiled a big, wide grin and his teeth looked incredibly white and even. He cocked his head to one side and I noticed that his neck had scarring on it. I remembered Beulah Stofer, a witness to Lauren Wagner's abduction, claiming that one of the killers was dressed in a long leather coat and had acne scars.

'You know, Chris, I'd like to be friends first before anything else happens between us.'

'Oh.' I could barely think of a rejoinder. What *could* happen? 'Me too.'

'If you can't be friends first in any relationship, then when it goes further it crumbles to shit. That's what I've found anyway.'

I felt like laughing. He truly didn't seem to register that he was in prison.

I looked around the room and saw the woman I'd spoken to in the waiting room sitting nearby clutching the hand of her husband, Bob.

'What's that man with the woman here for?'

'Only robbery,' he said with a guarded smile, his brown eyes watching me, enjoying something about me.

'Oh, is that all?' I replied.

'Yes, it's hardly crime of the century, is it, Chris? Hey, Chris, just think of this, I've one robber on one side and I've one on the other. Hey, who does that make me?' He laughed.

I became very uncomfortable. I had a cold sensation of paranoia filling me up like water filling a jug. I felt that I wanted to leave immediately and I struggled to suppress it. I looked at him and thought this would make me feel worse but suddenly he seemed to be someone else entirely. His eyes became soft and feminine and looked baby-blue. I relaxed and wondered what had been wrong with me. I blinked. I could have sworn his eyes were brown or dark. It must have been the light, however, as now they were fairytale blue and looking at me with deep concern.

'You OK?'

'Yes, I'm fine.'

'Are you sure you're OK, Chris? You don't seem as if you're enjoying yourself with me.'

'I'm just jet lagged is all. It was a long old flight.'

He smiled. 'It would be different now if we had a coupla drinks in front of us, wouldn't it, Chris? We could completely relax with each other, instead of both of us feeling stressed. You know, you know what it would be like? We'd relax, laugh, maybe if we were in a bar, shoot some pool and then what?' He smiled at me, his hands relaxed on the table in front of him, cool as a cucumber.

I bit my lip. I didn't know how safe I would feel with him in a bar, though right at this moment I would have loved to have a drink.

I was just starting to relax a little, when . . .

'You know, Chris, that fucking cunt who you spoke with, who wrote that fucking bullshit book about me, Chris Berry-Dee? I want to take him down, know what I mean, Chris? Down, down. Know what I mean? Down, right down.' He leaned forward and was staring at me very, very angrily. He was watching me closely to see if I registered fear or rushed to the defence of Dee.

Not being the loyal type, I couldn't have cared less what he was saying about Dee.

'I barely know him!' I said.

Bianchi was watching me like a hawk. I was suddenly angry. He had gone on about Dee in his letters and he knew I didn't know him very well, but now he was making it clear that he thought I was lying. Not only that, he was talking street talk, nodding his head and being the tough guy, and presumably I was supposed to be afraid. I felt annoyed.

'Did you threaten him when he was with you? Did he shit himself?' I asked sarcastically.

'Yes, Chris, I threatened him.' He put his head on one side again and looked me in the eye. I noticed his eyes seemed darker again. 'And, yes, he did shit himself.'

I looked down at the desk and let my sweaty fingers play with each other. 'What did you say to make him afraid?'

We held each other's gaze for a whole minute without speaking.

'I told the fucking cunt that I'd smash his skull in.' He leaned back in his chair and stared at me hard.

'That's what he said you'd said.'

It was no good. I was afraid. My breath felt shallow. I wished I wasn't sitting in an American prison; I wished I was at home in England watching a DVD. Bianchi was speaking in a quiet but menacing voice as if I was guilty of something.

'I don't like people who write lies about me, Chris. Dee wrote that I confessed to murder to him. I have stated my innocence since my arrest. You understand me? Apart from when they hypnotised me after showing me the files day after day until I thought I had done it. They told me I was a multiple, but I am not, Chris. It was a set-up to get someone for the Hillside atrocities.'

'I thought you said you weren't violent?'

'Not to a string of innocent girls, but to a man that acts like Dee – hell, yes I can be.' He sat with his hands folded in front of him on the table.

But then his piercing eyes seemed to get lighter again and my fear of his anger diminished a little. His eyes seemed to go from dark to light; they were like Catherine wheels, silver and spinning, throwing off tiny, hot sparks of fire.

'So! Now! How are you?' He leaned forward on his elbows and was smiling again.

'Good.' But I was lying.

'You look damn good.'

'I'm tired – I don't look great. I . . . often . . . look good, just not today.'

'What?'

'I often look good but not today!' I was babbling due to the strain of the conversation.

He laughed. 'You do now, Chris, just relax.'

Silence fell. I looked at the table and noticed my expensive gold bracelet was lying there, as they had made me take it off as I went through the metal detector.

'Will you help me put my bracelet back on?' I realised that he would have to touch me as he did it. I knew he wouldn't have touched a woman in years, decades maybe. Our bare skin would touch bare skin and then maybe he would like me and open up.

He picked up the heavy gold chain. I had bought it for two thousand pounds in an exclusive jeweller's back when I had money. I knew he would feel the value of the gold and treat me accordingly.

He tried to put it around my wrist and fumbled with my arm for a while. It was odd to feel his touch after corresponding for so long in letters. His perfectly shaped fingers with their clean pink nails shook as he fastened the clasp securely. I noted that he was now on the back foot. He didn't look up, which gave it away.

Bracelet fastened, I pulled my arm away. He looked at me as if we had just done something really intimate. His eyes were thick with need and they were back to baby-blue. I felt smug.

'Talking of beautiful women, you remind me of that British actress, Chris.'

'Some people used to say I looked like Michelle Pfeiffer, not now I'm so old! Mind you, so's she!'

'No, you're a Kate Winslet, you're so well rounded.'

'Have you seen her on TV?'

'I have my own little TV in my cell and I watch all of her films. I like her British accent. You're one of the few Limey woman I've ever met, Chris.'

I laughed. 'Limey!'

He grinned. 'You've called me a Yank enough times.'

I blushed and looked away.

'I really like Kate,' he went on. 'It's those meandering curves.' He smiled at me slowly and looked at my figure.

'I don't. God, she's so British. I like Angelina Jolie.'

'Oh no, too American. I'm into Limey broads – Winslet, I also like Keira Knightley.'

I laughed. 'Really?'

'No, not really.' His voice was soft and he was gazing at me.

My mouth twisted as I tried to not smile; he had just taken all the power back and I was a geeky, shy schoolgirl and he the older boy. He was a very charismatic and good-looking man, and he both knew it and wielded it. I mustn't be flattered by him or he would treat me like trash.

I had flown thousands of miles to see the real Bianchi. I knew it wouldn't be easy; it was like being on a safari and waiting to see the dangerous lion or the rampaging elephant, keeping quiet in the jeep and hiding my binoculars.

The friendly woman, Phyllis, whom I had spoken to in the waiting room before I came in, smiled at me. She was still holding hands with her husband and had been gazing into his eyes. They looked like they were in love. Bianchi and I watched them both carefully for a while and neither of us spoke. He was still hardened to me, I could tell.

I looked into Bianchi's eyes. Was he dying to hold hands with me, I wondered, just to touch a person after all those decades in a cement box all alone, deprived of human closeness? Was he trying to smell me and to breathe me in? He wouldn't stop staring at me and it was hard for me to study him because when I did I was met by a pair of almond-shaped blue eyes staring back at me intently.

The room was crowded. The guards paced around and at one point one of them aggressively told me to put my black stilettos 'Back on your feet, please.'

I went barefoot to get us cold water from the drinking fountain in two white plastic cups, then remembered as I returned and quickly stuffed my hot feet back into my Jimmy Choos.

I heard Bianchi's stomach rumbling.

'What's the food like in here?'

'It's OK. I follow a kosher diet. It's healthier.' He rubbed at his arms that were pale and hairless.

'I don't like sausages myself much either,' I lied.

'Well, that's a very good thing, Chris. You don't smoke either, do you?'

'Never have,' I lied again. 'Do you work out?'

'Not now, I used to. Too many gang-bangers in the gym now. They holler to each other and it gets on my nerves – *hey you yo, hey buddy yo* – it's just so annoying! The level of intelligence of the men isn't that high in prison and I don't want it rubbed in by hearing that gang bullshit. All you can do in there is run around in a circle anyway; they took the weight machines. I do about a hundred sit-ups and press-ups in my cell each day after breakfast. I don't get out to the exercise yard, haven't been out there for over 15 years.'

'Why not?'

'The gangs out there, Chris, all doing the same thing – playing ball and shouting. I can't stand it, the noise is deafening. I stay in my cell for about 22 hours a day most days. Not that sitting in my cell isn't like sitting in Grand Central Station with the men banging on the doors, the shouting, and the needy men screaming in their cells. I lie on my bed with the pillow over my ears and pray for some peace. It goes on day after day, year after year, but I just take it – nothing else I can do. The cement walls start to talk to me some days but I count my blessings, Chris. I could be on the street, at least I'm warm. I could be dead, at least I'm alive.'

'I'd rather be dead than suffer that.' I put my elbow on the table and leant my chin on my hand. 'Aren't you bored stuck in a tiny cell all day on your own?'

'Of course I get bored, Chris. I read when it goes quiet. I'm reading *The Road*, which is good. I read a lot of Clive Cussler – do you read him?'

'I've never heard of Cussler.'

'What do you read, Chris?'

'D.H. Lawrence, Graham Greene, Virginia Woolf. I love the Brontës.'

'You're so English! I've never heard of Graham Greene, is he good?'

'Yes, he's good,' I laughed. 'I can't believe you've never even heard of Greene, especially as you're a Catholic.'

'Sorry, Chris. I stick to Boy's Own stuff. Cussler is a boys' thing, right! I think that's it. I read a lot of his books then I do my legal stuff, then I sleep. I feel real weird about life at the moment. It sure as hell sucks.'

'Well, it would do, being in prison. You can't expect it to feel good.'

'I get lonely and I feel the alienation, but I count my blessings, Chris. If I look hard enough in each day, I can see at least one blessing. I have joy. I share that with you in my letters.'

'I know. Thank you.' I felt embarrassed, *No, he didn't – what joy?*

'I sent some more of my new memoir to you two weeks ago. Did you get it?'

'I got the first few chapters before I left.'

'I've sent up to chapter five – get that?'

'No.'

'But you read the first four chapters? Was I – am I a good writer?'

Bianchi's writing had been sensual and lush as velvet. He had written with a shocking intensity and power. He wrote with the passion of Shelley but I wasn't very good at giving praise.

'I – well – after I read it I stopped liking Greene and you became my favourite.'

'What?'

'You – you're my favourite writer.'

He stared at the air in front of him and looked puzzled. I didn't know what to say but I knew I hadn't said it right.

I changed the subject.

'Do you want me to get you a drink or maybe food from the machines? Do you want a burger? Ted said he bought you a burger when he last came to see you and you said it was the first burger you'd had in decades. He said you wolfed it down.'

He looked at me blankly. He was so private. I could feel the high brick walls he had erected.

The prisoners weren't allowed to move out of their seats once they were sitting, unless it was to approach the guards' table. There were red lines painted all over the floor that the convicts weren't allowed outside of.

'I don't want food, thanks, Chris. You can get me a cold drink. Just make it whatever,' he said. 'I'm not allowed to cross the red line in front of the machines.'

There was a thick red line painted on the floor in front of the machines to stop the convicts getting close to the ten heavy, clanking machines that lined up along one wall of the hall.

'Oh, sorry, of course. I'll get us drinks. Do you want tea or coffee? I'll go to the hot machine.' I pointed to the large machine at the end of the hall.

'Chris, just please get me the water. I hate the machines, I know the machines, I clean them every day – it is my job for ten cents an hour. They let me out of my cell for an hour each day to clean those goddamn machines. I'm in my cell for 22 hours a day, I get breakfast for 20 minutes and lunch for 20 and then 20 for dinner and an hour to clean the machines.'

'OK.'

I browsed the drinks in the drinks machine, squatting down and looking through the clear glass. As I did so, I noticed that there was root beer in brown bottles. I stood up and looked back at Bianchi; he sat facing the guards' desk. I remembered that he had raped the dancer Lissa Kastin with a root-beer bottle before strangling her. I wanted to see what his reaction would be to seeing a matching bottle in the fingers of an attractive blonde who could have been her. Maybe that would startle him enough to let me catch a glimpse of the real Bianchi – a stroll down memory lane.

I came back to the table and casually put the root-beer bottle down in front of him. I moved it an inch or two to see how he would react.

His watchful blue eyes followed it, then looked at me impassively. Nothing.

He stared at me coolly. Then said, 'I don't much like root beer, but I'll drink it.' He stood up. 'I'll go and check at the guards' desk, Chris, and see what I can find for us to play with.' Bianchi shot me a hard look then stood up and swaggered over to the guards' table as if he was aware of his body, like a body builder.

As I sat waiting, I picked up his glasses, which he had left on the table and not worn the whole time we were together. They were silver rimmed. I ran my fingers over their edges; they were hard and cold like steel wire. He came back with a chess set. I quickly put the glasses down and noticed a flicker of a smile cross his face. He had noticed me fondling his glasses. I was trying to pick up his energy but I had picked up nothing. Mr Brick Walls.

'You play chess, Minerva?'

'I used to play with my brother as a kid. I'm OK, I'm clued-up.'

I suddenly realised that I was in an Ingmar Bergman situation: *Playing chess with Death*, I thought as I picked up one of the pieces.

He smiled again as he filled the board with large ivory and ebony chess pieces.

I leaned over, picked up his root-beer bottle and took a swig out of it. I banged it down on the table and stared at him hard.

'Yuk, that tastes like bleach.'

I suddenly remembered he had injected one of his victims with bleach. The word hung in the air between us. He leaned over to take the bottle and covered my hand with his. Not a flicker of a reaction. I let him have the drink and moved my hand from under his.

'Have it all, root beer tastes like medication.'

'You've never tasted root beer before?'

'No, it's an American thing, isn't it?'

His kneecap moved away from mine underneath the table.

'Don't tell me that you're a root-beer virgin, Minerva?' He swigged from the bottle like he was in a bar room and it was real ale.

'I've never had root beer before and I won't ever again.'

'But now you're no longer a virgin,' he grinned.

'I've had lovers, never been in love.'

'I've only truly loved women I knew back east – East-Coast women. Have you heard of a girl called Donna Duranso?'

271

'No.'

'I loved Donna and a girl called Janice and my wife Brenda Beck. Here, I lived with a girl, Kelli. I stayed with her for my baby. I fooled around on the side, hoping to meet "the one". Kelli wanted me to move out, so she got her way when I got arrested. She then went and slept with cops who were working on my case, Chris, and my social worker, which I think prejudiced my case. Not to mention she came in my cell and permed my hair – you know, with that bullshit perm you can see in shots of me? And she did that, Chris, as the cops told her that they wanted to see me with curls, as the witnesses had seen a man with curly hair trying to abduct a girl around the time of the Hillside Strangler. I never wore my hair in curls! Now what would you call that, Chris?'

He had no evidence for what he was saying but I decided to go along with it. 'Sneaky?'

'Yes, she was really sneaky. Yes, that's right. And I never got to see my son ever again. That cold bitch with ice flowing though her veins to a cold stone heart robbed me of my own fucking son.'

'I read she was upset about Veronica Compton, the woman who did that fake murder.'

'Oh no, Chris, she walked away from me a long time before that fruit and nut Compton came on the scene. Let me tell you about her, OK, Chris? Compton was a hooker, coke-head and housewife, and she met me once and it was through a glass screen. All that bullshit, Chris, about how I gave her my semen – sorry to sound crude – gave her my semen – how could I when there was a guard there and a glass screen? Yet year after year, whenever my parole comes up, she is brought up and it screws up my chances and keeps me in the joint. I fucking hate Compton, I can tell you.'

'She was a real looker, though – wow.'

'Beauty is only skin deep, Chris. I've turned down some real beauties in my time, as I think they can be trouble. I had a model in tears once in the reception of the visitors' room. She was just amazing looking, tall as hell, long blonde hair, great long legs, she visited me and then they said, no, you can't see him again, and she was on her knees in the foyer, screaming and crying.'

'Weird.'

'Yeah – that's not love!'

'What I don't understand is that when the cops in Bellingham came to arrest you, you denied you knew Karen Mandic, yet she worked in the store where you were a security guard. She was a real looker and how come you didn't notice this Amazonian princess?'

'There were loads of women in the store that looked hot, Chris. Ones that came into the store and ones that worked there. I knew Karen to say good morning to, that was it.'

'You don't remember asking her to house sit for you at the house on Bayside where she ended up strangled in the basement?'

'No, I did not ask her to house sit.'

He looked upset that I had started to interrogate him, so I changed the subject.

'What happened to the woman you married?'

'Shirlee? That was a bit of a pretence, Chris. It wasn't anything romantic or sensual at all, it was to help her with money. She was a pen pal and very poor. Many reporters found out she was writing to me. She asked me to marry her so that she could sell her story to them. I said, OK, then you can give them an interview and feed yourself. I haven't spoken to her since her mother died about 20 years ago. I don't bother with people on the outside – pen pals or otherwise. When I get a letter from a person who tells me they're a psychology student or interested in my case, or that they like me or some shit, I go to my toilet and I shred it into bits.'

'You replied to me.'

'I know – I don't know why. I broke all my own rules.'

'Why?'

'Who knows! Hey, Minerva, don't make me wish I hadn't.'

I was coming to realise that Bianchi only made me uncomfortable when his eyes went dark. Watching them change was like watching black ink being dripped into blue water. I stared back at him coolly. I was more dominant than the blue-eyed boy. But the dark-eyed one had me on the back foot.

A friendly-looking guard asked loudly if anyone wanted to leave. I had another glance at Bianchi. I could still feel the dark-eyed one watching me. I couldn't work out who he actually was; he was like a human maze.

I felt like a top psychiatrist who had just come across the patient of their dreams. I wanted to pin him down like one of Hugh's butterflies and put him in a glass case to keep him and observe him now and again, whenever I felt like it. I wanted to own him, like a collector with an unusual specimen. The dangerous, lesser-spotted Morpho.

'You want to go now, Minerva?' he sounded sarcastic. 'Had enough of me yet?'

'No – no, not at all. I'll stay.'

I watched his hands as he played chess. It was hard to believe he had killed.

When I looked up again he was staring at me. 'What's wrong, Minerva?' he asked.

'Nothing. I was thinking about how lovely the poetry is that you send to me.'

'It comes through me, I don't write it. Sorry,' he smiled.

'Who's your very favourite writer?'

'Well,' he said after some thought. 'I do like my Clive Cussler and I like Edgar Allan Poe.'

I felt uncomfortable. Ted Bundy had liked Poe.

'You look uncomfortable, Chris.'

'No, I'm not. I'm fine.'

'Chris, you're constantly trying to pin me down.' He started to laugh.

'I think that you're very into dark things, is all I was thinking.'

'Oh, Chris, no, I'm not. It makes me sad that you hunt that down in me constantly. You track down cops that don't even know me, like that senile cop who arrested me, Salerno. Chris, you won't ever find evil in me; it just isn't there.' His baby blues looked at me with sincerity. I was beginning to hate the blue-eyed version of him; it was like wading through a sugary marshmallow.

'Remember I asked you if you were ever into Satanism?'

'And I answered that honestly, Chris. It's my opinion that that Satan worshipping is sick.'

'I read in a book that you have a tattoo.'

He slowly rolled up his sleeve and revealed his pale left arm. He looked at me while he did so, as if he was hoping I would be aroused by the sight of his bare flesh and he was doing a slow striptease.

'Want to feel it?'

'OK.'

I ran my forefinger over his tattoo and felt his smooth, baby-like skin.

I looked up and he was grinning at me.

'That tickles me, Minerva.'

The faded tattoo said 'Satan's own'. He rolled his sleeve back down.

The Visiting Room

'Is Satan real, do you think?'

'The Devil is very real, Chris. I find him in Revelations. I'll send you some references.'

'Why mark yourself with a tattoo that says you're owned by Satan?'

'Chris, come on, I was in a motorcycle club.'

'I know, I read that when you were in this group of Hell's Angels they were all afraid of you and they called you Flash. You liked to fight and drive your bike too fast.'

'No, I was a pussy.' He looked like he was trying not to laugh.

I had seen pencil sketches Bianchi had drawn of demons and some were copies of the Doré illustrations of the Devil sitting in Hell, fallen from Heaven. A drawing of the four Horsemen of the Apocalypse had been for sale on a website with his name on it.

'Ralph Allison, the psychiatrist I spoke to who'd interviewed you, said that Steve is in fact your imaginary childhood friend. And the High Church says that invisible friends are demons.'

He got out his handkerchief and wiped his brow. 'Allison's a fucking idiot.' He looked at me, irritated. 'You and he really think I house a demon?'

'I don't know.' I moved my black rook to meet his white queen.

'You and that quack are crazy, Minerva.'

'Sorry.'

He stared at the chess board in front of us.

'You had an imaginary friend as a boy. It's written in your medical notes that at age seven you had an invisible friend who was bigger than you.'

He moved his white queen sideways five spaces to get away from me.

'Chris, all little kids have little invisible friends.' His cheek began to twitch. I moved my dark knight forward to chase his queen.

'Little kids get bigger and their little imaginary friends grow too.'

He pursed his lips, took a sip of root beer from the condensation-covered bottle and took my knight with his other white bishop, letting out a hoot of derision as he banged the bottle down.

'The hypnosis made me say all the stuff about Steve, Chris. Allison is a nut-bag.' He glanced at me and I saw a fire flare in his eyes – a hot silver flame that landed on my cheek and burnt me.

'Steve wasn't a demon, Chris. He wasn't real. It was an aberration brought on by the hypnosis.'

'How would you know?'

'Why would Steve be a demon?'

'All those evil things he said to the cops – *I killed the blonde cunt and the brunette cunt and that one fucks really badly.*' I stopped. I could feel him thinking.

'Those women who died had nothing to do with me.'

He looked at me steadily and a vein pulsed in his cheek.

'I listened to those tapes of me confessing, Chris, and I couldn't believe it. The hypnosis produced a chicken clucking on a stage. I was confessing to terrible crimes of an evil monster who committed horrendous murders. Those bent cops used to say, "What colour is the inside of the murder victim's car?" and push me over a photo of Cindy Hudspeth's car and I could see it was brown. I'd say, "Brown," and they'd say, "Yes, it was brown. You must have raped her, strangled her and then pushed her over the cliff in her car while she was in the back," but I did not kill Cindy Hudspeth, Chris.'

'You and Angelo gassed a girl.'

'I did not gas a girl. I told the cops what they forced me to confess to from the files they made me read day in, day out. No one saw me with Angelo Buono at the time of the Hillside murders.'

'Did you and he ever speak after you were both sent to prison?'

'I sent Ange a card just before he died in prison, Chris. It was a normal Hallmark greetings card. I wrote on it, "Hey there, Ange, I'm really sorry for everything!" Just that, you know, and I signed it, "No hard feelings – your cousin". I got him put into prison for life by what I said. But he didn't reply. I guess Hallmark didn't have the right card for sorry I got you put into the joint for the rest of your life.' He laughed.

'Angelo thought you were crazy.'

'I told you, Chris, I was a chicken clucking on a stage, like in a fairground sideshow.' He moved his king one square sideways. 'I confessed to things I'd read in the police reports. I was hypnotised into pretending to be the world's worst serial killer, Chris. I'm just not what the world thinks but I live with that in this place, day after day.'

'It must be hard.'

I moved my king and he took it with his rook.

'Checkmate, Minerva, you lose!'

'OK, I lose,' I admitted.

'Chris, could you get me a glass of water, please? My lips are dry as a bone.'

I stood up. He was tired. So was I. I used the card that I had bought at reception to buy myself another drink. I was confused about how I was feeling about Bianchi. I wanted to understand him. I returned to the table with a paper cup of steaming hot chocolate and some water for him.

'Hungry now? I'll get us something to eat. Want some popcorn?'

'Nothing really, thank you. I don't like eating in front of a woman. My manners from living in here are that of a pig.'

'Who cares?'

'I'm not in the mood for food.'

'OK.'

I felt a bit rejected by him. I stood up and let my fingers tail all along his back as I went past him. He looked around as I touched him and met my eyes, and I could see loneliness lodged in them. *Don't stroke the wild animals unless they let you*, I thought to myself.

I got some salted butter popcorn from the machines, heated it up in their microwave and put it in three white plastic bowls. I also got a tuna sandwich and a carton of juice. I brought two bowls of popcorn over to the table and put one down in front of him and the other for me. I forgot my shoes and sauntered over to the crèche area in bare feet and gave the other bowl to Charlie as well as the sandwich and drink. He was happily playing the Wii with one of the guards and the little boy from reception.

'We'll be out of here soon, baby.'

'Oh please, Mum, just let me have one more round of tennis. I'm beating Ethan!'

I ruffled his hair and stood up. The kind-looking guard in charge was with him and I smiled gratefully at him. How different this was from intimidating and unfriendly English prisons.

I went to the toilet at the left side of the large hall. Someone was in there, so I stood and looked over at Bianchi as I waited. He leaned over the table and was stuffing popcorn into his mouth from his half-clenched fists and then the bowl got picked up and licked. It was shocking, he looked like a lion feeding, snarling and licking the bowl.

The toilet was large and clean. I looked at myself in the small mirror. My face looked flushed and hot. *I have a strong reaction to him and I'm not sure why,* I thought to myself. *I sense the child deep within him. I want to reach it. Why? It's odd.* I sat and read aloud a metal plaque on the door that said 'Please – after using the bathroom – call a guard.'

I came out and spotted a prison officer lounging nearby and called him over to check I was OK.

'Permission to search,' asked the tall, dark-haired guard. He made me open my mouth and searched me all down my body.

'Don't touch the prisoner,' he said gruffly.

'What do you mean?'

'You touched his back as you went to the machines.'

'Did I?'

'Yes, you did. You ran your hand along his back.'

'I don't remember touching him.'

'Do it again, ma'am, and we'll immediately terminate the visit. No touching the prisoner, whatsoever, except for hand holding.'

I felt irritated. They acted like they owned him. I had flown thousands of miles for this. I owned this chameleon for the hours I was here. I had paid the entrance fee.

I made my way back through the many tables where families were playing cards, eating and drinking and chatting to join Bianchi, who was still studying the chess board.

He started to speak as soon as I sat down. 'I had an attic in my old home, I mean my mother's home, Chris, and it's full of novels I've written. I'm thinking of giving the lot to you so you can find a publisher for me.'

'What kind of novels are they?'

'My novels are called "Miss Cabala", "The Naked Dawn", "In Such a Twilight Hour of Breath", "Daunted" and "The Devil's Nose".'

He had told me he wasn't interested in the occult yet they sounded like a reading list for Edgar Allan Poe.

'In one of them, I wrote about a nun who had a very full, sensual sex life even though she lived in a cell.'

I held my breath. He leaned forward and spoke quietly.

'She had the power to come out of her body, Chris. She could just fly out into the night. Imagine that!' He raised his hand like a bird flying, and I saw beads of sweat glistening on his neck. 'She could visit anyone she wanted, in the dark of the night, Chris, even though she was locked in a cell. Do you believe that that's possible? Projection, I mean?'

The Visiting Room

My face coloured up. His eyes locked onto mine, dark as tea.

'No cell could ever hold her. Imagine having that kind of power.' He seemed to be smirking.

I had felt him in my house, watching me bathe, watching me cook, watching me in my private space. I didn't want this confirmed or I would freak out, so I decided to bring up Dee.

'Dee said you could come out of your cell. He said you've got paranormal powers to project yourself out of your cell and into the home or mind of anyone you wanted.'

'He's a fucking cunt. You listen to him?'

'No.'

'You fucking do listen to him – you've just now said what he said as if he's sitting here with me.'

'Sorry.'

'You listen to him, Chris, and forget me if you do – OK?'

'OK.'

'I'm angry you've said that. '

'I barely know him.'

'What?'

'I barely know the guy! I rang him because of you – Jesus.'

Our eyes held each other's. In his, I could see that he was powerful. He was also odd, somehow awake on another level of consciousness. I thought of the movie *Scanners*. It was like he was able to read minds, like one of the scanners, or gifted in some other way like that. His mind was better than others somehow, but in a really spooky way. What kind of shit had I waded knee-deep into, in my search for supernatural evil? Had I really wanted to find it? Was it a lark? Something to do in life, a *raison d'être*, a demon to kill my mother, who no longer bothered me as I had grown older? Now here I was sitting with this man who was somehow like the prisoner in *The Exorcist III*, panting as he lay in the corner of his cell. Would he at any moment be crawling upside down on the ceiling? This was all way, way over my head.

I accidentally knocked over a cup of cold water that was on the table.

'Don't worry, I'll get a cloth to clean it up.' He grabbed a tissue on the table and began to mop up the mess. He was used to cleaning and seemed to accept it humbly as he mopped. The chameleon again, turning humble-pie blue.

He sat down again after piling the wet tissues into a papier mâché mountain in front of us.

279

'I don't need to force myself on a woman who doesn't want me, Chris. Know what I'm saying?'

'Of course.'

'If I didn't want a real relationship with you then you'd not be here.'

'Oh, thanks.' I felt like laughing.

He went on. 'But I don't want shit on paper, Chris. That's not romantic at all. The guards read stuff and it's like I'm in bed with a broad and I'm just about to make my best move, then all of a sudden someone else's head pops up from underneath the duvet and says, "Oh that's a hot move, Ken. Go on, buddy." I don't like that, Chris. It puts me off my stride. Thing is, Chris, I'm not Mr Phone Sex Chat guy either. I've done a lot of that and now I don't. I feel used, Chris, talking away while the girl does her stuff, you know.' He looked at me curiously.

What did do her stuff mean? I wondered. I blushed deep red.

'I hate that kind of thing too.'

'We'll get there, Chris, after I know that you believe what I say when I tell you that I'm innocent. Some of the things you say, Chris, your insistence on bringing up Steve makes me pause. That's the reason we don't get on.'

He was promising me a carrot, yet I couldn't work out what the carrot actually was. His body? His soul? Or his undying love?

'I'm very wary of you, Chris. I sometimes ask myself, *What does Chris want from me? Does Chris just want material for a book?* Then I tell myself, *Hey, Ken, don't be a dope. Chris needs you. Chris is very, very lonely. Who would Chris have to talk to if it weren't for you, Ken? Stuck in that cold, snotty little village of hers in ol' Blighty?*'

I swallowed hard.

'So if Chris ever did write about me – when it's all written and done and dusted – she'd turn around and reach out for me, but Daddy wouldn't be there. I would never speak to Minerva ever, ever again – that's for damn sure.'

I felt my whole body shrink like Mrs Pepperpot and I felt like I was nine years old.

He watched me for a while, studying me. I saw him drinking me in, each twitch, each fragment of each painful feeling as it passed through me.

'So, if you did write about me, you'd send it to me first and I'd check that it was accurate and go over it myself, OK?'

The Visiting Room

'OK.'

He smiled at me as if he'd achieved something and leaned back in his seat. 'You know, I really like to paint, Chris.' He pushed at the pile of wet tissues. 'In fact, I'm going to send you one of my paintings as a gift to show you how much I think of you. I'll paint you a wolf. You said you love wolves, Minerva?'

'I love wolves.' I looked up at him.

'Me too, Chris! They're my favourite too. Wolves are so bright and clever.'

'What do you use to draw?'

'Sometimes watercolour paints but that's a bit messy. Crayon sometimes. I like crayon.'

Crayon!

He had sat back down and suddenly sounded like a boy. His legs were swinging under the table and it seemed to me that he had morphed into a ten-year-old kid and was looking to me for approval. I still felt as if I was nine years old, so I openly smiled at the boy and he smiled back.

I finally felt him right then in the back of my throat. It was what I had felt when I had heard his confession. A boy. He was a weird boy and I had seen him in dreams. An orphan with no parents, a *Lord of the Flies* wild boy who hated girls and liked to collect their skulls, to feel powerful and then run off into the night.

The guard called final time. I stood up. He came forward and gathered me into his arms without thought of my reaction. He clamped me tightly to his chest again; his rough-to-the touch beige shirt smelt of male sweat mixed with musk. I was so overwhelmed that my brain ceased to think. I felt for a moment like I was just there to be whatever he wanted me to be.

'You OK, Chris?'

'Yes.' I felt breathless being so tightly held.

'You coming back tomorrow? You said that you would.'

'Sure.'

He pressed the whole length of his hard body up against mine. I could feel his body and every bit of him. Later that night he would write me a ten-page erotic scene from his memoir, where he and an unnamed girl had sex in the back of his Cadillac. He wrote about how they lay naked 'pressed tightly naked flesh to naked flesh, heat to heat, sweating, jockeying for position, steaming up the Caddy's windows, rocking the Cadillac violently until – chest pressed to naked chest, they both climaxed magnificently in unison'.

As I put my coat on and watched him clearing up the table, I wondered what he wanted from me.

Thirty-four
Please Love Me

Carve about the sycamore and pick not the roses of summer, and melt the ice and feel the breeze caress your face and let me hold you tight.

Kenneth Bianchi

Rain started to lash down on us in the prison yard as we stood waiting for another guard to unlock the gate and let us out. I wiped at my wet face. When we got outside to the neatly manicured gardens, we waited for Rick, then he drove us into town to a French bistro called L'Escargot where we ate onion soup and crusty buttered bread, followed by steak and fries, and galettes with chocolate sauce in front of a hot fire that burned in the centre of the restaurant.

'What will he eat, Mummy, that man you interviewed?' Charlie looked at me with concern shining out of his blue-green round eyes.

'Rubbish, I expect!'

'Poor him, Mummy.'

'Perhaps.' I stopped eating and put down my knife and fork. 'He will eat. They have – something vile, I guess, nothing like this feast. Porridge, I think, cold.'

'We should thank Jesus for what we have,' Charlie said brightly. 'We should pray for all the prisoners too.'

'OK, let's pray!'

I put down my fork and joined my hands, and we said two prayers, one for prisoners and one in gratitude for our food. I pulled out my notebook to scrawl an account of the visit and quotes in shorthand, but ended up closing my pad and playing I-spy with Charlie as we enjoyed our extravagant supper.

Back at the hotel with Charlie fast asleep I was still feeling vulnerable. I got off the bed and locked the door before climbing out of the window to sit next to the swimming pool. It was directly outside our room, so I could keep an eye on Charlie. The pool was lit, so it looked turquoise and glimmered. I sat in a deck chair next to our window and spoke into my tape recorder about the visit. I didn't want to go back again. I wanted to accept defeat. I could write up something for *The Guardian* on the visit today alone, but I suddenly realised I had asked him very little about the case.

After making verbal notes on my Olympus, I went back in the window and lay on the bed. I looked at my watch. It showed 3 a.m. I had been working for four hours solid. The American countryside was sleeping. Not even the hooting of owls or scuttling noises disturbed the silence.

I feel asleep. In my dream I saw a man who looked like Bianchi. He spoke to me. 'Help me get out of that shithole. I know you care about the sap, but don't let that distract you.'

'Who are you?'

'Steve.'

'Steve?'

He was a twin of Ken, yet with a sheen to him of other-worldly glitter. His eyes were dark and black and radiated pure power. He was very pale, breathtaking and yet terrifying. My eyes followed him.

'Why are you a twin to him?'

'I've got no other body except for his. I'm a form-taker. I'm not him.'

'What are you?'

'You know what I am, bitch. You seek us here, you seek us there.'

I woke up in fright and leapt out of bed. I felt for the light and clicked it on. I had dreamed about him before. I thought of the quote, 'Call us legion for we are many.'

I fumbled in my handbag and pulled out the squashed packet of Silk Cut at the very bottom. I took out one of my emergency cigarettes and went into the bathroom, where I opened the window and puffed smoke out into the empty silence of the chilly dark night and felt fear purge through me like an ice-cold chill.

After finishing the cigarette, I got back into bed and cuddled under the blankets in the cold, strange bed and thought about the ghost in my dream; he really seemed to affect me. I rolled over and felt lonely. The Devil was an angel; I remembered. Lucifer, the great archangel who had fallen from Heaven, once the most special of angels. I rolled back over to my other side and felt anxious. My chest felt tight and I felt breathless. I sat up in bed, wiped the sweat off my face and reached again for the light. Oddly I felt cold, yet the sweat was hot.

I fell asleep again and was woken by the phone ringing. I jumped and opened my eyes, trying to work out where I was. I rolled over and picked up the cream phone beside my bed.

'Hey, Chris, it was great to meet you yesterday.' It was Kenneth Bianchi. He sounded as if he was reading off of a script card. I thought of those sickeningly sweet blue eyes.

'Are you still coming into the prison today? It's a lovely hot morning. I've just come back from the law library where I've been busy advising two of the guards about some legal problems they have.'

'I'm barely awake, Ken. In fact, I'm still in bed.' I remembered his aversion to dirty talk over the phone and smiled to myself.

'Don't forget it's Valentine's Day today, Minerva.'

'Well, I'll see.' I looked out of the window at a man who was letching at me lying in bed in my flimsy white cotton nightdress while he was cleaning out the pool. I turned away from the window.

'Try to come.'

'OK then.'

I put down the phone and lay back on the pillow. I was due to meet Ted Ponticelli that morning in my suite at 7 a.m., so I showered and then slipped on a dress. As it turned out, Ted couldn't make it to Walla Walla and so we had our interview over the phone. He was in his 60s and sounded crisp, like a lawyer.

'Well then, what did you think of him?'

'Interesting,' I said. 'He's just rung me and told me it's Valentine's Day.'

'I wonder what he's up to?'

'I don't know – you tell me.'

'Bianchi didn't kill anyone. I guess you know that now you've met him.'

I thought back to Bianchi. Something about Ted made me reluctant to discuss the fact that I felt Bianchi was a multiple personality. 'What makes you say that?'

In for the Kill

'I have interviewed the man who did it. He's a convicted killer called William Suff. He's on Death Row for a string of rapes and killings and he has already admitted to killing six of the Hillside Strangling victims but that's all been hushed up.'

I listened as I sipped some coffee.

'There was absolutely no physical evidence connecting Bianchi to the crimes. There was one single pubic hair from the victim Karen Mandic found on the stairs of the basement where she was strangled. How could Knudsen have found one of Bianchi's pubic hairs, when the crime scene was hoovered over by the first lot of cops who found nothing? None of Bianchi's DNA was found on the body.'

'He may have used a condom?'

'What serial killer uses a condom?'

'I don't know – a considerate one?' I mocked. 'Bianchi, under hypnosis and as Steve, had confessed to the cops saying he used a condom as he raped the last two girls.'

'It's unheard of and there was no evidence of one being used.'

'Steven Pennell and Richard Cottingham used condoms,' I told him. 'I've advised many British media outlets about serial killers. I've been asked for advice on cases where victims were still missing – profiling for the BBC News. I do know my stuff.'

'Well, I've never heard of it. Look, I'm an ex-cop. The confession was the only thing they convicted him on and it was full of incorrect details. I was with Internal Affairs for five years. I have investigated this thoroughly and have written a book on it called *Without Evidence*. It was a sensational case and I became interested in it. I left the book for you the night you flew in.'

'I've read it, or most of it, now. Thanks for leaving it in reception for me. I've also read the one by a private investigator at the time, Ron Crisp, in which he says he doesn't believe that Bianchi is the Hillside Strangler.'

'You Brits going to look into all this?' he asked.

'The Brits already are.' I put the phone down after saying goodbye. I wasn't sure whether I liked him or not but he was sharp, intelligent and his book had been an interesting read.

Valentine's Day morning had brought sun first thing but now there were only grey skies and it was pouring with rain. I looked out of our hotel window with a frown as I watched heavy plops of water fall in the swimming pool. Rain lashed from a bruised mauve sky over the jagged, snowcapped mountains. I shivered, pulled on a cardigan and looked over at Charlie, who was still asleep. I kissed him awake and he smiled and reached up to hug me. He sat up excitedly and then stared at the rain on the window with a frown.

'Oh no, I wanted to go out to the pool today but it's raining, Mummy.'

'Let's go to that wine-making place this morning then later the rain will clear and we can swim, darling.' I hugged him and kissed his warm mop of blond hair and enjoyed his smell of new-mown hay and shortbread biscuits.

'Come on, all is not lost, we have those hot American waffles and sweet syrup to indulge in, Charlie.'

We went down the corridor and picked out the freshest breakfast on hot white plates and ate in the restaurant, chatting happily.

After breakfast we drove out with Louise, the assistant manager of the hotel, to the rain-drenched vineyards to see the local winemaking. I bought a bottle of Nicholas Coles' finest red. Louise paid so much attention to Charlie and they laughed so much together it was heart-warming. She was rapidly becoming the kind of person you stay in touch with and invite to your house and I warmly extended that invitation.

Later on in the day we all sat in a trendy town-centre Mexican restaurant and sipped lemonade floats and ate beef tortillas. Louise then insisted I take Charlie to a sweet shop that made homemade chocolate and sold ice cream in exotic flavours. She let me take her car, so I drove along the highway to a second-hand clothes shop and bought a vintage tea dress in candy apple red with a virginal pink bow on the front. I tried it on in front of their floor-length mirror and bought some cream silk kitten heels to match. It was 1930s style. Madonna's 'Into the Groove' was playing on their radio and I relaxed. The heavy rain had cleared and a hot sun came booming out along with a huge rainbow. Traffic was light on the roads and the people were very friendly. I was starting to feel at home in Walla Walla.

After shopping in town, we went back to the hotel to hang out by the pool and swim. I rubbed sun cream onto Charlie's shoulders and placed a white sun hat on his blond head. The hot American sun beat down on our pale English skins.

Later on, I drove us in Louise's car out to a hamburger place to get Charlie a hamburger and me some fries. We sat in the car eating them, sipping on our peanut-butter milkshakes. I listened to the newly returned rain pattering down on the metal windowsill.

Valentine's Day was nearly over. I looked up at the sky. Across the street was the shop selling second-hand clothes where I had earlier bought my red dress. Next to it was an ice cream shop filled with children. The wide dusty street was full of old-fashioned trucks in beiges and browns, the like of which I had only seen in old movies. Outside the dress shop underneath a red striped awning were two white-silk tea dresses on mannequins with a long string of pearls around both. In the window I could see a little dog and I wasn't sure whether he was stuffed or real, but I hadn't seen him when I had purchased my red dress. I watched the traffic lights change colour and looked at the pink neon sign on Fast Eddie's roof. The air smelt fresh and clean with the hint of frying onions and hamburger. I thought of Bianchi as I watched the twilight gather over Walla Walla. I knew I had to go back a second time to solve the mystery.

Charlie was eager to play with Louise's children back at the hotel, so I left him in her care. Back in the suite I pulled on my red dress. I looked at myself in the mirror after applying red Dior lipstick. I wondered why I was getting all gussied up to go and see a killer. I undressed again and got into my jeans and a plain white T-shirt and rubbed off the lipstick. I put a CD on my Walkman – Abba, 'Name of the Game'.

I drove off to the prison in Louise's car and was just able to get in at the five o'clock opening. To my surprise, when I got into the visitors' room, Bianchi was already sitting at the same table, number 12, waiting for me. I took my coat off and hung it up. My new shoes were painfully rubbing and forming a blister as I limped over. Bianchi stood up and hugged me to his chest as tightly as he had done at our first meeting.

'Happy Valentine's Day, Minerva,' he whispered straight into my ear as he held me in his arms.

'Happy Valentine's Day.' I hated Valentine's Day and had never celebrated it in my life. It seemed like it was for schmucks. We scraped seats on the floor as we sat down next to each other in the same seats as the previous day.

'Hey, they let us make a present to give to our visitors. Can I give you the one I made for you this morning in the prison library?'

'Yes, thank you.' I didn't know what he was talking about.

Please Love Me

Bianchi swaggered over to the guards' desk and then came back with a Valentine's card with a crayon sketch of two roses covered in dew. On the other side it had a few lines of handwritten poetry.

Carve about the sycamore and pick not the roses of summer, and melt the ice and feel the breeze caress your face and let me hold you tight.

'For Valentine's Day, for you, Minerva.'

'Thank you. I'm sorry, I haven't got anything for you.'

'Doesn't matter.'

I looked at it. I pushed it across the table so it sat in the middle, then I tried not to stare at it.

The guards came round and offered large polythene bags to everyone. I thought of how the killers had tied one around Kristina Weckler's head and then filled it with gas. They had also strangled Jane King using a plastic bag to quicken her death. I felt it was an insult to both of these victims to touch one with him but Bianchi looked at me as if to say did I want one and I nodded a yes. To my embarrassment, I found they were packs with kits to make Valentine's cards for each other. It was too late. He was opening his, tugging out the contents of white card, cut-out hearts and glue, and I had to follow suit.

They keep them busy, I thought to myself. But in fact these kinds of activity were probably provided to help the prisoners and their families and friends relate to one another during the visits.

We sat in silence and made our Valentine's Day cards for each other. I decided that as he was so relaxed it was the time to bring up Steve again.

'I had a dream about Steve last night.'

I carried on colouring in but I could hear him put his pencil down.

'Chris, I don't believe you said that. Here we are, it's Valentine's Day and you and I are having a really nice time, then you go ahead and ruin that nice time. You're making me really very, very angry. You bring him up time and time again like a dog gnawing on a bone. Sorry you have this sick fascination with Steve but he's nothing to do with me.'

'You called him an aberration brought on by hypnosis?'

'That's right!'

'How come he's such a *real* aberration? As if invented by Stephen King? He's real – I feel him. But you know yesterday, when you were so angry with Dee, I kind of felt that you were being Steve.'

He took out his hanky and wiped his brow.

'I was *being* Steve?'

'Yes, you stopped being yourself and you were like Steve.'

'I don't know what you fucking mean.'

Bianchi had a candy red heart that said 'You are Beautiful' on his card and I had got stuck with a baby pink heart with the words 'Please Love Me' on it.

'I mean that maybe you go in and out of being Steve and maybe you've just got a shattered ego – that way it would explain how you can kill 12 girls and be OK with that. Dee said that you could project yourself into dreams and my head, so I think it's you that's Steve.'

He looked up at me, his eyes flashing bright blue.

'How fucking dare you accuse me of such ugly horrible things? You sit there with me like a friend and accuse me of that shit. You make out you're my friend then you attack me like that? I'm not your whipping boy, Chris, I'll react to that.'

'I'm sorry.'

I thought he was going to cry.

'You're either my friend, Chris, and you believe me, or the future isn't good for us, Chris, it really isn't.'

'I *am* your friend.'

'You try on roles with me all the time, Chris. Know why they don't fit, Chris? It's because I smell that you're a journalist with me and being close to me is unethical, Chris, for a professional journalist.'

Unethical? Did he assume journalists were cherubs? I had been News Corp's finest.

'I'm your friend.'

'How could you be if you think I've done what you accuse me of, Chris? Oh, I forgot, you sat with that monster Ian Brady! I've tried not to judge you for that. That *monster* should be given the death penalty.'

'We don't have it. Brady's trying to kill himself.'

'He's right.'

We put our heads down and silently coloured in around the edges of our love hearts with the tiny pencils in the kit. Outside it had got dark. I could hear nothing but the sound of pencils swiftly colouring in. He leaned over and placed his finger on the edge of my love heart, so it wouldn't move as I coloured over the edges of it.

He threw his across the table to me when he finished it.

'Thanks – here's yours.' I passed his back. He looked at it without smiling.

'I can't take it back through the door into the prison, you know. You keep it.'

'Oh, OK.'

I sat down and didn't know what to say or do now the cards had been exchanged. I picked up a pencil and out of embarrassment decided to sketch Bianchi so I could really study him. He noticed what I was doing and leaned back in his seat, arms folded to pose for me.

'Do you often do this?' he asked, lifting his head up and showing me his profile.

'Nope, never.' I was busy filling in his thick eyelashes with curly strokes of an HB pencil.

He looked exactly like he had in footage I had seen of him in court listening to the evidence being given against him. I drew the austere straight nose and the bump on it at the bridge and his long dark eyelashes and his sensitive but strong chin. The almond-shaped intense eyes and his slightly flared nostrils.

'There's a tiny hole in your ear lobe!'

'I used to have an earring in that ear, Chris.'

I leaned over and pinched his ear lobe with my fingers.

'Oh gosh, there's the little hole. I can feel it!' I exclaimed excitedly as I dug my thumbnail hard into his ear lobe.

'Ouch!'

He leaned over to look at my artwork.

'It looks nothing like me, Chris. You're no artist.'

'I don't remember ever saying that I was.' I took a dark grey pencil and made a cross through it.

He looked upset. 'Chris, come on, cheer up. Please can you let them take a photo of both of us together?'

I didn't want to – it seemed fake happy, like a donkey ride on a beach on a wet rainy day. 'No, I don't look my best.'

'Please. You have to give them a dollar off the card. The machine has a photo voucher. Please go and get it, I can't. You can send it to me as a beautiful reminder of my day of normality with you,

Minerva. I get no normal. You don't know what this day has meant to me. I feel so much lighter.'

He seemed to need it so much and seemed so sad about not having it that I relented and went to get the voucher. The guard went off and came back with a large heavy camera. Apparently there was an area where we had to be photographed, so we went over and stood under some white balloons. Bianchi put his arm around my waist to pose for the picture. I put my arm around his waist and tucked my thumb into the waistband of his trousers. He looked down, smiled at me and held me tighter. One of the guards took our photo with a flash as his hipbone crushed ever so tightly up against mine.

We went back to the table and waited for the photo to be given to us. When we got it, Bianchi flicked it across the table to me.

'You have it. I look too pale.' He was upset he looked less than lovely in the photo.

'Hey, will I ever see you again?' he asked.

'Do you want me to come back in the summer?'

'OK, I'll get a tan ready for you. I won't look so pale.'

'OK.'

'Did you enjoy the poetry I've been writing?'

I wanted to ask him if it was Steve who was the poet but knew he'd get too angry.

'You're a very talented poet.'

'Thanks. Hey, I'm going to start counting the days until my cell gets warmer. I'll go outside, get that tan and get myself looking better ready for your return.' He rubbed his pale arms as he stood up. 'Are you OK?'

'Yes,' I said.

'Sure? OK?'

He hugged me and then looked at me carefully.

'Come back then, Minerva.'

'OK.'

'Will you write to me?'

'Sure, I'll post a letter before I leave town.'

'You know, I felt you in my heart as soon as your plane landed in my country.'

He let go of me and moved away. It was six o'clock. Visiting hours ended at eight. It was chaos; visiting children were running around playing tag and some of the wives were saying goodbye to their husbands.

Please Love Me

I turned to try to see if Bianchi had gone back to his cell. He was standing near the table looking lost. I gave in to an impulse and went back over to him. I gave him a hug, watching over his shoulder at the guard who had told me not to touch him.

'Is there a problem? Are you OK?' He squeezed my waist tightly.

'It's such a pity all this. I feel bad for you,' I said sadly.

He looked foxed for a moment then he looked directly at me.

'Chris, I want you to know something. I'm not the same man.'

'The same man as what?'

'I'm not the same man as the young punk who walked in here all those years ago.'

Our eyes met.

'Thanks for telling me.'

He let me go and walked towards the door that led to the cells. I turned and was escorted through the three sets of locked iron gates. Outside it was dark and pouring with rain again. I fell down the steps and then ran to the car, fumbled with the key, got in and slammed the door. As I turned on the ignition, I glanced back through the wet window at the dark, looming prison. He had put on an act for me. He would be tired now after all that time being nice. Why? He wanted to get out was why.

All of a sudden I saw that I was utterly and incredibly alone, and had been all of my life. I felt like I was a tiny piece floating around the universe and belonged nowhere.

The next day I woke up and felt exhausted. I was also worried about what I would write. *The Guardian* had splashed out on my airfare and expenses, which meant my son's airfare. I felt a sense of panic. I had no idea what to say about him as it had been an odd two days. He wasn't a multiple; he was a man who hid.

Ken was not your average serial killer; his mind was very strange. I had more research to do, as I still hadn't solved the mystery. Bianchi had a mind like a house with many hidden rooms – but hit on the right room and I would shine in a torch and find him. I remembered the film *Hellraiser*, in which a man found a Chinese box, turned it and turned it and all of a sudden Pinhead the demon appeared. Once released, the demon wouldn't go back into the box. It was odd how films sometimes mirrored reality. But this wasn't the kind of story *The Guardian* would publish or thank me for.

I packed my case and Charlie's smaller yellow one. We made one last trip to the toy shop in the dusty roads of Walla Walla village. It was a beautiful village and so typically olde worlde America. We picked up three big shiny metal models of an old red truck, an open-topped blue Chevy and a yellow school bus. Charlie insisted on some metal figures of Confederate and Yankee soldiers on horses, then we got ice creams from the home-made ice cream shop. Charlie had black liquorice while I had a deep-brown peanut butter, then we dashed into a cab to take us to the tiny shack that doubled as an airport.

I couldn't get out of Walla Walla fast enough. As I got on the tiny plane I felt like everyone was talking about the English woman who had come to see Bianchi. Back on board, the red wine was at the ready but this time I declined. I decided to white-knuckle it, while Charlie, staring from the window at the jagged mountains, was enjoying it.

On the next plane from Seattle the seat in front of me kept falling back onto my knees. I complained to the British Airways steward, flashed my press pass and he kindly arranged for Charlie and me to transfer free of charge into first class.

We slept in these huge, soft, warm flying beds; it was an amazing experience. We both slept deeply for hours and then woke up, Charlie to chocolate milk and me to a glass of icy Bucks Fizz. Then we both excitedly watched our private TV screens for the rest of the flight and enjoyed the first-class cuisine in front of the blue curtain. As we flew over New York I snuggled down under the soft warm blankets as the sun blazed into my face and slept again, but this time I dreamed.

In the dream, an old gypsy was sitting at a table in a small red-lit room. She had a pack of Tarot cards in front of her and she began to turn them for me. Curious, I sat down opposite her. She pulled out one card and handed it to me; to my dismay it was the Grim Reaper. As I held the Death card of a skeleton in my hand, it grew larger and larger. I stood up and dropped the card and ran, my heart beating hard, down a dark alleyway that led to a very cold, icy place. I woke up and felt a sense of dread; it was a clear prophecy that someone close to me was going to die.

Charlie looked at me anxiously as I woke up. 'Bad dream?'
'Yeah.'

It was more than a bad dream; I knew it was foresight. I felt filled with dread. I stared out the window with fear and anxiety flowing through me, hiding it from Charlie by feigning sleep as he watched *Shrek* on his large private TV screen.

Thirty-five

Zapping

How quickly love forgets upon the flakes, atop the
peaks, we never see upon the breeze that kisses us,
amidst dark storms. We are not strangers you and I,
the trees I know, even the silvery lit I know, the rain
and the pompous shower I know, all your secrets I
know, and you, Minerva, you I know the best.

Kenneth Bianchi

We landed back in England after a 9-hour flight. As soon as
we got back I received calls from the news reporter Alistair
Jackson from BBC's *Panorama* and Nick Davies from *The
Guardian*. Stories about phone hacking at the *News of the World*
were all over the media and *Panorama* wanted me to appear on a
programme they were planning about the scandal, saying they
knew that I had been 'inner circle'. Even the Prime Minister had
been caught up in the affair, as he had hired Andy Coulson, a
former *News of the World* editor, as his media adviser.

The *Panorama* producer Stephen Scott wanted to meet me but
before I agreed I contacted an award-making filmmaker I knew
for her advice. Sylvia Jones and a producer called Clive Entwistle
had contacted me a few months previously to ask whether I
would be interested in making a film about my life for the BBC
or Channel 4, who had apparently both shown interest in the
story of my lifelong investigation into evil. Sylvia was positive
about the *Panorama* guys' honesty, so I arranged to meet the two
very persuasive BBC producers in the Petersham Hotel on
Richmond Hill.

In for the Kill

As soon as I walked into the cocktail bar, Stephen Scott, a good-looking, dark-haired man in his 40s, got up from his chair.

'So! I finally meet the legend.'

I blushed. 'Legend?'

'That's what they call you – and what you can do!'

'Well . . .'

'I've been told many things about you. You can get an arch criminal to pull over in his car and let you know where he is going so photographers can take a picture of him.'

I smiled. 'So, you've been talking to the *Mail*!'

Stephen smiled and went on, 'You're one of the most amazing investigators Fleet Street has ever known, and that's coming from an editor who calls your renowned ability "magic powers".'

They were out fishing, but I was enjoying the bait. The *Daily Mail* had often rung me to sort out this mess or that. They were always charming and would start by saying, 'We need your genius.' Consequently, I would always pull it out of the bag for them, getting them front page after front page.

Alistair, a blond in a smart suit, spoke up. 'One legend meets another. I'm honoured to sit in on this meeting of Fleet Street's finest. It's amazing you two meeting and it's great for me to be able to sit in on it.' He went to the bar to get us all cocktails and returned with the menu. A waitress appeared with our drinks and set them on the table. I sipped at the creamy cocktail I had ordered and found myself warming to a pleasant glow.

Stephen now said, 'I have been told many, many things about you. Some say you've got magic powers.'

'I've a very strong sixth sense,' I said, eyeing him over my frosted glass full of Screaming Orgasm.

'Give me an example.'

He seemed very curious about me and this was flattering as I had been a school-gate mother for the past few years, my son left out of play dates and parties over the bullying and because I didn't live in one of the village's mansions and have a grey-haired moneybags husband. I felt downtrodden and domesticated in my suburban hellhole but now I had the chance to re-live my years as a hotshot and show off my peacock plume of sought-after Fleet Street genius.

'Well, I would kind of know what to say to a subject of investigation to access their minds.'

He forked a piece of steak and put it into his mouth. 'Go on.'

Zapping

I sipped more of my cocktail. 'Well, when I phoned someone up to probe a story, I would have a script up my sleeve. You know, something to say to get them to open up to me. But as soon as they picked up the phone, I would be reading them. It wasn't what they said; it was what I could hear in their voices. I could know them in minutes. I would be reading and getting into their minds as each second passed, until I knew exactly what to say to access the information I was looking for.'

Alistair had gone quiet and was studying his drink. I felt embarrassed, as if I had exposed myself as a freak.

'It's my inner side that does the really spooky stuff. The interesting thing is it can only work for someone it likes. I mean, if it likes the person who was asking me to get the information. If I try to do it myself, I can't. She – or my inner – does it, but she's fickle. Oh, you must think I'm a weirdo.'

'I don't see it as weird; I see it as utterly fascinating.' Stephen beamed at me. 'Please would you agree to talk about your gift on screen?'

'OK.'

But then he told me that they wanted me to go into detail about the inner workings of the *News of the World*.

I sipped my Screaming Orgasm and felt a stab of dread in my gut. They wanted a lot.

'Is this going to upset Murdoch?'

'What's your problem with Murdoch?'

I thought of the rabbit dream I had had and all of a sudden my fillet steak tasted like cardboard, my cocktail like poison and I felt kind of breathless. I said that I would answer their questions on camera, in an attempt to buy myself time to think about what I was doing. They seemed to accept this and were very polite about it.

After dinner and hugs all round, I walked out of the restaurant and went straight to Hugh's, feeling full of dread as I banged on the front door.

He answered in his blue silk dressing gown, his face covered in stubble. He grinned at me good-naturedly.

'Didn't you bother to get up today?' I asked him.

'No! Does it bother you?'

'Yes, I'm jealous of you.'

'You can come and join me next time.'

I blushed as I went into his kitchen to get us drinks, hearing him shout from the drawing room, 'OK, what's up?'

In for the Kill

I opened a bottle of Sainsbury's red wine and poured it into two glasses, broke out some Green and Black's almond and milk chocolate I found lying on the side and brought the whole lot in on a tray.

'I've just agreed to being filmed by the BBC.' I told him the story as I supped the fruity stuff and sucked on broken shards of milk chocolate.

He crossed his legs and frowned at me as he positioned his glass on his knee. 'There's no way you should do it, Chris. Come on, there is so much more to this than just a newspaper. This will bring down the government. It's Britain's Watergate. Why did you talk to them?'

'Stephen, the *Panorama* producer, called me a queen and gave me three Screaming Orgasms, so I wanted to be nice to him back.'

'Sucker! He gave you the orgasms so you'd talk.' He raised his eyebrows and licked his lips. 'Did you flash your great legs like you're doing to me just now?'

'No!'

'Liar!'

I sighed. 'What should I do?'

'Tell him to get stuffed of course. Unless you want to find yourself with a poisoned umbrella up your bum one day. This is heavy stuff.'

I rang them the next day to tell them I'd changed my mind. A few weeks later I felt bad for letting them down, so I agreed to talk about fluff only. The segment was filmed in a library off Park Lane. Strong lights had been set up and I sat in a large leather chair with a bookcase as a backdrop while my son was waited on hand and foot by Stephen. As the cameras rolled and the clapper board snapped shut, I was asked about what Alex Marunchak was like as a man. I really liked Alex, so I sang his praises, saying, 'Alex is charming and intelligent.'

Then they asked what Greg was like. I had a flashback of caressing his hips as he lay fast asleep on my bed while rain lashed against the window on a wet Friday night.

'He was a good editor,' I heard myself saying.

In the end the whole thing was kept very light and lasted only half an hour. I was surprised but grateful that they kept their word and didn't bring up anything that would have made me uncomfortable.

Zapping

I drove back from Knightsbridge in the dark and the rain, analysing myself as Charlie slept in the back seat. *Why was my life directionless and empty?* I wondered. I had been commissioned to do my first investigative piece in two years on the Hillside Strangler for *The Guardian* and I was struggling with being brutally honest because I had got far too close to Kenneth Bianchi. Ken had made me into his long-lost sister, while I was obsessed with finding the demonic Steve, who Ken now said didn't exist.

I was swimming in dark waters and had no lamp by which I could see the way forward. What could I write up in my piece for *The Guardian*? I just didn't know what to say, as I couldn't see Ken clearly enough and I felt like a complete loser.

I opened the window of the car and shouted to the heavens, to God, 'I bloody HATE you.' Then I wound the window back up with a soaking wet face.

After we got home and I had bathed Charlie and settled him in bed I sat and tried again to tackle the story. But as I sat at the computer and wrote about Bianchi I felt depressed and I couldn't work out why.

I rang Chris Berry-Dee. 'You know, it's no good,' I told him. 'I can't write about Bianchi. It's an emotional feeling and I don't know what it is.'

Dee started to laugh. 'Oh, Mummy, Mummy, PLEASE help me! I'm stuck in a cell, Mummy. Oh God, Mummy – God, it's so bad. Oh, please, Mummy, help me.'

I started to cry.

'Are you crying over our Ken?'

'No.'

'Yes, you are. He's really suckered you by putting on the vulnerable little boy act!'

'Piss off. I'm not stupid!'

'I know you're not stupid, you're a very experienced journalist, but Reverend Bianchi is a whole different ball game than other serial killers, Chris. I'd not even attempt to get inside his head. I did a story on him and that was it. I take my hat off to you, I really do. Of all the serial killers I've met, Bianchi is the most evil and the most complex. '

'Yes, he's a chameleon. I haven't put any pieces of the jigsaw together.'

'I didn't go deep with him, Chris. I admire you for taking him on at such a depth, though it's dangerous, if you ask me.'

In for the Kill

'Why?'

'I don't know, just a feeling I get.'

I hung up and then went to get one of my emergency cigarettes. As I smoked I looked at the photos of the Hillside victims on my computer files. I didn't want to hurt them either. I could feel their presence sometimes and I needed to be true to them – they had lost their lives.

I tracked down another of the doctors who had diagnosed Bianchi, who told me, 'Kenneth Bianchi is a multiple personality – I still stand by it.'

'Can I interview you on this?' I asked hopefully.

'What? No! Look, I've retired. Bianchi didn't kill anyone, the malevolent alter did it. It's a fully fledged alter – the real deal.'

'What's the real deal?' I felt excited. I had struck gold.

'I'm sorry, I'm busy.'

'Is it a thing? Is it a person with no body? What exactly is a malevolent alter? Is it a demonic possession?'

'I'm sorry but I have no interest in this at all.'

He hung up angrily but he wasn't as angry as I was. It had taken me two hours to track him down. I rang him back three times and shouted at him aggressively.

'What exactly is a malevolent alter? Is it attached to him or a possessing entity? Why is it evil? Why did it want to kill?'

He kept hanging up until finally I gave up, trembling with temper, and poured myself a drink and lit another cigarette.

The next morning, after I had taken my son to school, I went into the garden for a five-minute break before I got back to work on my children's book. As I went back into the kitchen to get a coffee, I felt a sharp sting in my foot and I screamed. I could feel the filthy wasp poison go all the way up my leg and it made me feel sick. I looked up and to my horror I saw wasps swarming out of the light fitting. Their venomous bodies were dropping out and buzzing around the floor, half-dead. I stared at them for a while, their furry little bodies all mingling on the floor. Then for a second I could feel a presence beside me. I turned my head. Then I looked back at the filthy little wasps writhing on the floor and I felt afraid.

A few hours later, a pest expert arrived in a yellow van with a giant wasp on the side of it.

'It's a massive nest. It must be in the eaves,' he said as he examined the ground and saw the large pile of half-dead wasps. 'I'll get my kit.'

Zapping

I felt upset. My foot was throbbing and I hated insects, especially ones that stung.

Sienna rang. I drove round to The Priory in the heavy rain. She was sedated. We sat in the reception with its giant fish tank, coffee machine and endless armchairs.

'How are you?' I asked, looking around at the sanatorium. I handed her the mini Buddha I had bought for her in the shop near the entrance but she didn't look at it.

She sought out my weak point. 'I knew that Bianchi was your soulmate a long, long time ago. It's why you've acted so badly on this case.' She lay back in the massive leather armchair in her pink silk dressing gown with her dark bob and looked like an ageing princess. 'You can't write objectively about him because you're madly in love with him.'

'No, I'm not, Sienna. I wish you'd never started me off on this soulmates crap, I really do. I know you're in here but please don't talk like a mad person. He's evil.'

'I told you all we do in life is look for love and you've been searching like crazy, Chris. It was Kenneth Bianchi, the Hillside Strangler, you were searching for all the time. You love Bianchi, Chris, and the real Bianchi – the vampire he has become – because he loves you back, he's come for you in your home and is haunting it. You don't seek him to study him, you love him. You seek his soul as it's your soul.'

I stood up and frowned at her. 'Well, I'm glad I managed to keep *that* quiet from *The Guardian*.' I swallowed hard and wished I hadn't come. 'Ken isn't mine and nor is his malevolent alter! He's an insect I want to dissect, not make love to. I'm interested in him as I've been interested in evil all of my life.'

'I rest my case! Now you've found each other he's been coming into your dreams and into your head. He's in your house. You can feel him, I know you can. You've the second sight, just like I have. You know he's the undead, don't you? You don't care because you crave him like a drug, because his soul is your soul.'

I stood up and backed away from her. 'You bloody crazed witch, *nothing* you say is true. I hope they keep you in here.'

I ran down the stairs and out to the car park. I sat in the car for a while, feeling tired and anxious, and watched the rain stream down the windscreen.

I drove home just before Charlie got back from school and after supper we played draughts. I ran a hot bath after he had gone to bed, pouring all my best bath oil into the water and enjoying the scent as it rose up off the water. I undressed slowly, admiring my figure in the long mirror. Breasts, stomach – it was all tight and all in the right place – I was lucky. I opened the window naked, then lit tall, white, scented candles and placed them around the bath before turning off the light. It was relaxing and the glow was warming. I poured myself a glass of red wine from the bottle of Merlot I'd brought up to the bathroom and sipped it.

I was starting to feel guilty about being harsh on Sienna. She was ill, after all, and I shouldn't have been so nasty. I should have just ignored her, but it was hard.

I drank the Merlot and enjoyed the scent of frankincense from the cheap candles as it mingled with the lush scent of rose otto. It was getting cold outside, so I stood up and closed the window. I lay back in the water and admired my legs. The candles gave off a warm glow and flickered on the ceiling, making patterns that my lazy eyes followed. The condensation on the bathroom mirror began to drip and run in rivulets. I watched it dreamily as I relaxed in the hot water; it seemed to form shapes. Then suddenly I felt a sinister presence, almost as if someone was watching my naked body as I bathed. I sat up in the water and my heart began to thump. I wondered if the spooky stuff was going to start to happen to me again. It did. Images of naked, pale, dead bodies laid out on the ground, their faces half covered in wet, dead leaves, filled my mind.

I shot out of the bath and rubbed at the wet mirror with my hand, then stared at myself standing dripping wet with my heart beating hard in my chest. Sienna was driving me as mad as she was. Her hocus-pocus bullshit was making me see things. I felt a cold chill go through me. Soon I would be scared to be in my own home.

I dried off and covered myself up but I could still feel the presence of a man that hated, as if he was watching me with a need to murder me but he couldn't as he didn't have a body.

I put on a silk robe and went down to make some cocoa in the kitchen, pouring in a jot of brandy to calm myself. I looked out at the neatly trimmed garden as I stirred the milk then went back upstairs to bed, picking up *Lady Chatterley's Lover* on the way. I fell asleep reading it with the light on.

The next day I went around to see Hugh to discuss what had happened.

Zapping

'Bianchi's having an effect on you spiritually. Why didn't you write this up for the newspaper? It'd be fascinating. Maybe if you go near serial killers, this is what you get. Dee had the same.'

'No, it feels too personal. Anyway, it's not serial killers, it's Ken. He's somehow got himself powers like Dee suspected. I think he's got them as he's been devil worshipping.'

'Yet you held him in your arms when you met. Why?'

'To feel how much he needed me.'

'Did he need you?'

'Maybe.'

'What did you feel in the prison?'

'Nothing, and he was laughing at me as he felt me futilely trying to penetrate him.'

'What did you think of Bianchi as a journalist?'

I took a deep breath. 'Ken is a medium-dominance male. You've heard of Maslow's theory of dominance?'

'Vaguely – do go on.'

'Well, society is divided into three groups of humans – low dominance, medium dominance and high. They all mate within their groups. The high doms need to self-actualise and are often leaders. A high-dom male would turn his nose up at a medium-dom woman – it's like wolves.

'Ken gave me his memoirs and in all three volumes that I have he waxes lyrical about his girlfriend who was a medium-dominance female. Bianchi's ex-wife Shirlee was also the same type. His ex-partners are all medium dominance – both of the aforementioned aren't clever women yet Bianchi is very intelligent, *ipso facto* Ken must squash who he is to be with them. It must mean his real self is constantly hidden.'

'And? Carry on.'

'Well, serial killers are always high dominance. They are thwarted, resentful outsiders because they haven't obtained a "position of power" over the flock. This frustrates the high dom. But he may not have the tools – the education or social polish – to achieve his rightful position. It's like having an alpha wolf that is forced to feed last – life becomes a series of humiliations. They vent. They mostly murder women, as the one who has thwarted them is Mother. Mother has usually been violent and or emotionally abusive, which has made them unable to assert or socialise and hence the alpha wolf with the broken leg.'

'And the Hillside Murders?'

In for the Kill

'Carried out by a high dom – the way the bodies are littered like so much rubbish is an attack on society. The killer is sadistic – anger excitation. I've studied reports on Buono and believe he was a rapist and woman hater but wouldn't have killed as he did. No, it wasn't Buono that led the way. Bianchi was the more dominant in the *folie à deux*. The Hillside Murders are a heinous attack on humanity, even the way the desecrated human bodies are lain out in the middle of society to be "found" on happy sunny days. He gets to do a *double kill* – once on the victim and once on society as they find the horror. He also terrorised society.'

I paused to feel Bianchi. 'He's getting orders from another level. I can feel it. Hang on – didn't one of the psychiatrists say that Ken told him he received orders from Steve? Yes, he did. But maybe it wasn't Steve he got orders from, maybe it was just a demonic entity. This thing hates humanity, hates the world – it's his sworn enemy.'

I looked out of Hugh's leaded window to the wet lawn in his walled front garden. I thought of the two victims I most identified with, the first being the vulnerable runaway Judy Miller with her sweet face and stringy brown hair. She had no parents and no one who cared. She hated herself and probably thought she deserved to die. Then there was Karen – the brainy beauty who was raped and then strangled to death.

I rubbed my forehead. I thought of the blue-eyed Bianchi and how I had hated him – his smiley, nice persona. I thought of how I had moved the beer bottle back and forth in front of him to remind him how he had raped Lissa Kastin with a beer bottle.

I stared out of the window. I was confused by Bianchi. He was a maze and I was lost in him, walking round and round, and there was no sign of anything human, only fake dummies everywhere. He was a chameleon, enjoying the game of hide and seek.

Since I could not see him, I used my sixth sense and tried to feel him. There it was! He was hard and jagged. He could cut like glass into soft female flesh. I could feel his hate – hate like that had brewed in a dark room for decades and had enjoyed communing with the dark. It would mash my bones and chop up my limbs. Yet it hid – it was as carefully concealed as a crocodile in the bushes of a swamp.

I needed to know why Bianchi killed not only in Los Angeles but also in Bellingham, and why the timing? What was the trigger to kill? His mother, Frances, a very sharp, intelligent and plain-speaking woman whom I had got to know over the phone, had said to the cops that she blamed his girlfriend Kelli Boyd for making her son Kenny into a murderer. She said, 'Every time Kelli threw Kenny out or ended it there would be a murder.'

During my visit, I had asked Ken about his mother's comments and he replied, 'Sure, you could find a trigger here or there and say me and Kelli argued here or there, but I'm not the killer, so it's irrelevant. Anyway, how would Mom know when we argued?'

Ken had usually rung her is why. I checked his mother's version of events.

In LA, Boyd had contracted gonorrhea and given it to Ken. She told him that she had been raped only when it was found out about the disease. The rape was not reported. Ken was suspicious but when she told him she was pregnant he hugged her and seemed overjoyed.

Gonorrhea is a dirty, degrading sexual disease that takes a long time to heal and involves sticks being inserted in the male penis. This painful treatment must have reminded him of the times as a child when Frances had subjected him to numerous painful sticks in his genitals to try to halt his bed wetting. Only a few months after the day he learned that he had caught gonorrhea from his idealised 'spiritual' lover, the terrifying rampage in the streets of Los Angles began. One of his *punishments* was to inject 'cleaning' fluid into the girls.

The plan Salerno said Bianchi had to shoot the girls in the head in the Santa Monica mountains seemed to me to be like retribution for an offence.

When they lived together in Bellingham, Boyd told him that she was sick of him and that he would have to leave after the Christmas holiday. Karen Mandic and Diane Wilder both were murdered by Bianchi in early January. Boyd wanted Bianchi out of her life. The beauty Karen Mandic and her friend Diane Wilder were strangled to death in a dimly lit basement after being viciously raped by Bianchi in reaction to his girlfriend throwing him out.

In his confession, Bianchi had said to the cops, 'The rope was tied so tightly my knuckles went white. I was so full of anger as I strangled Karen Mandic but I had no idea why I was so angry.'

Was Frances correct? Boyd was also very like his mother, Frances, in appearance and height, both spoke in a noticeably high-pitched voice, and both are in their own words 'take-charge types'.

In books and movies about the Hillside Stranglers Boyd has been portrayed as weak and exploited by Bianchi but this just isn't correct or anywhere near the truth. Boyd told the cops after her lover's arrest, 'Ken loves me very deeply, a whole lot more than I love him. He still does. He sought approval from me all the time and was forever doing kind things for me and the baby.'

This was the truth. Bianchi told me, 'She'll always be the mother of our son. We had a deep spiritual love.' He describes her in his memoir as nothing short of Vivien Leigh.

What goes up must come down. With all this idealisation going on he had to redress the balance. Other women became shit and filth he could murder and vent on – it just didn't matter as long as he kept his precious relationship going.

Some may call this love, but love does not exist where others cry out in agony. This was something sick.

Bianchi was so upset at the idea of his live-in lover ending it one time he pretended he had cancer and was dying so she wouldn't throw him out. It has been twisted in books to show how much of a cruel husband he was but he acted this way out of fear. To him the end of their relationship meant death and brought on his killing rage.

Bianchi had spent his entire childhood with a domineering, yet medium-dominance adoptive mother whom psychiatrists said had not allowed him to express negative emotions or anger. He saw relationships with women as ones where he had to lie prostrate before them as he bleated like a lamb.

It was Kelli Boyd's power over him he was raging against but that relationship was only a weak reflection of the power his mother had over him in his childhood. When Bianchi was under hypnosis, Steve said on tape that he not only hated Boyd, he was *afraid of her.*

Bianchi was a high-dominance male but his mother had crushed his masculinity so he had to take abuse from women less dominant and less intelligent than him. This caused a powder keg of rage for the high-dominance male that he truly was. Ken couldn't feel anger. It was siphoned off into Steve – his ousted real self – who then went off with no controls in place and expressed the anger to women by killing them.

When Bianchi got addicted to a woman, he slipped into the role of a very meek, self-effacing slave. I received a letter from Bianchi after the visit to say that he had received the postcard I sent him before leaving town. He said he held it in his 'unworthy hands'. He included another photograph of himself in his cell with the letter, saying I could use it for mopping up spilt tea or as toilet paper.

When Bianchi likes a woman, he lies on the ground in front of her and makes her into a goddess. After we met he transferred this onto me and worshipped me as if I were a goddess. This repressed character defect caused a powder-keg personality that the serial -killer had to periodically release when it was triggered by rejection.

Ken the blue-eyed family man was a hologram. The real Ken who I had first sensed and heard was a man who had never grown up. A wild, unsocialised *Lord of the Flies* boy – needy, lonely, angry and half in this world and half in the next. He was what FBI serial-killer profilers call a diphasic personality – the outer persona is a fake cardboard cut-out. The real person has retreated so far from this world that it's like a ghoul. The ghoul never showed his face. He only carried around his sack of skulls and at times when he felt the most rage over his life in which women had massive power over him, when they dumped him, gave him gonorrhoea, betrayed him or rejected him, another skull was added to the sack.

This *Lord of the Flies* boy killer was interesting. I wanted to name this creature of the night. He was like the undead – a ghoul, a blood-lusting vampire, barely human. I believe Angelo saw the ghoul and it scared him, so he told Ken to leave him alone. Angelo told his family in the last few weeks that Ken was around, 'Stay away from Ken, he's nutty.'

Some say Angelo Buono took the lead in the murders and was more dominant than Bianchi. This is false. The cops pointed out that no killing had taken place before Bianchi turned up. Bianchi was the more dominant personality. There can be no question. Journalists who met Buono reported that just before he died Angelo confessed just how ashamed he was over the Hillside stranglings and how it had been Bianchi that led the way into serial murder. He would say that, yes, but Bianchi's dominance is phenomenal. No one could ever control him. This was what made him so very angry when women who were less than him pulled his strings.

I thought of my dream of another lifetime and a boy called Jack. Of how I had vowed to him that I would search for him high and low. I'd said I'd never give up on him. But this, this creature, even if it was once Jack, my beloved brother in a previous lifetime, now he was a murdering, blood-lusting ghoul. I wanted to run for miles from him. I had finally found true evil and it was an energy that engendered great fear – a primal terror. And I had hunted evil to challenge it! Such conceit!

Hugh was looking at me with such interest that I picked up his pipe off the mantelpiece, shoved it into my mouth and pretended to smoke it while warming my backside on his fire. 'You see, Watson, it's like this,' I said, mocking myself.

'Carry on, Chris, you've worked very hard. Now pin him down like I pin down my butterflies and collect him for yourself.' He gestured to the butterflies and moths pinned down in glass cases on his walls.

'No glass case can hold a Bianchi. He's become something and it's non-human. He's the undead, Hugh.'

'A vampire?'

'A something. A something that is more at home in another world and only comes into this one for human blood.'

I left Hugh's to go and pick up Charlie from school. Times were hard financially and I needed money to support us. I had only forty pounds in my current account and that month's rent was already late. I decided to write a book, expanding on the still unpublished investigation on Bianchi I had written for *The Guardian*.

I sat for six months writing this book, working through the night as Charlie slept and I woke up to do the school run at seven then slept for a few hours till midday and then got started again. I gave it to Hugh to read.

'It's great, Chris, but you've no title! I say, why not call it *In for the Kill*? Everyone in it is in for the kill. The only thing is, the last chapter's empty. You need some great happening – some big event, a real ending, you know?'

I worked on it all through the stuffy hot month of July and would go over to Hugh's to sit in his front garden and eat strawberries, or sit in his shady drawing room eating ginger biscuits and drinking endless cups of Earl Grey with honey before and after the school run. He would shave or go about his business and I would sit working, sometimes just coming over for his company, enjoying the quiet of just us – living – breathing –

being. When Charlie came out of school Hugh would draw cartoons and get Charlie to copy him, encouraging him to draw and write childish storybooks, which he did.

I confessed to Hugh that I was completely drained and exhausted. The publisher I had found was also a hard task master. Not content with what I had written, he dragged more and more out of me until I felt I had turned myself inside out. The book on Hillside was too short and he felt I had to do another 100,000 words and include more about my life and work.

One drowsy late summer afternoon, Hugh spoke out of the silence. 'Hey, why not put me at the end of the last chapter? Let's talk about all this then put it in the book. Let me give you the ending – let it be me.'

'You just want fame!'

'If you think that, then get out now.'

'Oh, for God's sake, I was joking! You've had fame already! You've produced films for the BBC!'

'I'm trying to help, Chris, and you're going to put me into an early grave with worrying about you and Charlie and your financial predicament. Have you paid this month's rent?'

'Nope.'

"What'll you do?'

'Move in with you!' I winked at him and we both laughed.

That evening we all had dinner together and over the fried chicken, gravy and mash with rhubarb crumble and cream that I'd baked for us Hugh spoke to Charlie in a soft voice full of emotion.

'Look after your mother for me, won't you, Charlie?'

I eyed him over my glass of Merlot. He was being dramatic as usual – worrying about not being here to take care of us emotionally.

At the end of the unbearably hot summer of 2011, when Hugh's prize-winning pink roses were all looking parched and weary and the ground was dry as a bone, I felt emotionally exhausted by writing the book. I was claustrophobic in London but couldn't afford to take Charlie away. I rang around and finally managed to persuade a well-known French magazine to interview me about my research into evil and knowledge of serial killers. I had met with the Catholic Church and their representatives on evil and studied theology for a year in a seminary run by a Jesuit called Michael Barrow. Under his tuition I had read tomes on evil, studied Father Malachi Martin on exorcism, Merton and Aquinas. I felt I was ready to be interviewed about the nature of evil and share my experiences.

The magazine didn't have the budget to cover accommodation and pay me a fee, so I agreed to talk with no fee as long as they covered my expenses and put me up somewhere decent. They agreed and I flew to Paris at the end of summer to show my son the sights and give him a miniature summer holiday.

We stayed in the dazzling Shangri-La Hotel in Avenue d'Iéna. The owner, a big-hearted billionaire called Robert Kuok, had wanted to recreate the feel of a spiritual paradise that he had found in the book *Lost Horizon* by James Hilton. He had succeeded; I felt my own ego float away in the Shangri-La as I bathed in its spiritual atmosphere. Staff were taught all about selflessness and how to truly put others first, which were the values Kuok had schooled his own family in.

The elegant, historical hotel, much loved by French royalty, Madonna and Isabelle Adjani, was down a skinny Parisian street and behind tall nineteenth-century wrought-iron gates. The Eiffel Tower, lit up in gold at night, was only a hundred yards away from our spacious balcony. The unassuming staff put red roses by my bed in a vase and I pulled off the petals and threw them on the bed – the dark red against the white. Then I lay on them, the scent filling my nostrils. There were chocolate biscuits on his bedside table for Charlie and chilled Chablis ready for me in an ice bucket on the balcony.

I relaxed for the first time in a long time in Paris. It was what I needed, as I had become trapped in a mean, self-centred, selfish, little world. While there, I lay on the bed and studied a very recent photograph Bianchi had sent me of himself. The photo had been taken very close up and was unusual in that you could see every blemish on his skin, every line on his face. People didn't often send such revealing photographs of themselves.

He had enclosed a note that wasn't in his usual style. He said he was looking for a life partner. He didn't want a Madonna, he wanted a woman who would be loving and giving – a woman he could share his life with. The recent photo of Bianchi, who was standing, arms folded in his prison cell and smiling, had 'Your Yank' scrawled on the back of it. I wondered whether the comment about sharing a life related to me. Bianchi told me he had only sent the photo to two people– me and his mother, to be put in her grave as she had died a few weeks earlier.

310

Zapping

The photo didn't resemble the other one he had sent me in which he looked feminine. This time he seemed very male and strong. It was like looking at a male tiger. I knew it was savage and had to be behind bars but I felt a perverse longing to restrain him so I could touch him.

You could tell Bianchi didn't want a woman to be his life partner, but to rip and tear at one and then maul the dead body. I found it odd that he had put that particular photo in his mother's coffin – after all, it was a side of him he had kept hidden from her when she had been alive, but it was a dead woman he wanted this dominant photo to perch on top of.

I wrote to Bianchi from Paris to tell him about my idea to do a book on him. I knew he wouldn't like it. He wanted to use me to write his own memoir, not for me to dissect him. He had told me over and over that he was a very private person. He was also very wary about someone getting near to him and then telling the world what he was really like. Needless to say, his own memoir contained only what he wanted to show, which was very little. He had even told me that he didn't kiss and tell on his women, or ever reveal himself, so his memoir was all fiction.

After I posted that letter to the Hillside Strangler in the narrow Paris street I looked up at the Eiffel Tower and somehow caught sight of who I was as a person. To my surprise, my reflection had an ugly tinge to it. All of my life I had been hunting evil. It had been a long, arduous search, yet all along it had been right under my very nose. I was outwardly normal but I was definitely batting for the black team. I saw parts of my life as if it were flashing before me – the defrocking of a Catholic priest, bedding a Real IRA commander, a man wedded to violence.

I had introduced the aggressive newspaper to the secretive world of spying, little knowing that when two devils meet they surely start to fuck – the hacking scandal and the fall of News Corp appears to be the offspring. I hadn't known what I was hatching, nor am I making allegations of illegal activity by anyone I knew at News Corp, but there is a saying, fly with the crows and you get shot with them. What had I ever been doing in the murky smokescreens and mirrors, the world of the spy? What had I ever been doing in the dark world of News Corp? Failing professionally and financially had made me bitter and resentful, and I'd under achieved. I had been underpaid by men who had used me for sex as well as exploited me, betrayed me and kept me down. I was mistakenly resentful against humanity because I felt humanity was on the side of my parents, so I had unconsciously sought my own grand union with the Devil, like a nun seeking union with Christ. I had always assumed I was a warrior princess seeking to slay evil, yet all along I was a resentful she-devil who generated evil like a car plant pumped out new cars.

The fact was, I had been brought up in a dark, Godless, abusive, unloving home. Satan becomes the higher power in homes like that, no matter how many photos of Jesus there are on the walls. The abused child learns to hate and distrust God. The abused child learns that God has forsaken them. In their suffering it is then the Devil that creeps down and does his work with seductive whispers. *Where is your God now? He has abandoned you.* The Devil then whispers his final seduction, *Come follow me.* I had followed as I sought the succour and the power that I felt humanity had robbed from me. This is the trick that evil plays as it hides and pretends that it doesn't exist and humanity is the evil one who hurts. It gets many more followers that way, many of them unloved neglected and abused children.

I had been hunting for evil all of my life but all I had to do was look at my own reflection in the mirror.

I sank down on my knees and prayed for respite from the dark world where I had always been exiled. I was so sick of living in a world of terrorism and spying and murder. Yes, I was a crime reporter but I felt like a war correspondent who had seen too much blood. I wanted a taste of the lighter side of life. But where was God? I had no idea where to look for Him. He had shunned me. He had abandoned me and left me in the wilderness. Fuck God.

I dried my eyes and stood up. What was I doing praying? I knew I would never be listened to – it was for mugs and needy weak fools.

Later, on a fragrant late summer's evening in Paris, with the frangipani trees giving off their lovely scent, Charlie and I got dressed up, he in a little tux, me in my best floor-length Prada evening dress. We were chauffeured around the luminous city in a long open-top limousine. There was a fragrant soft breeze in the hot August night as Handel's *Messiah* played on CD and we gazed at the architectural splendour of Paris. We drove by Nôtre Dame and the Eiffel Tower, with Charlie excitedly agog at its golden, sparkly magnificence and shouting out joyfully to the wondrous monument.

Zapping

When we passed the Arc de Triomphe the carvings of angels made me catch my breath. Suddenly a hard lump appeared in my throat and hot tears began to fall as I watched my son enjoying his holiday. I suddenly saw myself as an intelligent, caring woman with her beautiful son enjoying this privilege in a lovely car seeing this magnificent city – how blessed was I? I had focused on all the negative things in life – I had focused on all the things I didn't have rather than the many blessings God had given me. I had been completely blind, like I was in a cave. Suddenly I knew that 'there' was God. God was beauty, art, music and love within and without for others and in selflessness. God had always been there, weaving his magic into my life. I had been the one ignoring God while I purposely hunted Satan with my bitter, closed, resentful mind full of self-obsession and self-pity. Yes, I had had a bad childhood; yes, I was an abuse victim and a rape victim, but many others had suffered and would suffer in life. Pain was a teacher on earth and it was only through challenge and adversity that we would come to know the shape of our own soul and let it grow.

I wanted to speak to God to thank him but I had no idea how. I spoke out from my hungry heart. *Father, help me. I'm in the darkness and I am so very, very afraid.*

I waited patiently for a reply and then I heard it loud and clear inside my head.

I HEAR YOU.

Back in our suite later that night I stared out at the illuminated Eiffel Tower and rang Hugh. He sounded croaky and bunged up.

'You're in Paris and I'm here with the damn flu.'

'Oh, don't fret, sweetheart. I'll bring you back a sparkly gold Eiffel Tower to soothe you!'

'How's he? Enjoying it?'

'Loves it!' I smiled down the phone. I could tell he cared for Charlie deeply.

'Is the angel asleep?'

'Yep, out like a light. We went to see the *Mona Lisa* this morning and he just about caught a glimpse of it through the crowds.'

'Have a good night's sleep.'

'You too.'

'I'm just about to go on up.'

'Hugh, do you believe in God?'

'God? No such thing. Sorry, Chris, and all the other weaklings who need to cling on to something. When you die, you die. That's it, lights OUT! Belief in an afterlife is for the weak minded.'

I had tears in my eyes. 'Today, in Paris, I finally had union with Him.'

'Who?'

'God.'

'There's no God. Tut, tut – stupid broad. You just haven't met the right man yet and enjoyed good sex.'

I let the phone go silent. I could just hear his breath down it.

He spoke again. 'Have you?'

I stayed silent and in the silence I felt him– he and I.

'By the way,' he said, 'I've been reading Bianchi's poetry.'

'Oh?' I had left a whole sheaf of Bianchi's poetry so Hugh could give me a second opinion on whether it was any good.

'All Eve she weeps her tears like sewers.'

'I didn't read that.'

'Thought not, you silly dame. It's a verse nestled within the mushy stuff for you to come across and enjoy.'

'Enjoy?'

'Oh yes, he wants you to read it, Chris. He wants you to know how much he enjoys who he really is. The monster is beginning to show itself. You're going to get a sighting if you crouch down in the undergrowth and keep really still. You've done very, very well.'

'Email me the verses you've found.'

'You'll be the death of me. I left them upstairs, now I'll have to go all the way upstairs and then down again, then sit here scanning them in.'

'But you'll do it because you love me!'

'Bloody dame.'

'Night night.'

'Wait, wait, when are you coming back from Paris?'

'Three more days – stop pining!'

I hung up. I had to or I'd have been on the phone with him all night long.

I wandered back onto the balcony. The air was balmy and I felt warm even in my flimsy nightdress. I sprawled on a sofa which I dragged over to the open French windows leading onto the balcony and, as the Eiffel Tower flashed like a firework sparkler, I wrote a gratitude list for all I had seen that day. Charlie's smile, the sights of Paris, Hugh's love, this beautiful hotel room. As I wrote, I felt a light inside me warm the chill. God did love me. He kept telling me over and over – in my son's sweet smile, in today's warm breeze on my face, in the beautiful museums we had visited. *I love you. I truly love you*, he had whispered and I had never heard him. What a loser. What an idiot. My deep resentment and boiling hot rage with life had been my life-long prison bars, affecting no one but myself.

I stood up and walked naked along the balcony sipping a glass of cold champagne. This was God. God wasn't dull or boring or sadistic or vengeful or punishing like my staunch Catholic parents had made out. God was an open-top limousine ride around Paris on a hot summer night dressed in Prada. God was passionate lovemaking with a George Clooney lookalike, a bumper bottle of vintage champagne drunk naked on the balcony of the Shangri-La. The Devil and the Catholic Church had tricked us all into believing that God was a boring cunt.

Charlie and I stayed for three more days in Paris and on my return I got straight into finishing my book. The publisher I had found wanted to see a final draft. I remembered to let go and let God in, so I asked God to see that the book was published so I could pay my rent and feed and clothe Charlie.

One thing I didn't have to worry about was Charlie's school life. He had moved up to middle school and was finally enjoying the experience. He had a brilliant headmistress. She was totally fair-minded, and if I had a complaint it was seen to and sorted. I was in heaven! His teacher was nurturing and truly cared for my son.

I began to make friends with the other mothers and I found them interesting and fun, and I began to get to the school gate early so I could stand and chat to them. Then a miraculous thing happened. The village was the same place but I began to warm to it. It was like someone had painted it in bright, warm colours and I saw that it was a really clean, nice place with a lot of beautiful people and lovely Edwardian villas. And if I felt jealous when I saw a Stepford wife with a parasol and a mansion I told myself that it was OK. Didn't every woman, deep inside, want to lie around wearing silk dresses in a lovely villa, kept like a child and worshipped by some schmuck of a guy with too much money . . .?

Charlie was thriving both socially and academically, and he was growing so beautiful, strong and tall! One day I went to the school to drop off some cakes I had baked for their sale. It was the middle of playtime and I caught sight of Charlie playing football, running and joining in with the other boys, his face rosy pink and his eyes joyful and shining. For that I had his new head and teachers to thank.

Charlie was all that mattered to me – he was my life. He was now eight and all long legs, wide toothy smiles and joyful blue eyes flecked with a summery gold. One day he would leave home and I would be all alone, but I had him *now* and I was his sun, moon and stars.

The following week I went round to see Hugh. I was excited and there was a spring in my step. I had not seen him for over a month and I was pining for him. Hugh would make me laugh as soon as I sat down with him in his shady drawing room. With his sharp intelligence and wicked sense of humour he was my rock and I still had sneaking hopes of marriage even though he was far older than me. He had been ill and I feared germs because I was a single mother. Illness just wasn't allowed, so I had kept away and got on with my book. Then the days had gone on and I had just not seen him.

I arrived at his wrought-iron gate straight after school drop-off. I found to my amazement that the gate had a heavy padlock on it but it wasn't locked. His front door was wide open too. I barged into the drawing room, wondering with a sinking feeling in my stomach whether the flu had got so bad that he had had to go into hospital. I felt guilty that I hadn't gone round to cook for him. Why was I so selfish?

I found Hugh's best friend Rick sitting in the cosy patchwork armchair where Hugh always sat. I thought of the Death card in the Tarot and it grew larger and larger inside my mind until I thought I would scream.

I stood in Hugh's drawing room where he always sat and been there for me for the past 20 years. My stomach churned. Tears spilled down my face. He had been ill and I had given him a wide berth until he got better, but instead of getting better Hugh had died.

Rick spoke. 'We tried to contact you but we had no phone number. It all happened so suddenly. His flu turned to pneumonia and took him quickly.'

I thought if I screamed it would make it all OK but the scream wouldn't come. Death had come and snatched my soul away.

He's gone, he's gone, he's gone, he's gone.

I held on to my stomach as it lurched and churned.

Zapping

When someone leaves you for another dimension where you cannot follow, they rip out a part of you. I lay and sobbed all night in bed in an agony of need. Who would I run to now in times of need? My best friend was dead.

I can't remember if it was that night or the next when he came to me in a dream from the other side.

'Chris, don't mourn me. You'll be here soon – 30 years or so and it goes so fast, so, so fast. It's another dimension here – similar but not like earth. Life's different. It's a stage, Chris. Play your part. It's a test. And, Chris, I'm *here*! No more running up a big phone bill to speak to me all the time!'

I woke up, lay in bed and blinked at the ceiling. *So much for lights out, huh?* I listened hard, but he'd gone. Tears of loss and sadness coursed down my cheeks. *Haunt me, please haunt me. Never let me go. I miss you ever so much.*

Rick had given me Hugh's checked cashmere scarf and I slept with it pressed up to my nose as it smelt of him. I drenched his scarf with my salty tears and slept with it night after night pressed up against my breast.

Hugh came into my dream the next night and spoke to me. 'I'm in a room, Chris. There's no light – nothing. It's very, very dark. I'm forced to re-live all the things that I'm not proud of that I did in my lifetime over and over again. I blame you, Chris. It's a Catholic version of purgatory.'

I woke up to find it was still dark outside and my wolf-themed clock showed 3 a.m. I sat up in bed and finally took the time to study the poetry from Bianchi that Hugh had marked up for me in the file I'd given him. I started to read the lines.

All Eve she weeps grievously her tears but sewers over run upon her cheeks – make up smearing, all her lovers look on, but none comfort her, those friends false doors exposed, those betrayers betrayed, solemn, they have become malignant spirits.

    Her tall limbs upward stretched, while resting on her back, naked, reposed, teasing, her boundless energy released, from mortal zippers broken, down pouring within my winter shattered mind, playing visions where no one else sees.

I held the poems in my fists. I'd been hunting for the monster for three whole years and it had been right underneath my nose all along.

In for the Kill

I had reached the heart of darkness and I could sense it. It had eyes everywhere, it was as ancient as all time and it had the power of Christ.

There was no Ken, there was only the vampire lusting for the blood of beautiful young girls and waiting, hiding in the shadows.

I wanted to hang up my black cape and give up my role as huntress of evil.

I had no choice as a child but to try to comprehend evil because I had been thrown into it at birth, but I loathed its stink and came to know its utter banality. I had finally come across pure evil in the body of the Hillside Strangler and it sickened me. Yet I knew I couldn't get this far and turn around, give up my life's work and let someone else carry on while I found some cushions to loll on. If we didn't find and fight evil it would prevail.

That night I finally typed up my American notes for my book.

I got an email from the eminent Dr Ralph Allison, the psychiatrist who had examined Bianchi after his arrest and who I had spoken to the previous year.

I told him about the experience both Dee and I had had of Bianchi's spooky mind intrusion.

He sent a one-line reply.

'It's about time you learned what dangerous multiples and people with Imaginary Companions like Kenneth are capable of.'

My anxiety surged, so I sent an immediate response.

'What do you mean by capable of?'

Doctor Allison replied in an hour with a paper he had written for the Association of Anthropological Study of Consciousness, published in their journal *Anthropology of Consciousness,* Vol. 2, No. 4, 1986.

The paper explained that the feelings of being watched and the vile images I had described were a common occurrence in doctors who had treated people like Ken. Doctor Allison said that he had experienced the same haunting phenomena as both Dee and me.

Amazingly, both men seemed to take it in their stride, but I had never heard of this power of projection that certain serial killers wielded over others from their cells.

Dr Allison informed me that it was a 'known phenomenon' called 'zapping', and it had been reported for many years by doctors and therapists of dangerous multiples and serial killers with imaginary companions.

Zapping

He said: 'These people have cut off from a part of themselves and it disassociates and splits off because of some violent trauma they experienced before the age of seven. Ken only shows a fake part of himself that he feels can placate Mother (Ken's diphasic personality). These abused children can often develop minds that become far stronger than the average because of the amount of time that they spend alone, because they feel rejected from this world and because only the "place marker personality" is the one living. They are, however, functional in another world, where their real self has gone into hiding to avoid the fear of their physical reality which contains a constant threat. It is in this other world that they garner their paranormal powers.'

He warned me: 'They can do a lot more damage to you than just get inside a victim's mind; they can inject unwanted emotions into another person, they can inject a foreign belief system into a victim. Worse still, zapping can cause physical injury to another person. This could mean anything from headache to broken bones – the ultimate would be death. Like in voodoo deaths.'

So! Was this true? Was I the hunted instead of the hunter?

I thought about what I had learned from knowing Ken Bianchi, America's notorious Hillside Strangler.

I had dragged him out into the sunlight so the world could see just what a victim of his mother Kenneth Bianchi was. How tied to his common-law wife's apron strings, and this had been the reason the 12 beauties had to die.

This creature that Ken had created was pure evil. Is it we on earth who make demons? I think we do. There is no other place evil comes from apart from earth. We have to face the fact that 'earth' is a bad-apple planet, spinning around the universe, polluting the stratosphere. Earth is a seething pit of paedophilia, where people murder for pleasure, a place where vulnerable, innocent youngsters are abused and portrayed naked on websites, where unnecessary and bloody wars rage and half the world starves while the other half enjoys obscene riches. We look the other way and tell ourselves we've captured the evil and put it in a cell and now we are clean, but we are not clean at all.

I wanted to drag out the vampire I had located and stick him with my pin. I needed to 'collect' this creature, this 'vampire of the night'. I wanted to put the devil in a display case and share him with you, the reader, so you could see what the earth had created and perhaps be proud of it. Some would admire it – why not? We are made up of evil, so why not admire that which is within us all even when we most deny it?

The repulsive, brutal creature doesn't come from elsewhere – not Transylvania, not the pits of a fiery Hell – but from a suburban semi, born of Woman.